Spurgeon's
Gems

GREAT CHRISTIAN BOOKS
LINDENHURST, NEW YORK

Spurgeon's Gems

Brilliant Passages from the Discourses of C. H. Spurgeon

A Spurgeon Classic

Great Christian Books

is an imprint of Rotolo Media
160 37th Street Lindenhurst, New York 11757
(631) 956-0998

Spurgeon, Charles Haddon, 1834—1892
Spurgeon's Gems / by Charles Haddon Spurgeon
p. cm.
A "A Great Christian Book" book
GREAT CHRISTIAN BOOKS an imprint of Rotolo Media
ISBN 978-1-61010-028-1
Recommended Dewey Decimal Classifications: 200, 240
Suggested Subject Headings:
1. Religion—Christianity literature—Theology
2. Christianity—Theology—Devotional
I. Title

Book and cover design are by Michael Rotolo, www. michaelrotolo.com. This book is typeset in the Minion typeface by Adobe Inc. and is quality-manufactured on acid-free paper stock. To discuss the publication of your Christian manuscript or out-of-print book, please contact us.

Manufactured in the United States of America

PUBLISHERS' PREFACE

The popularity of Mr. Spurgeon's sermons in this country has been equaled only by the popularity of the preacher himself in his own land. Over a hundred and twenty thousand volumes of his writings have been already circulated here, and the demand for them is constant, showing that they have taken a strong and abiding hold upon the public mind. Their usefulness, we have reason to believe, has been, in a great measure, commensurate with their popularity.

The call has been repeatedly made for a volume giving the characteristics of Mr. Spurgeon's style, revealing the secret of his mighty power as a preacher of truth, with the peculiarities of manner which arrest the attention, rouse the sympathies, excite the admiration, and impress the feelings of his vast audiences. This cannot be done by giving simply detached sentences from his sermons. Mr. Spurgeon is not remarkable for terseness, nor does he deal in laconic phrases. He is rhetorical, descriptive, flowing and glowing He blazes and burns along the pathway of his subject, rising in flights of imagination and carrying his hearers along with him in earnest, overwhelming appeals. He is pungent in his applications, strong in his doctrinal opinions, and powerful in his exhibition of the divine Word. Such a preacher's *forte* is not to be presented in single sentences. We have therefore gathered from scores of his sermons many of the most striking passages, and set them in these pages, without regard to the order of subject, or their relations to each other: a series of earnest thoughts and graphic pictures, all of them revealing the true greatness of the preacher's conceptions, his individuality and strength. No one can read the first page of this volume without feeling that the speaker is no common man.

The publishers present this selection from the pages of Mr. Spurgeon, as a specimen of his happiest thoughts, gems from his discourses, which will glow in the mind of the reader, and quicken in him a desire to read and hear more of this remarkable youthful preacher of the unsearchable riches of Christ.

Spurgeon's Gems

Note to the reader:

Each of the passages in this volume are separated by a thin line except when they begin at the top of a new page; however you will still distinguish these from another by the fact that each passage also begins with at least the first word in all capital letters.

SPURGEON'S GEMS

ALL my springs are in thee, said David. If thou hast all thy springs in God, thy heart will he full enough. If thou dost go to the foot of Calvary, there will thy heart he bathed in love and gratitude. If thou dost frequent the vale of retirement, and there talk with thy God, it is there that thy heart shall be full of calm resolve. If thou goest out with thy master to the hill of Olivet, and dost with him look down upon a wicked Jerusalem, and weep over it with him, then will thy heart he full of love for never-dying souls. If thou dost continually draw thine impulse, thy life, the whole of thy being from the Holy Spirit, without whom thou canst do nothing, and if thou d»st live in close communion with Christ, there will be no fear of thy having a dry heart. He who lives without prayer—he who lives with little prayer—he who seldom reads the Word—he who seldom looks up to heaven for a fresh influence from on high—he will be the man whose heart will become dry and barren; but he who calls in secret on his God—who spends much time in holy retirement— who delights to meditate on the words of the Most High—whoso soul is given up to Christ—who delights in his fullness, rejoices in his all-sufficiency, prays for his second coming, and delights in the thought of his glorious advent—such a man, I say, must have an overflowing heart; and as his heart is, such will his life be. It will be a full life; it wilt be a life that will speak from the sepulcher, and wake the echoes of the future. "Keep thine heart with all diligence," and entreat the Holy Spirit to keep it full; for, otherwise, the issues of thy life will be feeble, shallow, and superficial; and thou mayest as well not have lived at all.

I AM certain thou needest no exhortation to love thyself, thine own case will be seen to, thine own comfort will be a very primary theme of thine anxiety. Thou wilt line thine own nest well with downy feathers, if thou canst. There is no need to exhort thee to love thyself. Thou wilt do that well enough. Well, then, as much as thou lovest thyself, love thy neighbor.

A MAN'S force in the world, other things being equal, is just in the ratio of the force and strength of his heart. A full-hearted man is always a powerful man: if he be erroneous, then he is powerful for error; if the thing is in his heart, he is sure to make it notorious, even though it may be a downright falsehood. Let a man be never so ignorant, still if his heart be full of love to a cause, he becomes a powerful man for that object, because he has heart-power, heart-force. A man may be deficient in many of the advantages of education, in many of those niceties which are so much looked upon in society; but once give him a good strong heart, that beats hard, and there is no mistake about his power. Let him have a heart that is right full up to the brim with an object, and that man will do the thing, or else he will die gloriously defeated, and will glory in his defeat. Heart is power.

WHEN the sunlight of God's mercy rises upon our necessities, it casts the shadow of prayer far down upon the plain; or, to use another illustration, when God piles up a hill of mercies, he himself shines behind them, and he casts on our spirits the shadow of prayer, so that we may rest certain, if we are in prayer, our prayers are the shadows of mercy.

OMNIPOTENCE may build a thousand worlds, and fill them with bounties; Omnipotence may powder mountains into dust, and burn the sea, and consume the sky, but Omnipotence cannot do an unloving thing toward a believer. Oh! rest quite sure, Christian, a hard thing, an unloving thing from God toward one of his own people is quite impossible. He is kind to you when he casts you into prison as when he takes you into" a palace; He is as* good when he sends famine into your house as when he fills your barns with plenty. The only question is, Art thou his child? If so, he hath rebuked thee in affection, and there is love in his chastisement.

PRAYER is the rustling of the wings of the angels that are on their way bringing us the boons of heaven. Have you heard prayer in your heart? You shall see the angel in your house. When the chariots that bring us blessings do rumble, their wheels do sound with prayer. We hear the prayer in our own spirits, and that prayer becomes the token of the coming blessings. Even as the cloud foreshadoweth rain, so prayer foreshadoweth the blessing; even as the green blade is the beginning of the harvest, so is prayer the prophecy of the blessing that is about to come.

YOU have seen the great reservoirs provided by our water companies, in which the water which is to supply hundreds of streets and thousands of houses is kept. Now, the heart is just the reservoir of man, and our life is allowed to flow in its proper season. That life may flow through different pipes— the mouth, the hand, the eye; but still all the issues of hand, of eye, of lip, derive their source from the great fountain and central reservoir, the heart; and hence there is no difficulty in showing the great necessity that exists for keeping this reservoir, the heart, in a proper state and condition, since otherwise that which flows through the pipes must be tainted and corrupt.

THERE is not a spider hanging on the king's wall but hath its errand; there is not a nettle that groweth in the corner of the churchyard but hath its purpose; there is not a single insect fluttering in the breeze but accomplisheth some divine decree; and I will never have it that God created any man, especially any Christian man, to be a blank, and to be a nothing. He made you for an end. Find out what that end is; find out your niche, and fill it. If it be ever so little, if it is only to be a hewer of wood and drawer of water, do something in this great battle for God and truth.

SUPPOSE you see a lake, and there are twenty or thirty streamlets running from it: why, there will not he one strong river in the whole country; there will he a number of little brooks which will be dried up in the summer, and will be temporary torrents in the winter. They will every one of them be useless for any great purpose, because there is not water enough in the lake to feed more than one great stream. Now, a man's heart has only enough life in it to pursue one object fully. Ye must not give half your love to Christ, and the other half to the' world. No man can serve God and mammon, because there is not enough life in the heart to serve the two.

HOW easy it is for you and I to fly up! How hard to keep down! That demon of pride was born with us, and it will not die one hour before us. It is so woven into the very warp and woof of our nature, that till we are wrapped in our winding-sheets we shall never hear the last of it.

ANY man who trusts so much as a single hair's breadth to his works, is a lost soul. He who trusts to the least atom of works, though it be so small that he himself cannot discern it, will be lost.

KEEP not back part of the price. Make a full surrender of every motion of thy heart; labor to have but one object, and one aim. And for this purpose give God the keeping of thine heart. Cry out for more of the divine influences of the Holy Spirit, that so when thy soul is preserved and protected by him, it may be directed into one channel, and one only, that thy life may run deep and pure, and clear and peaceful; its only banks being God's will, its only channel the love of Christ and a desire to please him.

THERE never was a saint yet, that grew proud of his fine feathers, but what the Lord plucked them out by and by. There never yet was an angel that had pride in his heart, but he lost his wings, and fell into Gehenna, as Satan and those fallen angels did; and there shall never be a saint who indulges self-conceit, and pride, and self-confidence, but the Lord will spoil his glories, and trample his honors in the mire, and make him cry out yet again, "Lord have mercy upon me," less than the least of all saints, and the "very chief of sinners."

MEN who have no brains are always great men; but those who think, must think their pride down, if God is with them in their thinking.

NEVER, never neglect the word of God; that will make thy heart rich with precept, rich with understanding; and then thy conversation, when it flows from thy mouth, will be like thine heart, rich, unctious, and savoury. Make thy heart full of rich, generous love, and then the stream that flows from thy hand will be just as rich and generous as thine heart. Above all, get Jesus to live in thine heart, and then out of thy belly shall flow rivers of living water, more rich, more satisfying than the water of the well of Sychar of which Jacob drank. Oh! go, Christian, to the great mine of riches, and cry unto the Holy Spirit to make thy heart rich unto salvation. So shall thy life and conversation be a boon to thy fellows; and when they see thee, thy face shall be as the angel of God. Thou shalt wash thy feet in butter and thy steps in oil: they that sit in the gate shall rise up when they see thee, and men shall do thee reverence. GOD hath said it; men must serve him—they must serve him in his own way, and they must serve him in his own strength too, or he will never accept their service. That which man doth, unaided by divine strength, God never can accept. There must be a consciousness of weakness before there can be any victory.

LIFE is but death's vestibule; and our pilgrimage on earth is but a journey to the grave. The pulse that preserves our being beats our death march, and the blood which circulates our life is floating it onward to the deeps of death. Today we see our friends in health, tomorrow we hear of their decease. We clasped the hand of the strong man but yesterday, and today we close his eyes. We rode in the chariot of comfort but an hour ago, and in a few more hours the last black chariot must convey us to the home of all living. Oh, how closely allied is death to life! The lamb that sporteth in the field must soon feel the knife. The ox that loweth in the pasture is fattening for the slaughter. Trees do but grow that they may be felled. Yea, and greater things than these feel death. Empires rise and flourish; they flourish but to decay, they rise to fall. How often do we take up the volume of history, and read of the rise and fall of empires. We hear of the coronation and the death of kings. Death is the black servant who rides behind the chariot of life. See life! and death is close behind it. Death reacheth far throughout this world, and hath stamped all terrestrial things with the broad arrow of the grave. Stars die; it is said that conflagrations have been seen far off in the distant ether, and astronomers have marked the funerals of worlds—the decay of those mighty orbs that we had imagined set forever in sockets of silver, to glisten as the lamps of eternity. But, blessed be God, there is one place where death is not life's brother—where life reigns alone; "to live" is not the first syllable which is to be followed by the next, "to die." There is a land where death-knells are never tolled, where winding-sheets are never woven, where graves are never dug. Blessed land beyond the skies! To reach it, we must die.

MY GOD! when I survey the boundless fields of ether, and see those pondrous orbs rolling therein—when I consider how vast are thy dominions —so wide that an angel's wing might flap to all eternity and never reach a boundary—I marvel that thou shouldst look on insects so obscure as man. I have taken to myself the microscope and seen the ephemera upon the leaf, and I have called him small. I will not call him so again: compared with me, he is great, if I put myself in comparison with God. I am so little that I shrink into nothingness when I behold the almightiness of Jehovah—so little that the difference between the animalculæ and man dwindles into nothing, when compared with the infinite chasm between God and man.

ALAS, alas, that the good should die! alas, that the righteous should fall! Death, why dost thou not hew the deadly upas? Why dost thou not mow the hemlock? Why dost thou touch the tree beneath whose spreading branches weariness hath rest? Why dost thou touch the flower whose perfume hath made glad the earth? Death, why dost thou snatch away the excellent of the earth, in whom is all our delight? If thou wouldest use thine axe, use it upon the cumber-grounds, the trees that draw nourishment, but afford no fruit; thou mightest be thanked then. But why wilt thou cut down the cedars, why wilt thou fell the goodly trees of Lebanon? O Death, why dost thou not spare the church? Why mast the pulpit be hung in black; why must the missionary station be filled with weeping? Why must the pious family lose its priest, and the house its head? O Death, what art thou at? touch not earth's holy things; thy hands are not fit to pollute the Israel of God. Why dost thou put thy hand upon the hearts of the elect? Oh, stay thou, stay thou; spare the righteous, Death, and take the bad! But no, it must not be; death comes and smiles the goodliest of us all; the most generous, the most prayerful, the most holy, the most devoted must die. Weep, weep, weep, O church, for thou hast lost thy martyrs; weep, O church, for thou hast lost thy confessors, thy holy men are fallen. Howl, fir tree, for the cedar hath fallen, the godly fail, and the righteous are cut off. But stay awhile; I hear another voice. Say ye thus unto the daughter of Judah, spare thy weeping. Say ye thus unto the Lord's flock, Cease, cease thy sorrow; thy martyrs are dead, but they are glorified; thy ministers are gone, but they have ascended up to thy Father and to their Father; thy brethren are buried in the grave, but the archangel's trumpet shall awake them, and their spirits are ever now with God.

DEATH was the devil's chief entrenchment; Christ bearded the lion in his den, and fought him in his own territory; and when he took death from him, and dismantled that once impregnable fortress, he took away from him, not only that, but every other advantage that he had over the saint. And now Satan is a conquered foe, not only in the hour of death, but in every other hour and in every other place. He is an enemy, both cruel and mighty; but he is a foe who quakes and quails when a Christian gets into the lists with him; for he knows that though the fight may waver for a little while in the scale, the balance of victory must fall on the side of the saint, because Christ by his death destroyed the devil's power.

SEE that man drowning, there—there is another in the water too, I see. He in the distance thinks he can swim: a plank is thrown to him; he believes himself to be in no danger of sinking. Well, he clutches the plank very leisurely, and does not seem to grasp it firmly. But this poor creature here, he knows he cannot swim, he feels that he must soon sink. Now put the means of escape near him, how desperately he clutches it; how he seems as if he would drive his fingers through the plank! He clutches it for life or death; that is his all, for he must perish if he is not saved by that. Now, in this case, he that fears the most believes the most; and I do think it is so sometimes with poor desponding spirits.

HERE we see through a glass darkly, but there face to face. There, what "eye hath not seen nor ear heard" shall be fully manifest to us. There, riddles shall be unraveled, mysteries made plain, dark texts enlightened, hard providences made to appear wise. The meanest soul in heaven knows more of God than the greatest saint on earth.

The greatest saint on earth may have it said of him, "Nevertheless he that is least in the kingdom of heaven is greater than he." Not our mightiest divines understand so much of theology as the: lambs of the flock of glory. Not the greatest master-minds of earth understand the millionth part of the mighty meanings which have been discovered by souls emancipated from clay. Yes. "To die is gain." Take away, take away that hearse, remove that shroud; come, put white plumes upon the horses' heads, and let gilded trappings hang around them. There, take away that fife, that shrill sounding music of the death march. Lend me the trumpet and the drum. O hallelujah, hallelujah, hallelujah; why weep we the saints to heaven; why need we lament? They are not dead, they are gone on. Stop, stop that mourning, refrain thy tears, clap your hands, clap your hands.

> "They are supremely blessed,
> Have done with care and sin and woe,
> And with their Savior rest."

What! weep! weep! for heads that are crowned with coronals of heaven? "Weep, weep for hands that grasp the harps of gold? What, weep for eyes that see the Redeemer? What, weep for hearts that are washed from sin, and are throbbing with eternal bliss? What, weep for men that are in the Savior's bosom? No; weep for yourselves, that you are here. Weep that the mandate has not come which bids *you* to die. Weep that you must tarry. But not for them. I sec them turning back on you with loving wonder, and they exclaim, "Why weepest thou?" What, weep for poverty that it is clothed in riches? What, weep for sickness, that it hath inherited eternal health? What, weep for shame, that it is glorified; and weep for sinful mortality, that it hath become immaculate? Oh, weep not, but rejoice. "If ye knew what it was that I have said unto you, and whither I have gone, ye would rejoice with a joy that no man should take from you."

WHEN the Lord Jesus came down to earth, Satan knew his errand. He knew that the Lord Jesus was the Son of God, and when he saw him an infant in the manger, he thought if he could kill him and get him in the bonds of death, what a fine thing it would be! So he stirred up the spirit of Herod to slay him; but Herod missed his mark. And many a time did Satan strive to put the personal existence of Christ in danger, so that he might get Christ to die. Poor fool as he was, he did not know that when Christ died he would bruise the devil's head. Once, you remember, when Christ was in the synagogue, the devil stirred up the people, and made them angry; and he thought, "Oh! what a glorious thing it would be if I could kill this man; then there would be an end of him, and I should reign supreme forever." So he got the people to take him to the brow of a hill, and he gloated over the thought that now surely he would be cast down headlong. But Christ escaped. He tried to starve him, he tried to drown him; he was in the desert without food, and he was on the sea in a storm; but there was no starving or drowning him, and Satan no doubt panted for his blood, and lodged that he should die. At last the day arrived; it was telegraphed to the court of hell that at last Christ would die. They rung their bells with hellish mirth and joy. "He will die now," said he; "Judas has taken the thirty pieces of silver. Let those Scribes and Pharisees get him, they will no more let him go than the spider will a poor unfortunate fly. He is safe enough now." And the devil laughed for very glee, when he saw the Savior stand before Pilate's bar. And when it was said, "Let him be crucified," then his joy scarce knew bounds, except that bound which his own misery must ever set to it. As far as he could, he reveled in what was to him a delightful thought, that the Lord of glory was about to die. In death, as Christ was seen of angels, he was seen of devils too; and that dreary march from Pilate's palace to the cross, was one which devils saw with extraordinary interest. And when they saw him on the cross, there stood the exulting fiend, smiling to himself. "Ah! I have the King of Glory now in my dominions; I have the power of death, and I have the power over the Lord Jesus." He exerted that power, till the Lord Jesus had to cry out in bitter anguish, "My God, my God, why hast thou forsaken me?" But ah! how short-lived was hellish victory! How brief was the Satanic triumph! He died; and "It is finished!" shook the gates of hell. Down from the cross the conqueror leaped, pursued the fiend with thunderbolts of wrath; swift to the shades of hell the fiend did fly, and swift descending went the conqueror after him; and we may conceive him exclaiming—

> "Traitor! this bolt shall find and pierce thee through,
> Though under hell's profoundest wave thou div'st,
> To find a sheltering grave."

And seize him he did—chained him to his chariot-wheel; dragged him up the steeps of glory; angels shouting all the while, "He hath led captivity captive, and received gifts for men." Now, devil, thou saidst thou wouldst overcome me, when I came to die. Satan, I defy thee, and laugh thee to scorn! My master overcame thee, and I shall overcome thee yet. You say you will overcome the saint, do you? You could not overcome the saint's Master, and you will not overcome him. You once thought you had conquered Jesus: you were bitterly deceived. Ah! Satan, thou mayest think thou shalt overcome the little faith and the faint heart; but thou art wondrously mistaken—for we shall assuredly tread Satan under our feet shortly; and even in our last extremity, with fearful odds against us, we shall he "more than conquerors through him that loved us."

THE river of God is full of water; but there is not one drop of it that takes its rise in earthly springs. God will have no strength used in his own battles but the strength which he himself imparts; and I would not have you that are now distressed in the least discouraged by it. Your emptiness is but the preparation for your being filled; and your casting down is but the making ready for your lifting up.

DEAL gently, deal kindly, deal lovingly, and there is not a wolf in human shape but will be melted by kindness; and there is not a tiger in woman's form but will break down and sue for pardon, if God should bless the love that is brought to bear upon her by her friend.

IF THE devil comes to my door with his horns visible, I will never let him in; but if he comes with his hat on as a respectable gentleman, he is at once admitted. The metaphor may be very quaint, but it is quite true. Many a man has taken in an evil thing, because it has been varnished and glossed over, and not apparently an evil; and he has thought in his heart, there is not much harm in it; so he has let in the little thing, and it has been like the breaking forth of water—the first drop has brought after it a torrent. The beginning has been but the beginning of a fearful end.

IF WE could see things as they are—if we were not deceived by the masquerade of this poor life—if we were not so easily taken in by the masks and dresses of those who act in this great drama, be it comedy or tragedy—if we could but see what the men are behind the scenes, penetrate their hearts, watch the inner motions, and discern their secret feelings, we should find but few who could bear the name of "blessed."

TOUCH not the persons of men; but smite their sin with a stout heart and with strong arm. Slay both the little ones and the great; let nothing be spared that is against God and his truth; but we have no war with the persons of poor mistaken men.

IF we had the blessings without asking for them, we should think them common things; but prayer makes the common pebbles of God's temporal bounties more precious than diamonds; and in spiritual prayer, cuts the diamond, and makes it glisten more. After a long chase, the hunter prizes the animal, because he has set his heart upon it, and is determined to have it; and yet more truly, after a long hunger, he that eateth findeth more relish in his food. So prayer doth sweeten the mercy. Prayer teaches us its preciousness. It is the reading over of the bill, the schedule, the account, before the estate and the properties are themselves transferred. We know the value of the purchase by reading over the will of it in prayer, and when we have groaned out our own expression of its peerless price, then it is that God bestows the benediction upon us. Prayer goes before the blessing, because it shows us the value of it.

WE hear, sometimes, a great deal said about possessing a full assurance of being a child of God; and then, every now and then, we hear of a doubt, a hope. As good Joseph Irons used to say, "They keep hope, hope, hoping—hop, hop, hopping —all their lives, because they can't walk." Little faith is always lame.

IF there were such a thing as national salvation; if it could be possible that we could be saved in the gross and in the bulk, that so, like the sheaves of corn, the few weeds that may grow with the stubble, would be gathered in for the sake of the wheat, then, indeed, it might not be so foolish for us to neglect our own personal interests; but if the sheep must, every one of them, pass under the hand of him that telleth them, if every man must stand in his own per son before God, to be tried for his own acts—by everything that is rational, by everything that conscience would dictate, and self-interest would command, let us each of us look to our own selves, that we be hot deceived, and that we find not ourselves, at last, miserably cast away.

THE great King, immortal, invisible, the Divine person, called the Holy Ghost, the Holy Spirit: it is he that quickens the soul, or else it would lie dead forever; it is he that makes it tender, or else it would never feel; it is he that imparts efficacy to the Word preached, or else it could never reach further than the ear; it is he who breaks the heart, it is he who makes it whole; he, from first to last, is the great worker of Salvation in us, just as Jesus Christ was the author of Salvation for us.

AS SURE as God is God, if you this day are seeking him aright, through Christ, the day shall come when the kiss of full assurance shall be on your lip, when the arms of sovereign love shall embrace you, and you shall know it to be so. Thou mayest have despised him, but thou shalt know, him yet to be thy Father and thy friend. Thou mayest have scoffed his name; thou shalt one day come to rejoice in it as better than pure gold. Thou mayest have broken his Sabbaths and despised his Word; the day is coming when the Sabbath shall be thy delight, and his Word thy treasure. Yes, marvel not; thou mayest have plunged into the kennel of sin and made thy clothes black with iniquity; but thou shalt one day stand before his throne white as the angels be; and that tongue that once cursed him shall yet sing his praise. If thou be a real seeker, the hands that have been stained with lust shall one day grasp the harp of gold, and the head that has plotted against the Most High shall yet be girt with gold. Seemeth it not a strange thing that God should do so much for sinners? But strange though it seem, it shall be strangely true.

WE do not care about 50,000 aphorisms, or syllogisms, or anything else. God's word against man's any day.

OUR God is no god who sits in one perpetual dream; nor doth he clothe himself in such thick darkness that he cannot see; he is not like Baal who heareth not. True, he may not regard battles; he cares not for the pomp and pageantry of kings; he listens not to the swell of martial music; he regards not the triumph and the pride of man; but whenever there is a heart big with sorrow, wherever there is an eye suffused with tears; wherever there is a lip quivering with agony, wherever there is a deep groan, or a penitential sigh, the ear of Jehovah is wide open; he marks it down in the registry of his memory; he puts our prayers, like rose leaves, between the pages of his book of remembrance, and when the volume is opened at last, there shall be a precious fragrance springing up therefrom.

GOD'S good pleasure is, that this world shall one day be totally redeemed from sin; God's good pleasure is, that this poor planet, so long swathed in darkness, shall soon shine out in brightness, like a newborn sun. Christ's death hath done it. The stream that flowed from his side on Calvary shall cleanse the world from all its blackness. That hour of mid-day darkness was the rising of a new sun of righteousness, which shall never cease to shine upon the earth. Yes, the hour is coming when swords and spears shall be forgotten things, when the harness of war and the pageantry of pomp shall all be laid aside for the food of the worm or the contemplation of the curious. The hour approacheth when old Rome shall shake upon her seven hills, when Mohammed's crescent shall wane to wax no more, when all the gods of the heathens shall lose their thrones and be cast out to the moles and to the bats; and then, when from the equator to the poles Christ shall be honored, the Lord paramount on earth, when from land to land, from the river even to the ends of the earth, one King shall reign, one shout shall be raised, "Hallelujah, hallelujah, the Lord God Omnipotent reigneth."

WITHOUT bread, I become attenuated to a skeleton; and, at last, I die. Without thought, my mind becomes dwarfed, aye, and dwindles itself until I become the idiot, with a soul that hath just life, but little more. And without Christ, my new born spirit must become a vague, shadowy emptiness. It cannot live unless it feeds on that heavenly manna which came down from heaven. Now the Christian can say, "The life that I live is Christ;" because Christ is the food on which he feeds, and the sustenance of his newborn spirit.

SINNER, let this be thy comfort, that God sees thee when thou beginnest to repent. He does not see thee with his usual gaze, with which he looks on all men, but he sees thee with an eye of intense interest. He has been looking on thee in all thy sin, and in all thy sorrow, hoping that thou wouldst re, pent; and now he sees the first gleam of grace, and he beholds it with joy. Never warder on the lonely castle top saw the first grey light of morning with more joy than that with which God beholds the first desire in thy heart. Never physician rejoiced more when he saw the first heaving of the lungs in one that was supposed to be dead, than God doth rejoice over thee, now that he sees the first token for good.

I HAVE seen the Christian man in the depths of poverty, when he lived from hand to mouth, and scarcely knew where he should find the next meal, still with his mind unruffled, calm, and quiet. If he had been as rich as an Indian prince, yet could he not have had less care; if he had been told that his bread should always come to his door, and the stream which ran hard by should never dry—if he had been quite sure that ravens would bring him bread and meat in the morning, and again in the evening, he would not have been one whit more calm.

OH, I reckon on the clay of death if it were for the mere hope of seeing the bright spirits that are now before the throne; to clasp the hand of Abraham, and Isaac, and Jacob, to look into the face of Paul the apostle, and grasp the hand of Peter; to sit in flowery fields with Moses and David, to bask in the sunlight of bliss with John and Magdalene. Oh, how blessed! The company of poor imperfect saints on earth is good; but how much better the society of the redeemed. Death is no loss to us by way of friends. We leave afew, a little band below, and say to them, "Fear not, little flock," and we ascend and meet the armies of the living God—the hosts of his redeemed. "To die is gain."

IF any one should ask me for an epitome of the Christian religion, I should say, it is in that one word—"prayer." If I should be asked, "What will take in the whole of Christian experience?" I should answer, "prayer." A man must have been convinced of sin before he could pray; he must have had some hope that there was mercy for him before he could pray. In fact, all the Christian virtues are locked up in that word, prayer. Do but tell me, you are a man of prayer, and I will reply at once, "Sir, I have no doubt of the reality, as well as the sincerity, of your religion."

IN the very beginning, when this great universe lay in the mind of God, like unborn forests in the acorn-cup; long ere the echoes walked the solitudes; before the mountains were brought forth; and long ere the light flashed through the sky, God loved his chosen creatures. Before there was creatureship— when the aether was not fanned by the angel's wing; when space itself had not an existence; when there was nothing save God alone; even then, in that loneliness of Deity, and in that deep quiet and profundity, his bowels moved for his chosen. Their names were written on his heart, and then were they dear to his soul.

THERE is an elect out of the elect, I will acknowledge, as to gifts and standing, and as to the labor they may accomplish in this world; but there is no election out of the elect as to a deeper extent of love. They are all loved alike; they are all written in the same book of eternal love and life.

WHEN I hear of a church where they are all gentlemen, I always say farewell to that, for where there are no poor, the ship will soon sink. If there are no poor, then, Christ will soon give them some, if they are a real Gospel church.

OH! it is a glorious fact, that prayers are noticed in heaven. The poor broken-hearted sinner, climbing up to his chamber, bends his knee, but can only utter his wailing in the language of sighs and tears. Lo! that groan has made all the harps of heaven thrill with music;

that tear has been caught by God, and put into the lachrymatory of heaven, to be perpetually preserved. The supplicant, whose fears prevent his words, will be well understood by the Most High.

YE lame! fear not; you will not be cast out. Two snails entered the ark; how they got there, I cannot tell. It must have taken them a long time. They must have set off rather early, unless is be that Noah took them part of the way. So, some of you are snails; you are on the right road, but it will take a long while, unless some blessed Noah helps you into the ark.

JESUS recognizes his family when they are black as the tents of Kedar, and he knows they shall be fair as the curtains of Solomon. He knows his children when they do not know themselves; when they fancy they are lost beyond rescue, or when they foolishly conceive that they can save themselves.

GIVE me the comforts of God, and I can well bear the taunts of men. Let me lay my head on the bosom of Jesus, and I fear not the distraction of care and trouble. If my God will give me ever the light of his smile, and glance his benediction—it is enough. Come on foes, persecutors, fiends, ay, Apollyon himself, for "the Lord God is my sun and shield." Gather, ye clouds, and environ me, I carry a sun within; blow, wind of the frozen north, I have a fire of living coal within yea, death, slay me, but I have another life—a life in the light of God's countenance.

BACKSLIDERS! fallen ones! God will have mercy if you are penitent. Glorious fact! the sorrowing backslider shall not be left behind. Backsliders shall sing above, as God's restored children, he ever has loved. Blind and lame ones! believe in the Lord, and you shall be found amongst the children of the Lamb at last.

YE may erect little thrones for those whom ye rightly love; but God's throne must be a glorious high throne; you may set them upon the steps, but God must sit on the very seat itself. He is to be enthroned, the royal One within your heart, the king of your affections.

DESPISE the world, rate its jewels at a low price, estimate its gems as paste, and its solidities as dreams. Think not that thou shalt thus lose pleasure, but rather remember the saying of Chrysostom, "Contemn riches, and thou shalt be rich; contemn glory, and thou shalt be glorious; contemn injuries, and thou shalt be a conqueror; contemn rest, and thou shalt gain rest; contemn earth, and thou shalt gain heaven!"

I GAZE on beauty, and may be myself deformed. I admire the light, and may yet dwell in darkness; but if the light of the countenance of God rests upon me, I shall become like unto Him: the lineaments of His visage will be on me, and the great out lines of His attributes will be mine. Oh, wondrous glass, which thus renders the beholder lovely! Oh, admirable mirror, which reflects not self with its imperfections, but gives a perfect image to those that are uncomely.

YOU cannot get to heaven by your works. You might as well seek to mount the stars on a treadwheel, as to go to heaven by works; for as you get up a step, you will always come down as low as before. If you cannot be perfect, God will not save you by works.

THE worm is not to murmur, because God did not make it an angel, and the fish that swims the sea must not complain because it hath not wings to fly into the highest heavens. God had a right to make his creatures just what he pleased, and though men may dispute his right, he will hold and keep it inviolate against all comers.

That he may hedge his right about and make vain man acknowledge it, in all his gifts he continually reminds us of his sovereignty.

DO you not know that God is an eternal self-existent Being; that to say he loves now, is, in fact, to say he always did love, since with God there is no past, and can be no future. What we call past, present, and future, he wraps in one eternal now. And if you say he loves you now, you say he loved yesterday; he loved in the past eternity; and he will love forever; for *now* with God is past, present, and future.

THEY that go forth to fight, boasting that they can do it, shall return with their banners trailed in the dust, and with their armor stained with defeat; for God will not go forth with the man who goeth forth in his own strength.

LET your mind rove upon the great doctrines of the Godhead: consider the existence of God from before the foundations of the world; behold Him who is, and was, and is to come, the Almighty; let your soul comprehend as much as it can of the Infinite, and grasp as much as possible of the Eternal, and I am sure, if you have minds at all, they will shrink with awe. The tall archangel bows himself before his Master's throne; and we shall cast ourselves into the lowest dust when we feel what base nothings, what insignificant specks we are when compared with our all-adorable Creator.

FAITH is the gift of God. Does my natural father love me because he fed me, and because he clothed me? Nay, he clothed and fed me because he loved me, but his love was prior to his gift. His gifts did not draw his love to me, because he loved me before he gave them. And if any man says, "God loves me because I can do this or that for him," he talks nonsense.

PEACE is the flowing of the brook, but joy is the dashing of the cataract when the brook is filled, bursts its banks, and rushes down the rocks.

MEN have said of many of their works, "they shall endure forever;" but how much have they been disappointed! In the age succeeding the flood, they made the brick, they gathered the slime, and when they had piled old Babel's tower, they said, "This shall last forever." But God confounded their language; they finished it not. By his lightnings he destroyed it, and left it a monument of their folly. Old Pharaoh and the Egyptian monarchs heaped up their pyramids, and they said, "They shall stand forever," and so indeed they do stand; but the time is approaching when age shall devour even these. So with all the proudest works of man, whether they have been his temples or his monarchies, he has written "everlasting" on them; but God has ordained their end, and they have passed away. The most stable things have been evanescent as shadows and the bubbles of an hour, speedily destroyed at God's bidding. Where is Nineveh, and where is Babylon? Where the cities of Persia? Where are the high places of Edom? Where are Moab, and the princes of Ammon? Where are the temples of the heroes of Greece? Where the millions that passed from the gates of Thebes? Where are the hosts of Xerxes, or where the vast armies of the Roman Emperors? Have they not passed away? And though in their pride they said, "This monarchy is an everlasting one; this queen of the seven hills shall be called the eternal city," its pride is dimmed; and she who sat alone, and said, "I shall be no widow, but a queen forever," she hath fallen, hath fallen, and in a little while she shall sink like a millstone in the flood, her name being a curse and a byword, and her site the habitation of dragons and of owls. Man calls his works eternal—God calls them fleeting; man conceives that they are built of rock—God says, "Nay, sand, or worse than that—they are air." Man says he erects them for eternity—God blows but for a moment, and where are they? Like baseless fabrics of a vision, they are passed and gone forever.

GOD'S Holy Spirit and man's sin cannot live to peaceably; they may both be in the same heart, but they cannot both reign there, nor can they both be quiet there; for "the Spirit lusteth against the flesh, and the flesh lusteth against the Spirit;" they cannot rest, but there will be a perpetual warring in the soul, so that the Christian will have to cry, "O wretched man that I am! who shall deliver me from the body of this death?" But in due time: the Spirit will drive out all sin, and will present us blameless before the throne of his Majesty with exceeding great joy.

———————————

WITHIN a hundred and fifty years how has the boasted power of reason changed! It has piled up one thing, and then another day it has laughed at its own handiwork, demolished its own castle, and constructed another, and the next day a third. It has a thousand dresses. Once it came forth like a fool with its bells, heralded by Voltaire; then it came out a braggard bully, like Tom Paine; then it changed its course, and assumed another shape, till, forsooth, we have it in the base, bestial secularism of the present day, which looks for naught but the earth, keeps its nose upon the ground, and like the beast, thinks this world is enough; or looks for another through seeking this. Why, before one hair on his head shall be grey, the last secularist shall have passed away; before many of us are fifty years of age, a new infidelity shall come, and to those who say "Where will saints be?" we can turn round and say, "Where are you?" And they will answer, "We have altered our names." They will have altered their name, assumed a fresh shape, put on a new form of evil, but still their nature will be the same; op posing Christ, and endeavoring to blaspheme his truths. On all their systems of religion, or non-religion—for that is a system too—it may be written "Evanescent; fading as the flower, fleeting as the meteor, frail and unreal as a vapor." But of Christ's religion, it shall be said, "His name shall endure forever." Let me now say a few things—not to prove it, for that I do not wish to do—but to give you some hints whereby, possibly, I may one day prove it to other people, that Jesus Christ's religion must inevitably endure forever.

YOU know, when we have been taking some kind of medicine, and our mouth has been impregnated with a strong flavor, whatever we eat acquires that taste. You have got your mouth out of taste with some of the world's poor dainties; you have some of the powder of the apples of Sodom hanging on your lips, that spoils the glorious flavor of your meditation on Jesus. In fact, it prevents your meditating on Christ at all. It is only a hearing of the meditation with your ears, not a receiving it with your hearts.

WARN the boatman before he enters the current, and then, if he is swept down the rapids, he destroys himself. Warn the man before he drinks the cup of poison, tell him it is deadly: and then, if he drinks it, his death lies at his own door. And so, let us warn you before you depart this life; let us preach to you while as yet your bones are full of marrow, and the sinews of your joints are not loosed.

FRIEND, thou hast not the Spirit. Then thou art nothing better— be thou what thou art, or what soever thou mayest be—than the fall of Adam left thee. That is to say, thou art a fallen creature, having only capacities to live here in sin, and to live forever in torment; but thou hast not the capacity to live in heaven at all, for thou hast no Spirit; and therefore thou art unable to know or enjoy spiritual things. And mark you, a man may be in this state, and be a sensual man, and yet he may have all the virtues that could grace a Christian; but with all these, if he has not the Spirit, he has got not an inch further than where Adam's fall left him—that is, condemned and under the curse. Aye, and he may attend to religion with all his might—he may take the sacrament, and be baptized, and may be the most devout professor; but if he hath not the Spirit he hath not started a solitary inch from where he was, for he is still in "the bonds of iniquity," a lost soul. Nay, further, he may pick up religious phrases till he may talk very fast about religion; he may read biographies till he seems to be a deep-taught child of God; he may be able to write an article

upon the deep experience of a believer; but if this experience be not
his own, if he hath not received it by the Spirit of the living God,
he is still nothing more than a carnal man, and heaven is to him
a place to which there is no entrance. Nay, further, he might go so
far as to be come a minister of the gospel, and a successful minister
too, and God may bless the word that he preaches to the salvation
of sinners, but unless he has received the Spirit, be he as eloquent
as Apollos, and as ear nest as Paul, he is nothing more than a mere
soulish man, without capacity for spiritual things. Nay, to crown all,
he might even have the power of working miracles, as Judas had—he
might even be received into the Church as a believer, as was Simon
Magus, and after all that, though he had cast out devils, though
he had healed the sick, though he had worked miracles, he might
have the gates of heaven shut in his teeth, if he had not received the
Spirit. For this is the essential thing, without which all others are in
vain—the reception of the Spirit of the living God.

SOME persons say they cannot bear to be an hour in solitude;
they have got nothing to do, nothing to think about. No Christian
will ever talk so, surely; for if I can but give him one word to think
of—Christ—let him spell that over forever; let me give him the word
Jesus, and only let him try to think it over, and he shall find that
an hour is naught, and that eternity is not half enough to utter our
glorious Savior's praise.

WHEN God sends rain upon the church, he "sends showers of
blessings." There are some ministers who think, that if there is a
shower on their church, God will send a shower of work. Yes, but if
he does, he will send a shower of comfort. Others think that God
will send a shower of gospel truth. Yes, but if he sends that, he will
send a shower of gospel holiness. For all God's blessings go together.
They are like the sweet sister graces that danced hand in hand. God
sends showers of blessings. If he gives comforting grace, he will also

give converting grace; if he makes the trumpet blow for the bankrupt sinner, he will also make it sound a shout of joy for the sinner that is pardoned and forgiven. He will bend "showers of blessings."

THE hour is coming, and it may be even now is, when the Holy Ghost shall be poured out again in such a wonderful manner, that many shall run to and fro, and knowledge shall be increased— the knowledge of the Lord shall cover the earth as the waters cover the surface of the great deep; when his kingdom shall come, and his will shall be done on earth even as it is in heaven. We are not going to be dragging on forever like Pharoah, with the wheels off his chariot. My heart exults, and my eyes flash with the thought that very likely I shall live to see the out-pouring of the Spirit; when "the sons and the daughters of God again shall prophesy, and the young men shall see visions, and the old men shall dream dreams." Perhaps there shall be no miraculous gifts—for they will not be required; but yet there shall be such a miraculous amount of holiness, such an extraordinary fervor of prayer, such a real communion with God, and so much vital religion, and such a spread of the doctrines of the cross, that every one will see that verily the Spirit is poured out like water, and the rains are descending from above. For that let us pray; let us continually labor for it, and seek it of God.

THE imagination will sometimes fly up to God with such a power that eagles' wings cannot match it. It sometimes has such might that it can almost see the King in his beauty, and the land which is very far off. With regard to myself, my imagination will sometimes take me over the gates of iron, across that infinite unknown, to the very gates of pearl, and discovers the blessed glorified. But, if it is potent one way, it is another: for my imagination has taken me down to the vilest kennels and sewers of earth. It has given me thoughts so dreadful, that, while I could not avoid them, yet I was thoroughly horrified at them. These thoughts will come; and when I feel in the holiest frame, the most devoted to God, and the most earnest in prayer, it often happens that that is the very time when the plague breaks out the worst. But I rejoice and think of one thing, that I can cry out when this imagination comes upon me. I know it is said in the Book of Leviticus, when an act of evil was committed, if the maiden cried out against it, then her life was to be spared. So it is with the Christian. If he cries out, there is hope. Can you chain your imagination? No; but the power of the Holy Ghost can. Ah, it shall do it! and it does do it at last, it does it even on earth.

ONCE I, like Mazeppa, bound on the wild horse of my lust, bound hand and foot, incapable of resistance, was galloping on with hell's wolves be hind me, howling for my body and my soul, as their just and lawful prey. There came a mighty hand which stopped that wild horse, cut my bonds, set me down, and brought me into liberty. Is there power? Aye, there is power; and he who has felt it, must acknowledge it. There was a time when I lived in the strong old castle of my sins, and rested on my works. There came a trumpeter to the door, and bade me open it. I with anger chid him from the porch, and said he ne'er should enter. There came a goodly personage, with loving countenance; his hands were marked with scars, where nails were driven, and his feet had nail-prints too; he lifted up his cross, using it as a hammer; at the first blow the gate of my prejudice shook; at the second it trembled more, at the third down it fell, and in he came; and he said, "Arise, and stand upon thy feet, for I have loved thee with an everlasting love."

JUST before I die sanctification will be finished; but not till that moment shall I ever claim perfection in myself. But at that moment when I depart, my spirit shall have its last baptism in the Holy Spirit's fire. It shall be put in the crucible for its last trying in the furnace; and then, free from all dross, and fine, like a wedge of pure gold, it shall be presented at the feet of God without the least degree of dross or mixture. O glorious hour! O blessed moment! Methinks I long to die if there were no heaven, if I might but have that last purification, and come up from Jordan's stream most white from the washing. Oh, to be washed white, clean, pure, perfect! Not an angel more pure than I shall be—yea, not God himself more holy! And I shall be able to say, in a double sense, "Great God, I am clean—through Jesus' blood I am clean, through the Spirit's work I am clean too!"

IF this earth could but have its mantle torn away for a little while, if the green sod could be cut from it, and we could look about six feet deep into its bowels, what a world it would seem! What should we see? Bones, carcasses, rottenness, worms, corruption. And you would say, Can these dry bones live? Can they start up? Yes! "in a moment! in the twinkling of an eye, at the last trump, the dead shall be raised." He speaks; they are alive! See them scattered! bone comes to his bone! See them naked; flesh comes upon them! See them still lifeless; "Come from the four winds, O breath, and breathe upon these slain!" "When the wind of the Holy Spirit comes, they live; and they stand upon their feet an exceeding great army.

THEOLOGY hath nothing new in it except that which is false. The preaching of Paul must be the preaching of the minister today. There is no advancement here. We may advance in our know ledge of it; but it stands the same, for this good reason, that it is perfect, and perfection cannot be any better.

THE resurrection of Christ was effected by the agency of the Spirit! and here we have a noble illustration of his omnipotence. Could you have stepped, as angels did, into the grave of Jesus, and seen his sleeping body, you would have found it cold as any other corpse. Lift up the hand; it falls by the side. Look at the eye; it is glazed. And there is' a death-thrust which must have annihilated life. See his hands: the blood distills not from them. They are cold and motionless. Can that body live? Can it start up? Yes; and be an illustration of the might of the Spirit. For when the power of the Spirit came on him, as it was when it fell upon the dry bones of the valley, "he arose in the majesty of his divinity, and, bright and shining, astonished the watchmen so that they fled away; yea, he arose no more to die, but to live forever, King of kings and Prince of the kings of the earth."

GOD is love in its highest degree. He is love rendered more than love. Love is not God, but God is love; he is full of grace, he is the plenitude of mercy—he delighteth in mercy. As high as the heavens are above the earth, so high are his thoughts of love above our thoughts of despair; and his ways of grace above our ways of fear. This God, in whom these three great attributes harmonize— illimitable sovereignty, inflexible justice, and unfathomable grace— these three make up the main attributes of the one God of heaven and earth whom the Christians worship.

I BID you take the meditation upon Christ, as a piece of scented stuff that was perfumed in heaven. It matters not what thou hast in thy house; this shall make it redolent of Paradise—shall make it smell like those breezes that once blew through Eden's garden, wafting the odor of flowers. Ah! there is nothing that can so console your spirits, and relieve all your distresses and troubles, as the feeling that now you can meditate on the person of Jesus Christ.

METHINKS, if you had a free pass to heaven's palace, you would use it very often; if you might go there and hold communion with some per son whom you dearly loved, you would often be found there. But here is your Jesus, the king of heaven, and he gives you that which can open the gates of heaven and let you in to hold company with him, and yet you live without meditating upon his work, meditating upon his person, meditating upon his offices, and meditating upon his glory.

JUST as the tiny shells make up the chalk hills, and the chalk hills together make up the range, so the trifling actions make up the whole account, and each of these must be pulled asunder separately. You had an hour to spare the other day—what did you do? You had a voice—how did you use it? You had a pen—you could use that—how did you employ it? Each particular shall be brought out, and there shall be demanded an account for each one.

IT IS well to be the sheep of God's pasture, even if we have been wandering sheep. The straying sheep has an owner, and however far it may stray from the fold, it ceases not to belong to that owner. I believe that God will yet bring back into the fold every one of his own sheep, and they shall all be saved. It is something to feel our wanderings, for if we feel ourselves to be lost, we shall certainly be saved; if we feel ourselves to have wandered, we shall certainly be brought back.

VIRTUES in unregenerate men are nothing but whitewashed sins. The best performance of an unchanged character is worthless in God's sight. It wants the stamp of grace on it; and that which has not the stamp of grace is false coin.

GOOD old Simeon called Jesus the consolation of Israel; and so he was. Before his actual appearance, his name was the day-star; cheering the darkness, and prophetic of the rising sun. To him they looked with the same hope which cheers the nightly watcher, when from the lonely castle-top he sees the fairest of the stars, and hails her as the usher of the morn. When he was on earth, he must have been the consolation of all those who were privileged to be his companions. "We can imagine how readily the disciples would run to Christ to tell him of their griefs, and how sweetly, with that matchless intonation of his voice, he would speak to them, and bid their fears be gone. Like children, they would consider him as their

Father; and to him every want, every groan, every sorrow, every agony, would at once be carried; and he, like a wise physician, had a balm for every wound; he had mingled a cordial for their every care; and readily did he dispense some mighty remedy to allay all the fever of their troubles. Oh! it must have been sweet to have lived with Christ. Surely, sorrows were then but joys in masks, because they gave an opportunity to go to Jesus to have them removed. Oh! would to God, some of us may say, that we could have lain our weary heads upon the bosom of Jesus, and that our birth had been in that happy era, when we might have heard his kind voice, and seen his kind look, when he said, "Let the weary ones come unto me."

It behooved him to slumber in the dust awhile, that he might perfume the chamber of the grave to make it—

> "No more a charnel house to fence
> The relics of lost innocence."

It behooved him to have a resurrection, that we, who shall one day be the dead in Christ, might rise first, and in glorious bodies stand upon earth. And it behooved him that he should ascend up on high, that he might lead captivity captive; that he might chain the fiends of hell; that he might lash them to his chariot-wheels, and drag them up high heaven's hill, to make them feel a second overthrow from his right arm, when he should dash them from the pinnacles of heaven down to the deeper depths beneath. "It is right I should go away from you," said Jesus, "for if I go not away, the Comforter will not come." Jesus must go. Weep, yo disciples: Jesus must be gone. Mourn, ye poor ones, who are to be left with out a Comforter. But hear how kindly Jesus speaks: "I will not leave you comfortless, I will pray the Father, and he shall send you another Comforter, who shall be with you, and shall dwell in you forever." he would not leave those few poor sheep alone in the wilderness; he would not desert his children, and leave them fatherless. Albeit that he had a mighty mission which did fill his heart and hand; albeit he had be much to perform, that we might have thought that even his gigantic intellect would be overburdened; albeit he had so much to suffer, that we might suppose his whole soul to be concentrated upon the thought of the sufferings to be endured. Yet it was not so; before he left, he gave soothing words of comfort; like the good Samaritan, he poured in oil and wine, and we see what he promised: "I will send you another Comforter—one who shall be just what I have been, yea, even more; who shall console you in your sorrows, remove your doubts, comfort you in your afflictions, and stand as my vicar on earth, to do that which I would have done had I tarried with you.

LET thy face ever wear a smile; let thine eyes sparkle with gladness; live near thy Master; live in the suburbs of the celestial city, as by and by when thy time shall come thou shalt borrow better wings than angels ever wore, and out-soar the cherubim, and rise up where thy Jesus sits—sit at his right hand, even as he has overcome and has sat down upon his Father's right hand.

MANY a good old Jerusalem blade has been blunted against the hard heart. Many a piece of the true steel that God has put into the hands of his servants has had the edge turned by being set up against the sinner's heart. We cannot reach the soul, but the Holy Spirit can. "My beloved can put in his hand by the hole in the door, and my bowels will move for sin." He can give a sense of blood-bought pardon that shall dissolve a heart of stone.

THE very fact that you have troubles is a proof of his faithfulness; for you have got one half of his legacy, and you will have the other half. You know that Christ's last will and testament has two portions in it. "In the world ye shall have tribulation:" you have got that. The next clause is—"In me ye shall have peace." You have that too. "Be of good cheer; I have overcome the world." That is yours also.

THERE will be little else we shall want of heaven besides Jesus Christ. He will be our bread, our food, our beauty, and our glorious dress. The atmosphere of heaven will be Christ; everything in heaven will be Christ-like: yea, Christ is the heaven of his people.

REST thee well assured, O scorner, that thy laughs cannot alter truth, thy jests cannot avert thine inevitable doom. Though in thy hardihood thou shouldst make a league with death, and sign a covenant with hell—yet swift justice shall overtake thee, and strong vengeance strike thee low. In vain dost thou jeer and mock, for eternal verities are mightier than thy sophistries, nor can thy smart sayings alter the divine truth of a single word of this volume of Revelation. Oh! why dost thou quarrel with thy best friend, and ill-treat thy only refuge? There yet remains hope, even for the scorner. Hope in a Savior's veins. Hope in the Father's mercy. Hope in the Holy Spirit's omnipotent agency.

IT is true that you have no fiery chariot; but then the angels carry you to Jesus' bosom, and that is as well. It is true, no ravens bring you food; it is quite as true you get your food somehow or other. It is quite certain that no rock gushes out with water; but still your water has been sure. It is true your child has not been raised from the dead; but you remember that David had a child that was not raised any more than yours. You have the same consolation as he had: "I shall go to him; he shall not return to me."

MEN in the days of Toplady looked back to the days of Whitfield; men in the days of Whitfield looked back to the days of Bunyan; men in the days of Bunyan wept, because of the days of Wycliffe, and Calvin, and Luther; and men then wept for the days of Augustine and Chrysostom. Men in those days wept for the days of the Apostles; and doubtless men in the days of the Apostles wept for the days of Jesus Christ; and no doubt some in the days of Jesus Christ were so blind as to wish to return to the days of prophesy, and thought more of the days of Elijah than they did of the most glorious day of Christ. Some men look more to the past than the present. Best assured, that Jesus Christ is the same today as he was yesterday, and he will be the same forever.

THE old truth that Calvin preached, that Chrysostom preached, that Paul preached, is the truth that I must preach today, or else be a liar to my conscience and my God. I cannot shape the truth. I know of no such thing as paring off the rough edges of a doctrine. John Knox's gospel is my gospel. That which thundered through Scotland must thunder through England again. The great mass of our ministers are sound enough in the faith, but not sound enough in the way they preach it.

THE Holy Ghost advocates our cause with Jesus Christ, with groanings that cannot be uttered. O my soul! thou art ready to burst within me. O my heart! thou art swelled with grief. The hot tide of thy emotion would well-nigh overflow the channels of my veins. I long to speak, but the very desire chains my tongue. I wish to pray, but tho fervency of my feeling curbs my language. There is a groaning within that cannot be uttered. Do you know who can utter that groaning? who can understand it, and who can put it into heavenly language, and utter it in a celestial tongue, so that Christ can hear it? O yes; it is God the Holy Spirit; he advocates our cause with Christ, and then Christ advocates it with his Father. He is the advocate who maketh intercession for us, with groanings that cannot be uttered.

YE may take a corpse, ye may dress it in all the garments of external decency; ye may wash it with the water of morality; aye, ye may bedeck it with the crown of profession, ye may put on its brow a tiara of beauty, ye may paint its cheeks, until ye make it well-nigh like life itself. But remember, unless the Spirit be there, the worm shall feed on the painted cheek, and corruption will ere long seize upon the body. It is the Spirit that is the quickener.

OH! there is a voice in love; it speaks a language which is its own; it has an idiom and a brogue which none can mimic; wisdom cannot imitate it; oratory cannot attain unto it; it is love alone which can reach the mourning heart; love is the only hand kerchief which can wipe the mourner's tears away. And is not the Holy Ghost a loving comforter? Dost thou know, O saint, how much the Holy Spirit loves thee? Canst thou measure the love of the Spirit? Dost thou know how great is the affection of his soul towards thee? Go measure heaven with thy span; go weigh the mountains in the scales; go take the ocean's water, and tell each drop; go count the sand upon the sea's wide shore; and when thou hast accomplished this, thou canst tell how much he loveth thee. He has loved thee long, he has loved thee well, he loved thee ever, and he still shall love thee; surely he is the person to comfort thee, because he loves.

SPIRITUAL ploughman! sharpen thy ploughshare with the Spirit. Spiritual sower! dip thy seed in the Spirit, so shall it germinate; and ask the Spirit to give thee grace to scatter it, that it may fall into the right furrows. Spiritual warrior! whet thy sword with the Spirit, and ask the Spirit, whose word is a sword indeed, to strengthen thine arm to wield it.

THE young *may* die; the old *must!* To sleep in youth is to sleep in a siege; to sleep in old age is to slumber during the attack. What! man, wilt thou that art so near thy Maker's bar still put him off with a "Go thy way?" What! procrastinate now, when the knife is at thy throat—when the worm is at the heart of the tree, and the branches have begun to wither—when the grinders fail even now, because they are few, and they that look out of the windows are darkened? The sere and yellow leaf has come upon thee, and thou art still unready for thy doom!

THE canon of revelation is closed; there is no more to be added; God does not give a fresh revelation, but he rivets the old one. When it has been forgotten, and laid in the dusty chamber of our memory, he fetches it out and cleans the picture, but does not paint a new one. There are no new doctrines, but the old ones are often revived. It is not, I say, by any new revelation that the Spirit comforts. He does so by telling us old things over again; he brings a fresh lamp to manifest the treasures hidden in Scripture; he unlocks the strong chests in which the truth has long lain, and he points to secret chambers filled with untold riches; but he coins no more, for enough is done. Believer! there is enough in the Bible for thee to live upon forever. If thou shouldst outnumber the years of Methuselah, there would be no need for a fresh revelation; if thou shouldst live till Christ should come upon the earth, there would be no necessity for the addition of a single word; if thou shouldst go down as deep as Jonah, or even descend as David said he did, into the belly of hell, still there would be enough in the Bible to comfort thee without a supplementary sentence.

WISDOM had had its time, and time enough; it had done its all, and that was little enough; it had made the world worse than it was before it stepped upon it, and "now," says God, "foolishness shall overcome wisdom; now ignorance, as ye call it, shall sweep away science; now (saith God), humble, child like faith shall crumble to the dust all the colossal systems your hands have piled." He calls his warriors. Christ puts his trumpet to his mouth, and up come the warriors, clad in fishermen's garb, with the brogue of the lake of Galilee—poor humble mariners. Here are the warriors, O wisdom, that are to confound thee; these are the heroes who shall overcome thy proud philosophers; these men are to plant their standard upon thy ruined walls, and bid them fall forever; these men and their successors are to exalt a gospel in the world which ye may laugh at as ab surd, which ye may sneer at as folly, but which shall be exalted above the hills, and shall be glorious even to the highest heavens.

THERE are moments when the eyes glisten with joy: and we can say, "we are persuaded, confident, certain." I do not wish to distress any one who is under doubt. Often gloomy doubts will prevail; there are seasons when you fear you have not been called, when you doubt your interest in Christ. Ah! what a mercy it is that it is not your hold of Christ that saves you, but his hold of you! What a sweet fact that it is not how you grasp his hand, but his grasp of yours, that saves you.

THE book of nature is an expression of the thoughts of God. We have God's terrible thoughts in the thunder and lightning; God's loving thoughts in the sunshine and the balmy breeze; God's bounteous, prudent, careful thoughts in the waving harvest and in the ripening meadow. We have God's brilliant thoughts in the wondrous scenes which are beheld from mountain-top and valley; and we have God's most sweet and pleasant thoughts of beauty in the little flowers that blossom at our feet.

I RECOLLECT standing on a seashore once, upon J- a narrow neck of land, thoughtless that the tide might come up. The tide kept continually washing up on either side, and, wrapped in thoughts, I still stood there, until at last there was the greatest difficulty in getting on shore. You and I stand each day on a narrow neck, and there is one wave coming up there; see, how near it is to your foot; and lo! another follows at every tick of the clock; "our hearts, like muffled drums, are heating funeral marches to the tomb."

A MARTYR is going to the stake; the halbert men are around him; the crowds are mocking, but he is marching steadily on. See, they bind him, with a chain around his middle, to the stake; they heap fagots all about him; the flame is lighted up; listen to his words: "Bless the Lord O my soul, and all that is within me, bless his holy name." The flames are kindling round his legs; the fire is burning him even to the bone; see him lift up his hands and say, "I know that my Redeemer liveth, and though the fire devour this body, yet in my flesh shall I see the Lord." Behold him clutch the stake and kiss it, as if he loved it, and hear him say, "For every chain of iron that man girdeth me with, God shall give to me a chain of gold; for all these fagots, and this ignominy and shame, he shall increase the weight of my eternal glory." See all the under parts of his body are consumed; still he lives in the torture; at last he bows himself, and the upper part of his body falls over; and as he falls you hear him say, "Into thy hands I commend my spirit." What wondrous magic was on him, sirs? What made that man strong? What helped him to bear that cruelty? What made him stand unmoved in the flames? It was the thing of power; it was the cross of Jesus crucified. For "unto us who are saved it is the power of God."

THERE have been many, like infants, destroyed by elixirs, given to lull them to sleep; many have been mined by the cry of "peace, peace," when there is no peace; hearing gentle things, when they ought to be stirred to the quick. Cleopatra's asp was brought in a basket of flowers; and men's ruin often lurks in fair and sweet speeches. But the Holy Ghost's comfort is safe, and you may rest on it. Let him speak the word, and there is a reality about it; let him give the cup of consolation, and you may drink it to the bottom; for in its depths there are no dregs, nothing to intoxicate or ruin; it is all safe.

THE gospel is the sum of wisdom; an epitome of knowledge; a treasure-house of truth; and a revelation of mysterious secrets. In it we see how justice and mercy may be married; here we behold inexorable law entirely satisfied, and sovereign love bearing away the sinner in triumph. Our meditation upon it enlarges the mind; and as it opens to our soul in successive flashes of glory, we stand astonished at the profound wisdom manifest in it. Ah, dear friends! if ye seek wisdom, ye shall see it dis played in all its greatness; not in the balancing of the clouds, nor the firmness of earth's foundations; not in the measured march of the armies of the sky, nor in the perpetual motions of the waves of the sea; not in vegetation with all its fairy forms of beauty, nor in the animal with its marvelous tissue of nerve, and vein, and sinew; nor even in man, that last and loftiest work of the Creator. But turn aside and see this great sight!—an incarnate God upon the cross; a substitute atoning for mortal guilt; a sacrifice satisfying the vengeance of Heaven, and delivering the rebellious sinner. Here is essential wisdom; en throned, crowned, glorified. Admire, ye men of earth, if ye be not blind; and ye who glory in your learning bend your heads in reverence, and own that all your skill could not have devised a gospel at once so just to God, so safe to man.

WHAT is it that makes the young man devote himself, as a missionary, to the cause of God, to leave father and mother, and go into distant lands? It is a thing of power that does it; it is the gospel. What is it that constrains yonder minister, in the midst of cholera, to climb up that creaking staircase, and stand by the bed of some dying creature who has that dire disease? It must be a thing of power which leads him to venture his life; it is love of the cross of Christ which bids him do it. What is that which enables one man to stand up before a multitude of his fellows, all unprepared it may be, but determined that he will speak nothing but Christ, and him crucified? What is it that enables him to cry, like the war horse of Job, in battle, Aha! and move glorious in might? It is a thing of power that does it: it is Christ crucified. And what emboldens that timid female to walk down that dark lane some wet evening, that she may go and sit beside tho victim of a contagious fever? What strengthens her to go through that den of thieves, and pass by the profligate and profane?

What influences her to enter into that charnel house of death, and there sit down and whisper words of comfort? Does gold make her do it? They are too poor to give her gold. Does fame make her do it? She shall never be known nor written among the mighty women of this earth. What makes her do it? Is it love of merit? No; she knows she has no desert before high heaven. What impels her to it? It is the power, the thing of power; it is the cross of Christ: she loves it, and she therefore says,

> "Were the whole realm of nature mine,
> That were a present far too small;
> Love so amazing, so divine,
> Demands my soul, my life, my all."

O YOUNG man, build thy studio on Calvary! v7 there raise thine observatory, and scan by faith the lofty things of nature. Take thee a hermit's cell in the garden of Gethsemane, and lave thy brow with the waters of Siloa. Let the Bible be thy standard classic—thy last appeal in matters of contention. Let its light be thine illumination, and thou shalt become more wise than Plato, more truly learned than the seven sages of antiquity.

O MAN! of all fools, a fool with a grey head is the worst fool anywhere. With one foot in the grave, and another foot on a sandy foundation, how shall I depict you, but by saying to you as God said to the rich man, "Thou fool! a few more nights and thy soul shall be required of thee;" and then where art thou?

WHEN the Gospel was first preached, instead of being accepted and admired, one universal hiss went up to heaven; men could not hear it; its first preacher they dragged to the brow of the hill, and would have sent him down headlong; yea, they did more—they nailed him to the cross, and there they let him languish out his dying life in agony such as no man hath borne since. All his chosen ministers have been hated and abhorred by worldlings; instead of being listened to, they have been scoffed at; treated as if they were the offscouring of all things, and the very scum of mankind. Look at the holy men in the old times, how they were driven from city to city, persecuted, afflicted, tormented, stoned to death, wherever the enemy had power to do so. Those friends of men, those real philanthropists, who came with hearts big with love, and hands full of mercy, and lips pregnant with celestial fire, and souls that burned with holy influence; those men were treated as if they were spies in the camp, as if they were deserters from the common cause of mankind; as if they were enemies, and not, as they truly were, the best of friends. Do not suppose that men like the gospel any better now than they did then. There is an idea that you are growing better. I do not believe it. You are growing worse. In many respects men may be better—outwardly better; but the heart within is still the same. The human heart of today dissected, would he just like the human heart a thou sand years ago; the gall of bitterness within that breast of yours, is just as bitter as the gall of bitterness in that of Simon of old. We have in our hearts the same latent opposition to the truth of God; and hence we find men, even as of old, who scorn the gospel.

IF you feel at any time "death working in you," as doubtless you will, withering the bloom of your piety, chilling the fervor of your devotions, and quenching the ardor of your faith, remember, he who first quickened you must keep you alive. The Spirit of God is like the sap that flowed into your poor dry branch, because you were grafted into Christ, and as by that sap you were first made green with life, so it is by that sap alone you can ever bring forth fruit to God.

WHEN thou art wrestling, like Jacob with the angel, and art nearly thrown down, ask the Holy Spirit to nerve thine arm. Consider how the Holy Spirit is the chariot-wheel of prayer. Prayer may be the chariot, the desire may draw it forth, but the Spirit is the very wheel whereby it moveth.

A GOSPEL without a Trinity! it is a pyramid built upon its apex. A gospel without the Trinity! it is a rope of sand that cannot hold together. A gospel without the Trinity! then, indeed, Satan can overturn it. But, give me a gospel with the Trinity, and the might of hell cannot prevail against it; no man can any more overthrow it than a bubble could split a rock, or a feather break in halves a mountain. Get the thought of the three persons, and you have the marrow of all divinity. Only know the Father, and know the Son, and know the Holy Ghost to be one, and all things will appear clear. This is the golden key to the secrets of nature; this is the silken clue of the labyrinths of mystery, and he who under stands this, will soon understand as much as mortals e'er can know.

YOU know more about your ledgers than your Bible; you know more about your day-books than what God has written; many of you will read a novel from beginning to end, and what have you got? A mouthful of froth when you have done. But you cannot read the Bible; that solid, lasting, substantial, and satisfying food goes uneaten, locked up in the cupboard of neglect; while anything that man writes, a catch of the day, is greedily devoured.

THE science of Jesus Christ is the most excellent of sciences. Let no one turn away from the Bible because it is not a book of learning and wisdom. It is. Would ye know astronomy? It is here: it tells you of the Sun of Righteousness and the Star of Bethlehem. Would you know botany? It is here: it tells you of the plant of renown—the Lily of the Valley, and the Rose of Sharon. Would you know geology and mineralogy? You shall learn it here: for you may read of the Rock of Ages, and the White Stone with the name engraven thereon, which no man knoweth saving he that receiveth it. Would ye study history? Here is the most ancient of all the records of the history of the human race. Whate'er your science is, come and bend o'er this book; your science is here. Come and drink out of this fair fount of knowledge and wisdom, and ye shall find yourselves made wise unto salvation.

HAST thou now a sweet temper, whereas thou once wast passionate? Boast not of it; thou wilt be angry yet again if he leaves thee. Art thou now pure, whereas thou wast once unclean? Boast not of thy purity; it is a plant, the seed of which was brought from heaven; it never was within thy heart by nature; it is of God's gift, and God's alone.

OUR world has two forces; it has one tendency to run off at a tangent from its orbit; but the sun draws it by a centripetal power, and attracts it to itself, and so between the two forces it is kept in a perpetual circle. Oh! Christian, thou wilt never walk aright, and keep in the orbit of truth, if it be not for the influence of Christ perpetually attracting thee to the center. Thou feelest, and if thou dost not feel always, it is still there—thou feelest an attraction between thine heart and Christ, and Christ is perpetually drawing thee to himself, to his likeness, to his character, to his love, to his bosom, and in that way thou art kept from thy natural tendency to fly off and to be lost in the wide fields of sin. Bless God, that Christ lifted up draws all his people unto him in that fashion.

DO you see the cat? She sits there, and will lick her paws and wash herself clean. I see that, said the other. Well, said the first speaker, did you ever hear of one of the hogs taken out of the sty that did so? No, said he. But he could if he liked, said the other. Ah! verily he could if he liked; but it is not according to his nature, and you never saw such a thing done, and until you have changed the swine's nature, he cannot perform such a good action, and God's word says the same of man.

CAST your troubles where you have cast your sins; you have cast your sins into the depth of the sea, there cast your troubles also. Never keep a trouble half an hour on your own mind before you tell it to God. As soon as the trouble comes, quick, the first thing, tell it to your father. Remember, that the longer you take telling your trouble to God, the more your peace will be impaired. The longer the frost lasts, the more likely the ponds will be frozen.

HOW wise the Holy Spirit is! he takes the soul, lays it on the table, and dissects it in a moment; he finds out the root of the matter, he sees where the complaint is, and then he applies the knife where something is required to be taken away, or puts a plaster where the sore is; and he never mistakes. O, how wise is the blessed Holy Ghost; from every comforter I turn and leave them all, for thou art he who alone givest the wisest consolation.

CULTIVATE a cheerful disposition; endeavor, as much as lieth in you, always to bear a smile about with you; recollect that this is as much a command of God as that one which says, "Thou shalt love the Lord with all thy heart."

CHRIST JESUS was an attractive preacher; he sought above all means to set the pearl in a frame of gold, that it might attract the attention of the people. He was not willing to place himself in a parish church, and preach to a large congregation of thirteen and a-half, like our good brethren in the city, but would preach in such a style that people felt they must go to hear him. Some of them gnashed their teeth in rage and left his presence in wrath, but the multitudes still thronged to him to hear and to be healed. It was no dull work to hear this King of preachers, he was too much in earnest to be dull, and too humane to be incomprehensible.

IT WAS once said by Solon, "No man ought to be called a happy man till he dies," because he does not know what his life is to be; but Christians may always call themselves happy men here, because wherever their tent is carried, they cannot pitch it where the cloud does not move, and where they are not surrounded by a circle of fire. "I will be a wall of fire round about them, and their glory in the midst." They cannot dwell where God is not householder, warder, and bulwark of salvation.

> "All my ways shall ever be
> Order'd by His wise decree."

OH! ye that are not Christians, it were worth while to be Christians, if it were only for the peace and happiness that religion gives. If we had to die like dogs, yet this religion were worth having to make us live here like angels. Oh, if the grave were what it seems to be, the goal of all existence, if the black nails of the coffin were not bright with stars, if death were the end and our lamps were quenched in darkness, when it was said, "Dust to dust and earth to earth;" yet 'twere worth while to be a child of God, only to live here.

WE dream of everything in the world, and a few things more! If we were asked to tell our dreams, it would be impossible. You dream that you are at a feast; lo! the viands change into a Pegasus, and you are riding through the air; or, again, suddenly transformed into a morsel for a monster's meal. Such is life. The changes occur as suddenly as they happen in a dream. Men have been rich one day, they have been beggars the next. We have witnessed the exile of monarchs, and the flight of a potentate: or, in another direction, we have seen a man, neither reputable nor honorable in station, at a single stride exalted to a throne; and you who would have shunned him in the streets before, were foolish enough to throng your thoroughfares to stare at him. Ah! such is life. Leaves of the Sibyl were not more easily moved by tho winds, nor are dreams more variable:

"Boast not thyself of tomorrow, for thou knowest not what a day may bring forth."

BETTER have two lights than only one. The light of creation is a bright light. God may be seen in the stars; his name is written in gilt letters on the brow of night; you may discover his glory in the ocean waves, yea, in the trees of the field; but it is better to read it in two boots than in one. You will find it here more clearly revealed; for he has written this book himself, and he has given you the key to understand it, if you have the Holy Spirit. Ah, beloved, let us thank God for this Bible; let us love it; let us count it more precious than much fine gold.

HOW foolish are those men who wish to pry into futurity; the telescope is ready, and they are looking through; but they are so anxious to see, that they breathe on the glass with their hot breath, and they dim it, so that they can discern nothing but clouds and darkness.

EVERY now and then we turn up a fair stone which i lies upon the greeensward of the professing church, surrounded with the verdure of apparent goodness, and to our astonishment we find beneath all kinds of filthy insects and loathsome reptiles, and in our disgust at such hypocrisy, we are driven to exclaim, "All men are liars; there are none in whom we can put any trust at all." It is not fair to say so of all; but really, the discoveries which are made of the insincerity of our fellow creatures are enough to make us despise our kind, because they can go so far in appearances, and yet have so little soundness of heart.

OUR Bible is a blood-stained book. The blood of martyrs is on the Bible, the blood of translators and confessors. The pool of holy baptism in which ye have been baptized is a blood-stained pool: full many have had to die for the vindication of that baptism which is the answer of a good conscience towards God. The doctrines which we preach to you are doctrines that have been baptized in blood—swords have been drawn to slay the confessors of them; and there is not a truth which has not been sealed by them at the stake, or the block, or far away on the lofty mountains, where they have been slain by hundreds.

GOD might, if he pleased, wrap himself with night as with a garment; he might put the stars around his wrist for bracelets, and bind the suns around his brow for a coronet; he might dwell alone, far, far above this world, up in the seventh heaven, and look down with calm and silent indifference upon all the doings of his creatures; he might do as the heathens supposed their Jove did, sit in perpetual silence, sometimes nodding his awful head to make the fates move as he pleased, but never taking thought of the little things of earth, disposing of them as beneath his notice, engrossed within his own being, swallowed up within himself, living alone and retired; and I, as one of his creatures, might stand by night upon a mountain-top, and look upon the silent stars and say, "Ye are the eyes of God, but ye look not down on me; your light is the gift of his omnipotence, but your rays are not smiles of love to me. God, the mighty Creator, has for gotten me; I am a despicable drop in the ocean of creation, a sear-leaf in the forest of beings, an atom in the mountain of existence. He knows me not; I am alone, alone, alone." But it is not so, beloved. Our God is of another order. He notices every one of us; there is not a sparrow or a worm but is found in his decrees. There is not a person upon whom .his eye is not fixed. Our most secret acts are known to him. Whatsoever we do, or bear, or suffer, the eye of God still rests upon us, and we are beneath his smile—for we are his people; or beneath his frown—for we have erred from him.

ANY husbandman can get a good crop out of good soil; but God is the husbandman who can grow cedars on rocks, who cannot only put the hyssop upon the wall, but put the oak there too, and make the greatest faith spring up in the most unlikely position. All glory to his grace! the great sinner may become great in faith. Be of good cheer, then, sinner! If Christ should make thee repent, thou hast no need to think that thou shalt be the least in the family. Oh! no; thy name may yet be written among the mightiest of the mighty, and thou mayest stand as a memorable and triumphant instance of the power of faith.

IF we look on a thing in the dark, we cannot see it; but we have done what we were told. So, if a sinner only looks to Jesus, he will save him; for Jesus in the dark is as good as Jesus in the light; and Jesus, when you cannot see him, in as good as Jesus when you can.

THERE was an evil hour when once I shipped the anchor of my faith; I cut the cable of my belief; I no longer moored myself hard by the coasts of Revelation; I allowed my vessel to drift before the wind; I said to reason, "Be thou my captain;" I said to my own brain, "Be thou my rudder;" and I started on my mad voyage. Thank God, it is all over now; but I will tell you its brief history. It was one hurried sailing over the tempestuous ocean of free thought. I went on, and as I went, the skies began to darken; but to make up for that deficiency, the waters were brilliant with coruscations of brilliancy. I saw sparks flying upward that pleased me, and I thought, "If this be free thought, it is a happy thing." My thoughts seemed gems, and I scattered stars with both my hands; but anon, instead of these coruscations of glory, I saw grim fiends, fierce and horrible, start up from the waters, and as I dashed on, they gnashed their teeth, and grinned upon me; they seized the prow of my ship and dragged me on, while I, in part, glorified at the rapidity of my motion, but yet shuddered at the terrific rate with which I passed the old land-marks of my faith. As I hurried forward with an awful speed, I began to doubt my very existence; I doubted if there were a world, I doubted if there were such a thing as my self. I went to the very verge of the dreamy realms of unbelief. I went to the very bottom of the sea of Infidelity. I doubted everything. But here the devil foiled himself: for the very extravagance of the doubt, proved its absurdity. Just when I saw the bottom of that sea, there came a voice which said, "And can this doubt be true?" At this very thought I awoke. I started from that death-dream, which, God knows, might have damned my soul, and ruined this, my body, if I had not awoke. When I arose, faith took the helm; from that moment I doubted not. Faith steered me back; faith cried, "Away, away!" I cast my anchor on Calvary; I lifted my eye to God; and here I am, "alive, and out of hell."

THIS world is turning round on its axis once in four-and-twenty horn's; and besides that, it is moving round the sun in the 365 days of the year. So that we are all moving; we are all flitting along through space. And as we are traveling through space, so we are moving through time at an incalculable rate. Oh! what an idea it is could we grasp it! We are all being carried along as if by a giant angel, with broad outstretched wings, which he flaps to the blast, and flying before the lightning, makes us ride on the winds. The whole multitude of us are hurrying along—whither, remains to be decided by the test of our faith and the grace of God; but certain it is, we are all traveling. Do not think that you are stable things; fancy not that you are standing still; you are not. Your pulses each moment beat the funeral marches to the tomb. You are chained to the chariot of rolling time; there is no bridling the steeds, or leaping from the chariot; you must be constantly in motion.

CHRIST is the chariot in which souls are drawn to heaven. The people of the Lord are on their way to heaven, they are carried in everlasting arms; and those arms are the arms of Christ. Christ is carrying them up to his own house, to his own throne; by and by his prayer—"Father, I will that they, whom thou hast given me, be with me where I am," shall be wholly fulfilled. And it is fulfilling now, for he is like a strong courser drawing his children in the chariot of the covenant of grace unto himself. Oh! blessed be God, the cross is the plank on which we swim to heaven; the cross is the great covenant transport which will weather out the storms, and reach its desired heaven. This is the chariot, the pillars wherewith are of gold, and the bottom thereof silver, it is lined with the purple of the atonement of our Lord Jesus Christ.

THE Bible is the writing of the living God: each letter was penned with an Almighty finger; each word in it dropped from the everlasting lips; each sentence was dictated by the Holy Spirit. Albeit, that Moses was employed to write his histories with his fiery pen, God guided that pen. It may be that David touched his harp, and let sweet Psalms of melody drop from his fingers; but God moved his hands over the living strings of his golden harp. It may be that Solomon sang canticles of love, or gave forth words of consummate wisdom, but God directed his lips, and made the preacher eloquent. If I follow the thundering Nahum, when his horses plough the waters, or Habakkuk, when he sees the tents of Cushan in affliction; if I read Malachi, when the earth is burning like an oven; if I turn to the smooth page of John, who tells of love, or the rugged, fiery chapters of Peter, who speaks of fire devouring God's enemies; If I turn to Jude, who launches forth anathemas upon the foes of God, everywhere I find God speaking; it is God's voice, not man's; the words are God's words, the words of the Eternal, the Invisible, the Almighty, the Jehovah of this earth. This Bible is God's Bible, and when I see it, I seem to hear a voice springing up from it, saying, "I am the book of God; man, read me. I am God's writing; open my leaf, for I was penned by God; read it, for he is my author, and you will see him visible and manifest everywhere." "I have written to him the great things of my law."

A PILGRIM sets out in the morning, and he has to journey many a day before he gets to the shrine which he seeks. What varied scenes the traveler will behold on his way! Sometimes he will be on the mountains, anon he will descend into the valleys; here he will be where the brooks shine like silver, where the bird's warble, where the air is balmy, and the trees are green, and luscious fruits hang down to gratify his taste; anon he will find himself in the arid desert, where no life is found, and no sound is heard, except the screech of the wild eagle in the air, where he finds no rest for the sole of his foot—the burning sky above him, and the hot sand beneath him—no roof-tree, and no house to rest himself; at another time he finds himself in a sweet oasis, resting himself by the wells of water, and plucking fruit from palm trees. One moment he walks between the rocks in some narrow gorge, where all is darkness; at another time he ascends the hill, Mizar; now he descends into the valley of Baca; anon he climbs the hill of Bashan, "a high hill is the hill Bashan;" and yet again going into a den of leopards, he suffers trial and affliction. Such is life—ever changing. Who can tell what may come next? Today it is fair, the next day there may be the thundering storm; today I may want for nothing, tomorrow I may he like Jacob, with nothing but a stone for my pillow, and the heavens for my curtains. But what a happy thought it is, though we know not where the road winds, we know where it ends. It is the straightest way to heaven to go round about. Israel's forty years' wanderings were, after all, the nearest path to Canaan. We may have to go through trial and affliction; the pilgrimage may be a tiresome one, but it is safe; we cannot trace the river upon which we are sailing, but we know it ends in floods of bliss at last. We cannot track the roads, but we know that they all meet in the great metropolis of heaven, in the center of God's universe. God help us to pursue the true pilgrimage of a pious life!

THERE is no loss in being a Christian, and making God the first object; but make anything else your goal, and with all your running, should you run ever so well, you shall fall short of the mark; or if you gain it, you shall fall uncrowned, unhonored to the earth. "My soul, wait thou only upon God."

IF it would take me seven years to describe the way of salvation, I am sure you would all long to hear it. If only one learned doctor could tell the way to heaven, how would he be run after! And if it were in hard words, with a few scraps of Latin and Greek, it would be all the better. But it is a simple gospel that we have to preach. It is only "Look!" "Ah!" you say, "is that the gospel? I shall not pay any attention to that." But why has God ordered you to do such a simple thing? Just to take down your pride, and to show you that he is God, and that beside him there is none else. Oh, mark how simple the way of salvation is. It is, "Look! look! look!" Four letters, and two of them alike! "Look unto me, and be ye saved, all the ends of the earth."

FAITH is to say, that "mountains, when in darkness hidden, are as real as in day." Faith is to look through that cloud, not with the eye of sight, which seeth naught, but with the eye of faith, which seeth everything, and to say, "I trust him when I cannot trace him; I tread the sea as firmly as I would the rock; I walk as securely in the tempest as in the sunshine, and lay myself to rest upon the surging billows of the ocean as contentedly as upon my bed."

AS a man does not make himself spiritually alive, so neither can he keep himself so. He can feed on spiritual food, and so preserve his spiritual strength; he can walk in the commandments of the Lord, and so enjoy rest and peace, but still the inner life is dependent upon the Spirit as much for its after existence as for its first begetting. I do verily believe that if it should ever be my lot to put my foot upon the golden threshold of Paradise, and put this thumb upon the pearly latch, I should never cross the threshold unless I had grace given me to take that last step whereby I might enter heaven. No man himself, even when converted, hath any power, except as that power is daily, constantly, and perpetually infused into him by the spirit.

OH! IT IS a happy way of smoothing sorrow, when we can say, "We will wait only upon God." Oh, ye agitated Christians, do not dishonor your religion by always wearing a brow of care; come, cast your burden upon the Lord. I see ye staggering beneath a weight which He would not feel. What seems to you a crushing burden, would be to him but as the small dust of the balance. See! the Almighty bends his shoulders, and he says, "Here, put thy troubles here."

MOST of the grand truths of God have to be learned by trouble; they must be burned into us with the hot iron of affliction, otherwise we shall not truly receive them. No man is competent to judge in matters of the kingdom, until first he has been tried; since there are many things to be learned in the depths which we can never know in the heights. We discover many secrets in the caverns of the ocean, which, though we had soared to heaven, we never could have known. He shall best meet the wants of God's people as a preacher who has had those wants himself; he shall best comfort God's Israel who has needed comfort; and he shall best preach salvation who has felt his own need of it.

IF I desired to put myself into the most likely place for the Lord to meet with me, I should prefer the house of prayer, for it is in preaching, that the Word is most blessed; but still I think I should equally desire the reading of the Scriptures; for I might pause over every verse, and say, "Such a verse was blessed to so many souls; then, why not to me? I am at least in the pool of Bethesda; I am walking amongst its porches, and who can tell but that the angel will stir the pool of the Word, whilst I lie helplessly by the side of it, waiting for the blessing?"

OH! it is not some hectic flush upon the cheek of consumptive irresolution that God counts to be the health of obedience. It is not some slight obedience for an hour that God will accept at the day of judgment. He saith "continueth;" and unless from my early childhood to the day when my grey hairs descend into the tomb, I shall have continued to be obedient to God, I must be condemned. Unless I have from the first dawn of reason, when I first began to be responsible, obediently served God, until, like a shock of corn, I am gathered into my Master's garner, salvation by works must be impossible to me, and I must (standing on my own footing), be condemned. It is not. I say, some slight obedience that will save the soul. Thou hast not continued "in all things which are written in the book of the law," and therefore, thou art condemned.

REMEMBER to put thine eyes heavenward, and 'thine heart heavenward, too. Remember that thou bind round thyself a golden chain, and put one link of it in the staple in heaven. Look unto Christ; fear not. There is no stumbling when a man walks with his eyes up to Jesus. He that looked at the stars fell into the ditch; but he that looks at Christ walks safely.

BEHOLD the unpillared arch of heaven; see how it stretches its gigantic span; and yet it falleth not, though it is unpropped and unbuttressed, "He hangeth the world upon nothing." What chain is it that bindeth up the stars, and keepeth them from falling? Lo, they float in ether, upheld by his omnipotent arm, who hath laid the foundations of the universe. A Christian should be a second exhibition of God's universe; his faith should be an unpillared confidence, resting on the past, and on the eternity to come, as the sure groundwork of its arch. His faith should be like the world; it should hang on nothing but the promise of God, and have no other support but that; and he himself, like the stars, should float in the ether of confidence, needing nothing to uphold him but the right hand of the Majesty on high.

CHILDREN sometimes blow bubbles, and amuse themselves thereby. Life is even as that bubble. You see it rising into the air; the child delights itself by seeing it fly about, but it is all gone in one moment. "It is even a vapor, that appeareth for a little time, and then vanisheth away." But if you ask the poet to explain this, he would tell you that in the morning, sometimes at early dawn, tho rivers send up a steamy offering to the sun. There is a vapor, a mist, an exhalation rising from the rivers and brooks, but in a very little while after the sun has risen, all that mist has gone. Hence we read of the morning cloud and the early dew that passeth away. A more common observer, speaking of a vapor, would think of those thin clouds you some times see floating in the air, which are so light that they are soon carried away. Indeed, a poet uses them as the picture of feebleness:

> "Their hosts are scatter'd, like thin clouds
> Before a Biscay gale."

The wind moves them, and they are gone. "What is your life?"

SO mighty is the ever-rushing torrent of sin, that no arm but that which is as strong as Deity can ever stop the sinner from being hurried down to the gulf of black despair, and, when nearing that gulf, so impetuous is the torrent of divine wrath, that nothing can snatch the soul from perdition but an atonement which is as divine as God himself. Yet faith is the instrument of accomplishing the whole work. It delivers the sinner from the stream of sin, and so, laying hold upon the omnipotence of the Spirit, it rescues him from that great whirlpool of destruction into which his soul was being hurried.

MAN is like a great icicle, which the sun of time is continually thawing, and which is soon to be water spilt upon the ground that cannot be gathered up. Who can recall the departed spirit, or inflate the lungs with a new breath of life? Who can put vitality into the heart, and restore the soul from Hades? None. It cannot be gathered up. The place shall know it no more forever.

But here a sweet thought charms us. This water cannot be lost, but it shall descend into the soil to filter through the Rock of Ages, at last to spring up a pure fountain in heaven, cleansed, purified, and made clear as crystal. How terrible if, on the other hand, it should percolate the black earth of sin, and hang in horrid drops in the dark caverns of destruction!

AND all these—all this vast gathering of human souls, are joining in one cry—all moving in one direction. Oh, thought, at which the faithful well may weep; their cry is self, their course is sin. Here and there are the chosen few struggling against the mighty tide; but the masses, the multitude, still, as in the days of David, are hurrying their mad career in search of a fancied good, and reaping the fruit of the futile search in disappointment, death and hell.

PERHAPS the most miserable people in the world are the very careful ones. You that are so anxious about what shall happen on the morrow that you cannot enjoy the pleasures of today, you who have such a peculiar cast of mind that you suspect every star to be a comet, and imagine that there must be a volcano in every grassy mead, you that are more attracted by the spots in the sun than by the sun himself, and more amazed by one sear leaf upon the tree than by all the verdure of the woods— you that make more of your troubles than you could do of your joys—I say, I think you belong to the most miserable of men.

FROM the cross of Calvary, where the bleeding hands of Jesus drop mercy; from the garden of Gethsemane, where the bleeding pores of the Savior sweat pardons, the cry comes, "Look unto me, and be ye saved, all the ends of the earth." From Calvary's summit, where Jesus cries, "It is finished," I hear a shout, "Look, and be saved."

But there comes a vile cry from our soul, "Nay, look to yourself! look to yourself!" Ah, look to yourself, and you will be damned. That certainly will come of it. As long as you look to yourself there is no hope for you. It is not a consideration of what you are, but a consideration of what God is, and what Christ is, that can save you. It is looking from yourself to Jesus. Oh! there be men that quite misunderstand the gospel; they think that righteousness qualifies them to come to Christ; whereas sin is the only qualification for a man to come to Jesus. Good old Crisp says, "Righteousness keeps me from Christ: the whole have no need of a physician, but they that are sick. Sin makes me come to Jesus, when sin is felt; and in coming to Christ, the more sin I have the more cause I have to hope for mercy."

YOU cannot, though you may think you can, preserve a moderation in sin. If you commit one sin, it is like the melting of the lower glacier upon the Alps; the others must follow in time. As certainly as you heap one stone upon the cairn today, the next day you will cast another, until the heap, reared stone by stone, shall become a very pyramid. Set the coral insect at work, you cannot decree where it shall stay its work. It will not build its rock just as high as you please, it will not stay until it shall be covered with weeds, until the weeds shall decay, and there shall be soil upon it, and an island shall be created by tiny creatures. Sin cannot be held in with bit and bridle.

SOON, soon, the saints of the earth shall be saints in light; their hairs of snowy age shall be crowned with perpetual joy and everlasting youth; their eyes suffused with tears shall be made bright as stars, never to be clouded again by sorrow; their hearts that tremble now are to be made joyous and fast, and set forever like pillars in the temple of God. Their follies, their burdens, their griefs, their woes, are soon to be over; sin is to be slain, corruption is to be removed, and a heaven of spotless purity and of unmingled peace is to be theirs forever. But it must still be by grace. As was the foundation such must the top-stone be; that which laid on earth the first beginning must lay in heaven the topmost stone.

TO know one's-self to be foolish is to stand upon the doorstep of the temple of wisdom; to understand the wrongness of any position is halfway to wards amending it; to be quite sure that our self-confidence is a heinous sin and folly, and an offence towards God, and to have that thought burned into us by God's Holy Spirit, is going a great length to wards the absolute casting our self-confidence away, and the bringing of our souls in practice, as well as in theory, to rely wholly upon the power of God's Holy Spirit.

OH! how solemn will be that hour when we must struggle with that enemy, Death! The death-rattle is in our throat—we can scarce articulate— we try to speak; the death-glaze is on the eye: Death hath put his fingers on those windows of the body, and shut out the light forever; the hands well-nigh refuse to lift themselves, and there we are, close on the borders of the grave! Ah! that moment, when the spirit sees its destiny; that moment of all moments the most solemn, when the soul looks through the bars of its cage, upon the world to come! No, I cannot tell you how the spirit feels, if it be an ungodly spirit, when it sees a fiery throne of judgment, and hears the thunders of Almighty wrath, while there is but a moment between it and hell. I cannot picture to you what must be the fright which men will feel, when they realize what they often heard of!

TRUE friendship can only be made between true men. Hearts are the soul of honor. There can be no lasting friendship between bad men. Bad men may pretend to love each other, but their friendship is a rope of sand, which shall be broken at any convenient season; but if a man have a sincere heart within him, and be true and noble, then we may confide in him.

WHO can find a stain in the character of Jesus, or who can tarnish his honor? Has there ever been a spot on his escutcheon? Has his flag ever been trampled in the dust? Does he not stand the true witness in heaven, the faithful and just? Is ii not declared of him that he is God who cannot lie? Have we not found him so up to this moment; and may we not, knowing that he is "Holy, holy, holy Lord," confide in him, that he will stick closer to us than a brother? His goodness is the guaranty of his fidelity; he cannot fail us.

THIS Bible is the stone that shall break in powder philosophy; this is the mighty battering-ram that shall dash all systems of philosophy in pieces; this is the stone that a woman may yet hurl upon the head of every Abimelech, and he shall utterly be destroyed. O Church of God! fear not; thou shalt do wonders; wise men shall be confounded, and thou shalt know, and they too, that he is God, and that beside him there is none else.

HE who would be happy here must have friends; and he who would be happy hereafter, must, above all things, find a friend in the world to come, in the person of God, the Father of his people.

MERE profession, is but painted pageantry to go to hell in: it is like the plumes upon the hearse and the trappings upon the black horses which drag men to their graves, the funeral array of dead souls. Take heed above everything of a waxen profession that will not stand the sun; take care of a life that needs to have two faces to carry it out; be one thing, or else the other. If you make up your mind to serve Satan, do not pretend to serve God; and if you serve God, serve him with all your heart.

YOU may think of a doctrine forever, and get no good from it, if you are not already saved; but think of the person of Christ, and that will give you faith. Take him everywhere, wherever you go, and try to meditate on him in your leisure moments, and then he will reveal himself to you, and give you peace.

WHAT! is Christ thy Brother, and does he live in thine house, and yet thou hast not spoken to him for a month? I fear there is little love between thee and thy Brother, for thou hast had no conversation with him for so long. What! is Christ the Husband of his church, and has she had no fellowship with him for all this time?

YOU have seen mummies, wrapped round and round with folds of linen. Well, God's Bible is like that; it is a vast roll of white linen, woven in the loom of truth; so you will have to continue unwinding it, roll after roll, before you get the real meaning of it from the very depth; and when you have found, as you think, a part of the meaning, you will still need to keep on unwinding, unwinding, and all eternity you will be unwinding the words of this wondrous volume.

IT IS easy to find by hundreds those that have departed, but you must count those by ones who know how to groan over their departure. The true believer, however, when he discovers that he needs revival, will not be happy; he will begin at once that incessant and continuous strain of cries and groans which will at last prevail with God, and bring the blessing of revival down.

WHEN a man has fifty different desires, his heart resembles a pool of water, which is spread over a marsh, breeding miasma and pestilence; but when all his desires are brought into one channel, his heart becomes like a river of pure water, running along and fertilizing the fields.

SUPPOSING the innumerable company of the redeemed could perish, and their immortality were swallowed up in death, yet even then, daily Christ would he praised! If all of us had departed from the boundless sphere of being—look up yonder! See you starry host; bee the mighty cohorts of cherubs and seraphs? Let men begone and they shall praise him; let the troops of the glorified cease their notes, and let no sweet melodies ever come from the lips of sainted men and women; yet the chariots of God are twenty thousand, even many thousands of angels, who always in their motions chant his praise. There is an orchestra on high, the music of which shall never cease, even were mortals extinct and all the human race swept from existence. Again, if angels were departed, still daily would he be praised; for, are there not worlds on worlds, and suns on suns, and systems on systems, that could forever sing his praise? Yes! The ocean—that house of storms—would howl out his glories; the winds would swell the notes of his praise with their ceaseless gales; the thunders would roll like drums in the march of the God of armies; the illimitable void of ether would become vocal with song; and space itself would burst forth into one universal chorus—Hallelujah! Hallelujah! Hallelujah! still the Lord God omnipotent reigneth! And if these were gone; if creatures ceased to exist, he who ever liveth and reigneth, in whom all the fullness of the Godhead bodily dwells, would still be praised; praised in himself, and glorious in himself; for the Father would praise the Son, and the Spirit would praise him, and mutually blessing one another and rendering each other beatified, still "daily would he be praised."

THIS city of refuge had round it suburbs of a very great extent. Two thousand cubits were allowed for grazing land for the cattle of the priests, and a thousand cubits within these for fields and vineyards. Now, no sooner did the man reach the outside of the city, the suburbs, than he was safe; it was not necessary for him to get within the walls, but the suburbs themselves were sufficient protection. Learn, hence, that if ye do but touch the hem of Christ's garment, ye shall be made whole; if ye do but lay hold of him with "faith as a grain of mustard seed," with faith which is scarcely a believing, but is truly a believing, you are safe.

> "A little genuine grace ensures
> The death of all our sins."

Get within the borders; lay hold of the hem of Christ's garment, and thou art secure.

———

ALAS! for thee, that thy pulse should beat a ii march to hell. Alas! that yonder clock, like the muffled drum, should be the music of the funeral march of thy soul. Alas! alas! that thou shouldst fold thine arms in pleasure, when the knife is at thy heart. Alas! alas! for thee, that thou shouldst sing, and make merriment, when the rope is about thy neck, and the drop is tottering under thee! Alas! for thee, that thou shouldst go thy way, and live merrily and happily and yet be lost! Thou remindest me of the silly moth that dances round about the flame, singeing itself for a while, and then at last plunging to its death. Such art thou! Young woman, with thy butterfly clothing, thou art leaping round the flame that shall destroy thee! Young man, light and frothy in thy conversation, gay in thy life, thou art dancing to hell; thou art singing thy way to damnation, and promenading the road to destruction. Alas! alas! that ye should be spinning your own winding-sheets; that ye should every day by your sins be building your own gal lows; that by your transgressions ye should be digging your own graves, and working hard to pile the fagots for your own eternal burning. Oh! that ye were wise, that ye understood this, that ye would consider your latter end. Oh! that ye would flee from the wrath to come!

———

THE saints in Jesus, when their bodies sleep in peace, have perpetual fellowship with him—aye, better fellowship than we can enjoy. We have but the transitory glimpse of his face; they gaze upon it every moment. We see him "in a glass, darkly;" they behold him "face to face." We sip of the brook by the way; they plunge into the very ocean of unbounded love. We look up sometimes, and see our Father smile; look whenever they may, his face is always full of smiles for them. We get some drops of comfort; but they get the honeycomb itself. They have their cup filled with new wine, running over with perennial, unalloyed delights. They are full of peace, full of joy forever. They "sleep in Jesus." Such a description of death makes us wish to sleep too. O Lord, let us go to sleep with the departed! O happy hour! when a clod of the valley shall be our pillow! Though it be hard, we shall not be affected by it. Happy hour, when earth shall be our bed! Cold shall be the clay, but we shall not know it; we shall slumber and we shall rest. The worm shall hold carnival within our bones, and corruption shall riot o'er our frame; but we shall not feel it. Corruption can but feed on the corruptible; mortality can but prey upon the mortal. "We know 'tis common: all that live must die, passing through nature to eternity."

SALVATION is God's highest glory. He is glorified in every dewdrop that twinkles to the morning sun, He is magnified in every wood flower that blossoms in the copse, although it live to blush unseen, and waste its sweetness in the forest air. God is glorified in every bird that warbles on the spray; in every lamb that skips the mead. Do not the fishes in the sea praise him. From the tiny minnow to the huge Leviathan, do not all creatures that swim the water bless and praise his name? Do not all created things extol him? Is there aught beneath the sky, save man, that does not glorify God? Do not the stars exalt him, when they write his name upon the azure of heaven in their golden letters? Do not the lightnings adore him when they flash his brightness in arrows of light, piercing the midnight darkness? Do not thunders extol him when they roll like drums in the march of the God of armies? Do not all things exalt him, from the least even to the greatest? But sing, sing, O Universe, till thou hast exhausted thyself, thou canst not afford a song so sweet as the song of Incarnation. Though creation may be a majestic organ of praise, it cannot reach the compass of the golden canticle—Incarnation! There is more in that than in creation, more melody in Jesus in the manger, than there is in worlds on worlds rolling their grandeur round the throne of the Most High.

———————————

GOD would build for himself a palace in heaven of living stones: Where did he get them? Did he go to the quarries of Paros? Hath he brought forth the richest and the purest marble from the quarries of perfection? No, ye saints, look to "the hole of the pit whence ye were digged, and to the rock whence ye were hewn!" Ye were full of sin; so far from being stones that were white with purity, ye were black with defilement, seemingly utterly unfit to be stones in the spiritual temple, which should be the dwelling-place of the Most High. And yet he chose you to be trophies of his grace, and of his power to save. When Solomon built for himself a palace, he built it of cedar; but when God would build for himself a dwelling forever, he cut not down the goodly cedars, but he dwelt in a bush, and hath preserved it as his memorial forever, "The God that dwelt in the bush." Goldsmiths make exquisite forms from precious material; they fashion the bracelet and the ring from gold:—God maketh his precious things out of base material; and from the black pebbles of the defiling brooks he hath taken up stones, which he hath set in the golden ring of his immutable love, to make them gems to sparkle on his finger forever. He hath not selected the best, but apparently the worst of men, to be the monuments of his grace; and when he would have a choir in heaven that should with tongues harmonious sing his praises—a chorus that should forever chant hallelujahs louder than the noise of many waters, and like great thunders, he did not send Mercy down to seek earth's songsters, and cull from us those who have the sweetest voices: He said, "Go, Mercy, and find out the dumb, and touch their lips, and make them sing. The virgin tongues that never sang my praise before, that have been silent till now, shall break forth in rhapsodies sublime, and they shall lead the song; even angels shall but attend behind, and catch the notes from the lips of those who once were dumb." "The tongue of the dumb shall sing "God's praises hereafter in heaven.

"THE MANY"—what a thousand thoughts rise around these two words! The million-peopled city, the populous town, the wide-spread country, this isle, kingdoms, empires, continents, the world, all seem to issue forth like armies from the hundred-gated Thebes, at the mention of that word, "The many." Here we see the toiling peasant and his lordly squire, the artisan and the princely merchant, the courtier and the king, the young, the old, the learned and the unlearned, all gathered within the compass of a word.

O HYPOCRITE, thou thinkest that thou shalt excel, because the minister has been duped, and gives thee credit for a deep experience; because the deacons have been entrapped and think thee to be eminently godly; because the church members receive thee to their houses, and think thee a dear child of God too! Poor soul! thou mayest go to thy grave with the delusion in thy brain that all is right with thee; but remember, though like a sheep thou art laid in thy grave, Death will find thee out. He will say to thee, off with thy mask, man! away with all thy robes! Up with that whitewashed sepulcher! Take off that green turf; let the worms be seen. Out with the body; let us see the reeking corruption! and what wilt thou say when thine abominably corrupt and filthy heart shall be opened before the sun, and men and angels hear thy lies and hypocrisies laid bare before them? Wilt thou play the hypocrite then? Soul, come and sing God's praises in the day of judgment with false lip! Tell him now, while a widow's house is in your throat, tell him that you love him! Come, now, thou that devourest the fatherless, thou that robbest, thou that dost uncleanness! tell him now that thou didst make thy boast in the Lord! tell him that thou didst preach his word; tell him that thou didst walk in his streets; tell him thou didst make it known that thou wert one of the excellent of the earth! What! man, is thy babbling tongue silent for once? What is the matter with thee? Thou wast never slow to talk of thy godliness. Speak out, and say "I took the sacramental cup; I was a professor." Oh how changed! The whitewashed sepulcher has become white in another sense; he is white with horror. See now; the talkative has become dumb; the boaster is silent; the formalist's garb is rent to rags, the moth has devoured their beauty; their gold has become tarnished, and their silver cankered. Ah! it must be so with every man who has thus belied God and his own conscience.

THERE never shall come a day when the church shall be bereft of mighty champions for the truth, who shun not to declare the whole counsel of God; but continually, to the latest period of time, men shall be raised up to preach free grace in all its sovereignty, in all its omnipotence, in all its perseverance, in all its immutability. Until the sun grows dim with age, and the comets cease their mighty revolutions— till all nature doth quake and totter with old age, and, palsied with disease, doth die away—the voice of the ministry must and shall be heard, "and daily shall he be praised." Men cannot put out the light of Christianity; the pulpit is still the Thermopylæ of Christendom, and if there were but two godly ministers they would stand in the pass and repulse a thousand—yea, ten thousand. All the hosts of mankind shall never vanquish the feeble band of Christ's fol lowers, while he Bends forth his ministers. On this we rely as a sure word of prophecy: "Thy teachers shall no more be removed into a corner;" and we believe that by this ministry daily shall Christ be praised.

HEAVEN is *a place of complete victory and glorious triumph*. This is the battlefield; there is the triumphal procession. This is the land of the sword and the spear; that is the land of the wreath and the crown. This is the land of the garment rolled in blood and of the dust of the fight; that is the land of the trumpet's joyful sound—that is the place of the white robe and of the shout of conquest. Oh, what a thrill of joy shall shoot through the hearts of all the blessed when their conquests shall be complete in heaven, when death itself, the last of foes, shall be slain—when Satan shall be dragged captive at the chariot wheels of Christ—when he shall have overthrown sin and trampled corruption as the mire of the streets—when the great shout of universal victory shall rise from the hearts of all the redeemed!

THE eagle is a bird noted for its swiftness. I remember reading an account of an eagle attacking a fish-hawk, which had obtained some booty from the deep, and was bearing it aloft. The hawk dropped the fish, which fell towards the water; but before the fish had reached the ocean, the eagle had flown more swiftly than the fish could fall, and catching it in its beak, it flew away with it. The swiftness of the eagle is almost incalculable; you see it, and it is gone; you see a dark speck in the sky yonder; it is an eagle soaring; let the fowler imagine that by and by he shall overtake it on some mountain's craggy peak, it shall be gone long before he reaches it. Such is our life. It is like an eagle hasting to its prey; not merely an eagle flying in its ordinary course, but an eagle hasting to its prey. Life appears to be hasting to its prey—the prey is the body; life is ever fleeing from insatiate death; but death is too swift to be outrun, and as an eagle overtakes his prey, so shall death.

THERE is not a place beneath which a believer walks that is free from snares. Behind every tree there is the Indian with his barbed arrow; be hind every bush there is the lion seeking to devour; under every piece of grass there lieth the adder. Everywhere they are.

YOU saw but yesterday a strong man. in your neighborhood brought to the grave by sudden death; it is but a month ago that you heard the bell toll for one whom once you knew and loved, who procrastinated and procrastinated until he perished in procrastination. You have had strange things happen in your very street, and the voice of God has been spoken loudly through the lip of Death to you. Aye, and you have had warnings too in your own body, you have been sick with fever, you have been brought to the jaws of the grave, and you have looked down into the bottomless vault of destruction. It is not long ago since you were given up: all said they might prepare a coffin for you, for your breath could not long be in your body. Then you turned your face to the wall and prayed; you vowed that if God would spare you, you would live a goodly life, that you would repent of your sins; but to your own confusion you are now just what you were. Ah! let me tell you, your guilt is more grievous than that of any other man, for you have sinned presumptuously, in the very highest sense in which you could have done so. You have sinned against reproofs, but what is worse still, you have sinned against your own solemn oaths and covenants, and against the promises that you made to God. He who plays with fire must be condemned as careless; but he who has been burned out once, and afterwards plays with the destroying element, is worse than careless; and he who has himself been scorched in the flame, and has had his locks all hot and crisp with the burning, if he again should rush headlong into fire, I say he is worse than careless, he is worse than presumptuous, he is mad. But I have some such here. They have had warnings so terrible that they might have known better; they have gone into lusts which have brought their bodies into sickness, and perhaps this day they have crept up to this house, and they dare not tell to their neighbor who stands by their side what is the loathsomeness that even now doth breed upon their frame. And yet they will go back to the same lusts; the fool will go again to the stocks, the sheep will lick the knife that is to slay him. You will go on in your lust and in your sins, despite warnings, despite advice, until you perish in your guilt. How worse than children are grown-up men! The child who goes for a merry slide upon a pond, if he be told that the ice will not bear him, starteth back affrighted, or if he daringly creepeth upon it, how soon he leaves it, if he hears but a crack upon the slender covering of the water! But you men have conscience, which tells you that your sins are vile, and that they will be your ruin; you hear the crack of sin, as its thin sheet of pleasure gives way beneath your feet; aye, and some of you have seen your comrades sink in the flood, and lost; and yet ye go sliding on, worse than childish, worse than mad are you, thus presumptuously to play with your own everlasting state. O my God, how terrible is the presumption of some! How fearful is presumption in any! Oh! that we might be enabled to cry, "Keep back thy servant also from presumptuous sins."

OH! ye kind and affectionate hearts, who are not rich in wealth, but who are rich in love—and that is the world's best wealth—put this golden coin among your silver ones, and it will sanctify them. Get Christ's love shed abroad in your hearts, and your mother's love, your daughter's love, your husband's love, your wife's love, will become more sweet than ever. The love of Christ casts not out the love of relatives, but it sanctifies our loves, and makes them sweeter far. Remember the love of men and women is very sweet; but all must pass away; and what will you do, if you have no wealth but the wealth that fadeth, and no love but the love which dies, when death shall come? Oh! to have the love of Christ! You can take that across the river of death with you; you can wear it as your bracelet in heaven, and set it up as a seal upon your hand; for his love is "strong as death and mightier than the grave."

BEHOLD, him whom thou canst not behold! Lift up thine eyes to the seventh heaven; see where) in dreadful majesty, the brightness of his skirts makes the angels veil their faces, lest the light, too strong for even them, should smite them with eternal blindness. See ye him, who stretched the heavens like a tent to dwell in, and then did weave into their tapes try, with golden needle, stars that glitter in the darkness. Mark ye him who spread the earth, and created man upon it. And hear ye what he is. He is all-sufficient, eternal, self-existent, unchangeable, omnipotent, omniscient! Wilt thou not reverence him? He is good, he is loving, he is kind, he is gracious! See the bounties of his providence; be hold the plenitude of his grace! Wilt thou not love Jehovah, because he is Jehovah?

IT seems too costly for him who is the Prince of Life and Glory to let his fair limbs be tortured in agony; that the hands which carried mercies should be pierced with accursed nails; that the temples that were always clothed with love should have cruel thorns driven through them. It appears too much. Oh! weep, Christian, and let our sorrow rise. Is not the price all but too great, that your beloved should for you resign *himself*?

IT is marvelous that the men who most of all rail at faith are remarkable for credulity. One of the greatest unbelievers in the world, who has called himself a free-thinker from his birth, is to be found now tottering into his tomb, believing the veriest absurdity that a child might confute. Not caring to have God in their hearts, forsaking the living fountain, they have hewn out to themselves cisterns which are broken, and hold no water. Oh! that we may each of us be more wise, that we may not forsake the good old path, nor leave the way that God hath prepared for us. What wonder we should travel amongst thorns and briars, and rend our own flesh, or worse than that, fall among dark mountains, and be lost amongst the chasms thereof, if we despise the guidance of an unerring Father.

A CUNNING enemy we have to deal with; he knows our weak points; he has been dealing with men for these last six thousand years; he knows all about them. He is possessed of a gigantic intellect; though he be a fallen spirit; and he is easily able to discover where our sore places are, and there it is he immediately attacks us. If we be like Achilles, and cannot be wounded anywhere but in our heel, then at the heel he will send his dart, and nowhere else.

THERE are some that are like what is fabled of the swan. The ancients said the swan never sang in his lifetime, but always sang just when he died. Now, there are many of God's desponding children, who seem to go all their life under a cloud; but they get a swan's song before they die. The river of their life comes running down, perhaps black and miry with troubles, and when it begins to touch the white foam of the sea there comes a little glistening in its waters. So, beloved, though we may have been very much dispirited by reason of the burden of the way, when we get to the end we shall have sweet songs. Are you afraid of dying? Oh! never be afraid of that; be afraid of living. Living is the only thing which can do any mischief; dying never can hurt a Christian. Afraid of the grave? It is like the bath of Esther, in which she lay for a time, to purify her self with spices, that she might be fit for her lord. The grave fits the body for heaven. There it lieth: and corruption, earth, and worms, do but refine and purify our flesh. Be not afraid of dying; it does not take any time at all. All that death is, is emancipation, deliverance, heaven's bliss to a child of God. Never fear it; it will be a singing time. You are afraid of dying, you say, because of the pains of death. Nay, they are the pains of life—of life struggling to continue. Death has no pain; death itself is but one gentle sigh—the fetter is broken, and the spirit fled. The best moment of a Christian's life is his last one, because it is the one that is nearest heaven; and then it is that he begins to strike the key note of the song which he shall sing to all eternity.

———————————————

IT may be, that during a sermon two men are listening to the same truth; one of them hears as attentively as the other and remembers as much of it; the other is melted to tears or moved with solemn thoughts; but the one though equally attentive, sees nothing in the sermon, except, may be, certain important truths well set forth; as for the other, his heart is broken within him and his soul is melted. Ask me how it is that the same truth has an effect upon the one, and not upon his fellow: I reply, because the mysterious Spirit of the living God goes with the truth to one heart and not to the other. The one only feels the force of truth, and that may be strong enough to make him tremble, like Felix; but the other feels the Spirit going with the truth, and that renews the man, regenerates him, and causes him to pass into that gracious condition which is called the state of salvation. This change takes place instantaneously. It is as miraculous a change as any miracle of which we read in Scripture. It is supremely supernatural. It may be mimicked, but no imitation of it can be true and real. Men may pretend to be regenerated without the Spirit, but regenerated they cannot be. It is a change so marvelous that the highest attempts of man can never reach it. We may reason as long as we please, but we cannot reason ourselves into regeneration; we may meditate till our hairs are grey with study; but we cannot meditate ourselves into the new birth. That is worked in us by the sovereign will of God alone.

MARK ANTONY yoked two lions to his chariot; but there are two lions no man ever yoked together yet—the lion of the tribe of Judah, and the lion of the pit. These can never go together. Two opinions you may hold in politics, perhaps, but then you will be despised by everybody, unless you are of one opinion or the other, and act as an independent man. But two opinions in the matter of soul-religion you cannot hold. If God be God, serve him, and do it thoroughly; but if this world be God, serve it, and make no profession of religion. If you are a world ling, and think the things of the world the best, serve them; devote yourself to them, do not be kept back by conscience; spite your conscience, and run into sin. But remember, if the Lord be your God, you cannot have Baal too; you must have one thing or else the other. "No man can serve two *masters*." If God be served, he will be a master; and if the devil be served, he will not be long before he will be a master; and "ye cannot serve two *masters*." Oh! be wise, and think not that the two can be mingled together.

IF God be really worthy of worship, and you really think so, I demand that you either follow him, or else deny that he is God at all. Now, professor, if thou sayest that Christ's gospel is the gospel, if thou believest in the divinity of the gospel, and puttest thy trust in Christ, I demand of thee to follow out the gospel, not merely because it will be to thy advantage, but because the gospel is divine. If thou makest a profession of being a child of God, if thou art a believer, and thinkest and believest religion is the best, the service of God the most desirable, I do not come to plead with thee because of any advantage thou wouldst get by being holy; it is on this ground that I put it, that the Lord is God; and if he be God, it is thy business to serve him. If his gospel be true, and thou believest it to be true, it is thy duty to carry it out. If thou sayest, Christ is not the Son of God, carry out thy Jewish or thy infidel convictions, and see whether it will end well. If thou dost not believe Christ to be the Son of God, if thou art a Muslim, be consistent, carry out thy Muslim convictions, and see whether it will end well. But, take heed, take heed! If however, thou sayest God is God, and Christ the Savior, and the gospel true; I demand of thee, only on this account, that thou carry it out.

O CHILDREN of God! death hath lost its sting, because the devil's power over it is destroyed. Then cease to fear dying. Thou knowest what death is: look him in the face, and tell him thou art not afraid of him. Ask grace from God, that by an intimate knowledge and a firm belief of thy master's death, thou mayest be strengthened for that dread hour. And mark me, if thou so livest, thou mayest be able to think of death with pleasure, and to welcome it when it comes with intense delight. It is sweet to die: to lie upon the breast of Christ, and have one's soul kissed out of one's body by the lips of divine affection. And you that have lost friends, or that, may be bereaved, sorrow not as those that are without hope; for remember the power of the devil is taken away. "What a sweet thought the death of Christ brings us concerning those who are departed! They are gone, my brethren; but do you know how far they have gone?

The distance between the glorified spirits in heaven and the militant saints on earth seems great; but it is not so. We are not far from home.

> "One gentle sigh the spirit breaks,
> We scarce can say 'tis gone,
> Before the ransomed spirit takes
> Its station near the throne."

We measure distance by time. We are apt to say that a certain place is so many hours from us. If it is a hundred miles off and there is no railroad we think it a long way; if there is a railway, we think we can be there in no time. But how near must we say heaven is? For it is just one sigh and we get there. Why, my brethren, our departed friends are only in the upper room, as it were, of the same house; they have not gone far off; they are up stairs, and we are down below.

IT is said that where the most beautiful cacti grow, serpents are to be found at the root of every plant. And it is so with sin. Your fairest pleasures will harbor your grossest sins. Take care; take care of your pleasures. Cleopatra's asp was introduced in a basket of flowers; so are our sins often brought to us in the flowers of our pleasures.

GOD, the Almighty, though he might use instruments, was nevertheless the sole creator of man. Though he is pleased to bring us into the world by the agency of our progenitors, yet is he as much our Creator as he was the Creator of Adam, when he formed him of clay and made him man. Look at this marvelous body of thine: see how God hath put the bones together, so as to be of the greatest service and use to thee. See how he hath arranged thy nerves and blood-vessels: mark the marvelous machinery which he has employed to keep thee in life! O thing of an hour! wilt thou not love him that made thee? Is it possible that thou canst think of him who formed thee in his hand, and molded thee by his will, and yet wilt thou not love him who hath fashioned thee?

YOU may think to live very well without Christ, but you cannot afford to die without him. You can stand very securely at present, but death will shake your confidence. Your tree may be fair now, but when the wind comes, if it has not its roots in the Rock of Ages, down it must come. You may think your worldly pleasures good, but they will then turn bitter as wormwood in your taste; worse than gall shall be the daintiest of your drinks, when you shall come to the bottom of your poisoned bowl.

NO inferior hand hath sketched even so much as the most minute parts of providence. It was all, from its Alpha to its Omega, from its divine preface to its solemn finis, marked out, designed, sketched and planned by the mind of the all-wise, all-knowing God. Hence, not even Christ's death was exempt from it. He that wings an angel and guides a spar row, he that protects the hairs of our head from falling prematurely to the ground, was not likely, when he took notice of such little things, to omit in his solemn decrees the greatest wonder of earth's miracles, the death of Christ. No; the blood-stained page of that book, the page which makes both past and future glorious with golden words—that blood-stained page, I say, was as much written of Jehovah as any other.

YOU may well conceive how swiftly the mariner flies from a threatening storm, or seeks the port where he will find his home. You have sometimes seen how the ship cuts through the billows, leaving a white furrow behind her, and causing the sea to boil around her. Such is life, says Job, "like the swift ships," when the sails are filled by the wind, and the vessel dashes on, dividing a passage through the crowded water. Swift are the ships, but swifter far is life. The wind of time bears me along. I cannot stop its motion; I may direct it with the rudder of God's Holy Spirit; I may, it is true, take in some small sails of sin, which might hurry my days on faster than otherwise they would go; but nevertheless, like a swift ship, my life must speed on its way until it reaches its haven. Where is that haven to be? Shall it be found in the land of bitterness and barrenness, that dreary region of the lost? Or shall it be that sweet haven of eternal peace, where not a troubling wave can ruffle the quiescent glory of my spirit? Wherever the haven is to be, that truth is the same, we are "like the swift ships."

THERE is one great event, which every day at» tracts more admiration than do the sun, and moon, and stars, when they march in their courses. That event is, the death of our Lord Jesus Christ. To it the eyes of all the saints who lived before the Christian era were always directed; and backwards, through the thousand years of history, the eyes of all modern saints are looking. Upon Christ, the angels in heaven perpetually gaze. "Which things the angels desire to look into," said the apostle. Upon Christ, the myriad eyes of the redeemed are perpetually fixed; and thousands of pilgrims, through this world of tears, have no higher object for their faith, and no better desire for their vision, than to see Christ as he is in heaven, and in communion to behold his person. Beloved, we shall have many with us, whilst we turn our face to the Mount of Calvary. We shall not be solitary spectators of the fearful tragedy of our Savior's death: we shall but dart our eyes to that place which is the focus of heaven's joy and delight, the cross of our Lord and Savior Jesus Christ.

HAPPY is the nation which is blessed with the means of grace. No man was ever saved by the means of grace apart from the Holy Spirit. You may hear the sermons of the man whom God delighteth to honor; ye may select from all your divines the writings of the man whom God did bless with a double portion of his Holy Spirit; ye may attend every meeting for prayer; ye may turn over the leaves of this blessed book; but in all this, there is no life for the soul apart from the breath of the Divine Spirit. Use these means, we exhort you to use them, and use them diligently; but recollect that in none of these means is there anything that can benefit you unless God the Holy Spirit shall own and crown them. These are like the conduit pipes of the marketplace; when the fountain-head floweth with water then they are full, and we do derive a blessing from them; but if the stream be stayed, if the fountain head doth cease to give forth its current, then these are wells without water, clouds without rain; and ye may go to ordinances as an Arab turns to his skin bottle when it is dry, and with your parched lips ye may suck the wind and drink the whirlwind, but receive neither comfort, nor blessing, nor instruction, from the means of grace.

IF little things have done great things, let us try to do great things also. You know not, ye atoms, but that your destiny is sublime. Try and make it so by faith; and the least of you may be mighty through the strength of God. Oh for grace to trust God, and there is no telling what ye can do. Worms, ye are nothing, but ye have eaten princes; worms, ye are nothing, but ye have devoured the roots of cedars, and laid them level with the earth; worms, ye are nothing, but ye have piled rocks in the deep, deep sea, and wrecked mighty navies: worms, ye have eaten through the keel of the proudest ship that ever sailed the ocean. If ye have done this yourselves, what cannot we do? your strength lies in your mouths; our strength lies in ours too. We will use our mouths in prayer, and in constant adoration, and we shall conquer yet, for God is with us, and victory is sure.

IT would be presumption for any man to climb to the top of the spire of a church, and stand upon his head. "Well, but he might come down safe if he were skilled in it." Yes, but it is presumptuous. I would no more think of subscribing a farthing to a man's ascent in a balloon, than I would to a poor wretch cutting his own throat. I would no more think of standing and gazing at any man who puts his life in a position of peril, than I would of paying a man to blow his brains out. I think such things, if not murders, are murderous. There is suicide in men's risking themselves in that way; and if there be suicide in the risk of the body, how much more in the case of a man who puts his own soul in jeopardy just because he thinks he has strength of mind enough to prevent its being ruined and destroyed. Sir, your sin is a sin of presumption; it is a great and grievous one; it is one of the master pieces of iniquity.

WHILST thou hast a rag of thine own thou shalt never have Christ; whilst thou hast a farthing of thine own righteousness, thou shalt never have him; but when thou art nothing, Christ is thine; when thou hast nothing of thyself to trust to, Jesus Christ in the gospel is thy complete Savior; he bids me tell thee he came to seek and to save such as thou art.

THERE is no difference, by nature, between tho elect and others: those who are now glorified in heaven, and who walk the golden streets, clad in robes of purity, were by nature as unholy and defiled, and as far from original righteousness, as those who, by their own rejection of Christ, and by their love of sin, have brought themselves into the pit of eternal torment, as a punishment for their iniquities. The only reason why there is a difference between those who are in heaven and those who are in hell, rests with divine grace, and with divine grace alone. Those in heaven must inevitably have been cast away, had not everlasting mercy stretched out its hand and redeemed them. They were by nature not one whit superior to others. They would as certainly have rejected Christ, and have trodden under foot the blood of Jesus, as did those who were cast away, if grace—free grace—had not prevented them from committing this sin. The reason why they are Christians is not because they did naturally will to be so, nor because they did by nature desire to know Christ, or to be found of him; but they are now saints simply because God made them so. He gave them the desire to be saved; he put into them the will to seek after him; he helped them in their seekings, and afterward brought them to feel that peace which is the fruit of justification. But by nature they were just the same as others; and if there is any difference, we are obliged to say that the difference does not lie in their favor. In very many cases, we who now "rejoice in hope of the glory of God "were the very worst of men. There are multitudes that now bless God for their redemption who once cursed him; who implored, as frequently as they dare to do, with oaths and swearing, that the curse of God might rest upon their fellows and upon themselves. Many of the Lord's anointed were once the very castaways of Satan, the sweepings of society, the refuse of the earth, those whom no man cares for—who were called outcasts, but whom God hath now called desired ones, seeing he hath loved them.

DOUBT the Eternal, distrust the Omnipotent? O traitorous fear! thinkest thou that the arm which piled the heavens, and sustains the pillars of the earth, shall ever be palsied? Shall the brow which eternal ages have rolled over without scathing it, at last be furrowed by old age? What! shall the Eternal fail thee? God is too wise to err, too good to be unkind; leave off doubting him, and begin to trust him, for in so doing, thou wilt put a crown on his head, but in doubting him thou dost trample his crown beneath thy feet.

KEEP prayer going; do not neglect your prayer meetings. Christmas Evans gives us a good idea about prayer. He says, "Prayer is the rope in the belfry; we pull it, and it rings the bell up in heaven." And so it is. Mind you keep that bell going. Pull it well. Come up to prayer meetings. Keep on pulling it; and though the bell is up so high that you cannot hear it ring, depend upon it. It can be heard in the tower of heaven, and is ringing before the throne of God, who will give you answers of peace according to your faith. May your faith be large and plentiful, and so will your answers be!

THERE is enough tinder in the heart of the best men in the world to light a fire that shall burn to the lowest hell, unless God should quench the sparks as they fall. There is enough corruption, depravity, and wickedness in the heart of the most holy man that is now alive to damn his soul to all eternity, if free and sovereign grace does not prevent. O Christian! thou hast need to pray this prayer. But I think I hear you saying, "Is thy servant a dog that I should do this thing?" So said Hazael, when the prophet told him that he would slay Ins master; but he went home, and took a wet cloth and spread it over his master's face and choked him, and did the next day the sin which he abhorred before. Think it not enough to abhor sin; you may yet fall into it. Say not "I never can be drunken, for I have such an abhorrence of drunkenness;" thou mayest fall where thou art most secure. Say not "I can never blaspheme God, for I have never done, so in my life;" take care, you may yet swear most profanely. Job might have said, "I will never curse the day of my birth;" but he lived to do it. He was a patient man; he might have said, "I will never murmur; though he slay me yet will I trust in him;" and yet he lived to wish that the day were darkness wherein he was brought forth. Boast not then, O Christian! by faith thou standest. "Let him that thinketh he standeth take heed lest he fall."

WE never read that Joshua's hand was weary with wielding the sword, but Moses' hand was weary with holding the rod. The more spiritual the duty, the more apt we are to tire of it. We could stand and preach all day; but we could not pray all day. We could go forth to see the sick all day, but we could not be in our closets all day one half so easily. To spend a night with God in prayer would be far more difficult than to spend a night with man in preaching. Oh! take care, take care, Church of Christ, that thou dost not cease thy prayers!

ANGELS had been present on many august occasions, and they had joined in many a solemn chorus to the praise of their Almighty Creator. They were present at the creation: "The morning stars sang

together, and all the sons of God shouted for joy." They had seen
many a planet fashioned be tween the palms of Jehovah, and wheeled
by his eternal hands through the infinitude of space. They had sung
solemn songs over many a world which the Great One had created.
We doubt not, they had often chanted "Blessing and honor, and glory,
and majesty, and power, and dominion, and might, be unto him that
sitteth on the throne," manifesting himself in the work of creation. I
doubt not, too, that their songs had gathered force through ages. As
when first created, their first breath was song, so when they saw God
create new worlds else their song received another note; they rose
a little higher in the gamut of adoration. But this time, when they
saw God stoop from his throne, and become a babe, hanging upon
a woman's breast, they lifted their notes higher still; and reaching
to the uttermost stretch of angelic music, they gained the highest
notes of the divine scale of praise, and they sung, "Glory to God
in the highest" for higher in goodness they felt God could not go.
Thus their highest praise they gave to him in the highest act of his
godhead. If it be true that there is a hierarchy of angels rising tier
upon tier in magnificence and dignity—if the apostle teaches us that
there be "angels, and principalities, and powers, and thrones, and do
minions," amongst these blessed inhabitants of the upper world—I
can suppose that when the intelligence was first communicated to
those angels that are to be found upon the outskirts of the heavenly
world, when they looked down from heaven and saw the newborn
babe, they sent the news backward to the place whence the miracle
first proceeded, singing:

> "Angels from the realms of glory,
> Wing your downward flight to earth,
> Ye who sing creation's story,
> Now proclaim Messiah's birth;
> Come and worship,
> Worship Christ, the newborn King."

And as the message ran from rank to rank, at last the presence
angels, those four cherubim that perpetually watch around the

throne of God—those wheels with eyes—took up the strain, and gathering up the song of all the inferior grades of angels, surmounted the divine pinnacle of harmony with their own solemn chant of adoration, upon which the entire host shouted, "The highest angels praise thee."—"Glory to God in the highest." Aye, there is no mortal that can ever dream how magnificent was that song. Then, note, if angels shouted before and when the world was made, their hallelujahs were more full, more strong, more magnificent, if not more hearty, when they saw Jesus Christ born of the Virgin Mary to be man's redeemer—"Glory to God in the highest."

THE Bible is a vein of pure gold, unalloyed by quartz, or any earthly substance. This is a star without a speck; a sun without a blot; a light with out darkness; a moon without its paleness; a glory without a dimness. O Bible! it cannot be said of any other book, that it is perfect and pure; but of thee we can declare all wisdom is gathered up in thee, without a particle of folly. This is the judge that ends the strife, where wit and reason fail. This is the book untainted by any error; but is pure, unalloyed, perfect truth.

WE too often flog the church when the whip should be laid on our own shoulders. We drag the church, like a colossal culprit, to the altar; we bind her, and try to execute her at once; we bind her hands fast, and tear off thongful after thongful of her quivering flesh—finding fault with her where there is none, and magnifying her little errors; while we too often forget ourselves.

LOOK on the sleeper. He has been weary; he hath toiled all day long; but there is no weariness now. He breathes softly, sometimes a dream may disturb him, but he is not weary; he is resting in the unconsciousness of slumber. It is often pleasing to look upon the face of a weary sleeper. Have ye never passed along a country lane, and there, by the road-side, seen the harvest-man, as he is resting awhile from his toils, laid down upon the bank? What a heavy sleep he has, and what a blessed smile there is on his countenance while he is enjoying that rest! Such is the natural sleep t of the body; and is not this sleep of death a resting after toil? The poor limbs are weary; they are now stretched in the grave, and covered over with the green sod, that they may not hear the noise above their heads, nor be disturbed by the busy din. They are put in their quiet abodes, down deep there in the earth, that none may alarm them; and now let the cannon roar o'er their tomb, let the thunder shake the sky, let the lightning flash, no sight nor sound can startle them, or cause them dreams. In such still chambers of retirement, their troubles now are o'er: "There the wicked cease from troubling, and there the weary be at rest." The body has gone through its battle; the warrior sleeps, the conqueror rests; his brow shall soon be decked with laurels; the very brow which, now slumbers in the tomb awhile shall yet rise again to wear the crown of everlasting life; but now it rests awhile till the preparations are complete for the triumphant entry into the kingdom of God, when Christ shall come to receive body and soul into their everlasting resting-place.

I DO think that one of the worst sins a man can be guilty of in this world is to be idle. I can almost forgive a drunkard, but a lazy man I do think there is very little pardon for. I think a man who is idle has as good a reason to be a penitent before God as David had when he was an adulterer, for the most abominable thing in the world is for a man to let the grass grow up to his ankles and do nothing. God never sent a man into the world to be idle. And there are some who make a tolerably fair profession, but who do nothing from one year's end to the other.

SATAN is a fowler; he has been so and is so still; and if he does not now attack us as the roaring lion, roaring against us in persecution, he attacks us as the adder, creeping silently along the path, endeavoring to bite our heel with his poisoned fangs, and weaken the power of grace and ruin the life of godliness within us.

DEATH is a part of Satan's dominion; he brought sin into the world when he tempted our mother Eve to eat of the forbidden fruit, and with sin he brought also death into the world, with all its train of woes. There had been likely no death, if there had been no devil. If Satan had not tempted, may hap man had not revolted, and if he had not revolted, he would have lived forever, without having to undergo the painful change which is caused by death. I think death is the devil's masterpiece. With the solitary exception of hell, death is certainly the most Satanic mischief that sin hath accomplished. Nothing ever delighted the heart of the devil so much as when he found that the threatening would be fulfilled, "In the day that thou eatest thereof thou shalt surely die;" and never was his malicious heart so full of hellish joy as when he saw Abel stretched upon the earth, slain by the club of his brother. "Aha!" said Satan, "this is the first of all intelligent creatures that has died. Oh, how I rejoice! This is the crowning hour of my dominion. It is true that I have marred the glory of this earth by my guileful temptation; it is true the whole creation groaneth and travaileth in pain by reason of the evil that I have brought into it; but this, this is my masterpiece; I have killed man; I have brought death into him, and here lieth the first—the first dead man." Since that time Satan hath ever gloated over the death of the human race, and he hath had some cause of glory, for that death has been universal. All have died. Though they had been wise as Solomon, their wisdom could not spare their head; though they had been virtuous as Moses, yet their virtue could not avert the axe. All have died; and therefore the devil hath boasted in his triumph. But twice hath he been defeated; but two have entered heaven without dying; but the mass of mankind have had to feel the scythe of death; and he has rejoiced because this, his mightiest work, has had foundations broad as earth, and a summit that readied as high as the virtues of mankind could climb.

"OH!" cries one, "I wish I could escape the wrath of the law! Oh that I knew that Christ did keep the law for me!" Stop, then, and I will tell you. Do you feel today that you are guilty, lost, and ruined? Do you, with tears in your eyes, confess that none but Jesus can do you good? Are you willing to give up all trusts, and cast yourself alone on him who died upon the cross? Can you look to Calvary, and see the bleeding sufferer, all crimson with streams of gore? Then he kept the law for you, and the law cannot condemn whom Christ has absolved.

NONE of you can be the people of God without provoking envy; and the better you are, the more you will be hated. The ripest fruit is most pecked by the birds, and the blossoms that have been longest on the tree, are the most easily blown down by the wind. But fear not; you have naught to do with what man shall say of you. If God loves you, man will hate you; if God honors you, man will dishonor you. But recollect, could ye wear chains of iron for Christ's sake, ye should wear chains of gold in heaven; could ye have rings of burning iron round your waists, ye should have your brow rimmed with gold in glory; for blessed are ye when men shall say all manner of evil against you falsely, for Christ's name's sake; for so persecuted they the prophets that were before you.

DOTH the moon stay herself to lecture every dog that bayeth at her? Doth the lion turn aside to rend each cur that barketh at him? Do the stars cease to shine because the nightingales reprove them for their dimness? Doth the sun stop in its course because of the officious cloud which veils it? Or doth the river stay because the willow dipeth its leaves into its waters? Ah! no; God's universe moves on, and if men will oppose it, it heeds them not. It is as God hath made it; it is working together for good, and it shall not be stayed by the censure nor m6ved on by the praise of man. Let your bows, my brethren, abide. Do not be in a hurry to set yourselves right. God will take care of you. Leave yourselves alone; only be very valiant for the Lord God of Israel; be steadfast in the truth of Jesus and your bow shall abide.

CHRIST made the covenant to pay a price, and God made the covenant that he should have the people. Christ has paid the price and ratified the covenant; and I am quite sure that God will fulfill his part of it, by giving every elect vessel of mercy into the hands of Jesus. But all the power, all the grace, all the blessings, all the mercies, all the com forts, all the things we have, we have through the covenant. If there were no covenant; if we could rend the everlasting charter up; if the king of hell could cut it with his knife, as the king of Israel did the roll of Baruck, then we should fail indeed: for we have no strength, except that which is promised in the covenant. Covenant mercies, covenant grace, covenant promises, covenant blessings, covenant help, covenant everything—the Christian must receive, if he would enter into heaven.

YE have lost your friends some of you, ye have planted flowers upon their tombs, ye go and sit at eventide upon the greensward, bedewing the grass with your tears, for there your mother lies, and there your father or your wife. Oh! inpensive sorrow come with me to this dark garden of our Savior's burial; come to the grave of your best friend—your brother, yea, one who "sticketh closer than a brother." Come thou to the grave of thy dearest relative, O Christian, for Jesus is thy husband, "Thy maker is thy husband, the Lord of Hosts is his name." Doth not affection draw you? Do not the sweet lips of love woo you? Is not the place sanctified where one so well-beloved slept, although but for a moment? Surely ye need no eloquence; if it were needed I have none. I have but the power, in simple, but earnest accents, to repeat the words, "Come, see the place where the Lord lay."

"COME, see the place where the Lord lay." Surely ye need no argument to move your feet in the direction of the holy sepulcher; but still we will use the utmost power to draw your spirit thither. Come, then, for *'tis the shrine of greatness*, 'tis the resting-place of *the man*, the Restorer of our race, the Conqueror of death and hell. Men will travel hundreds of miles to behold the place where a poet first breathed the air of earth; they will journey to the ancient tombs of mighty heroes, or the graves of men renowned by fame; but whither shall the Christian go to find the grave of one so famous as was Jesus? Ask me the greatest man who ever lived—I tell you the man Christ Jesus was "anointed with the oil of gladness above his fellows." If ye seek a chamber honored as the resting-place of Jesus, turn in hither; if ye would worship at the grave of holiness, come ye here; if ye would see the hallowed spot where the choicest bones that e'er were fashioned lay for awhile, come with me, Christian, to that quiet gar den, hard by the walls of Jerusalem.

WHEN no eye seeth you except the eye of God, "when darkness covers you, when you are shut up from the observation of mortals, even then be ye like Jesus Christ. Remember his ardent piety, his secret devotion—how, after laboriously preaching the whole day, he stole away in the midnight shades to cry for help from his God. Recollect how his en tire life was constantly sustained by fresh inspirations of the Holy Spirit, derived by prayer. Take care of your secret life: let it be such that you will not be ashamed to read at the last great day.

VOLTAIRE said he lived in the twilight of Christianity. He meant a lie; he spoke the truth. He did live in its twilight; but it was the twilight before the morning—not the twilight of the evening, as he meant to say; for the morning comes, when the light of the sun shall break upon us in its truest glory. The scorners have said that we should soon forget to honor Christ, and that one day no man should acknowledge him. "His name shall endure forever," as to the honor of it. Yes, I will tell you how long it will endure. As long as on this earth there is a sinner who has been reclaimed by omnipotent grace, Christ's name shall endure; as long as there is a Mary ready to wash his feet with tears and wipe them with the hair of her head; as long as there breathes a chief of sinners who has washed himself in the fountain opened for sin and for uncleanness; as long as there exists a Christian who has put his faith in Jesus, and found him his delight, his refuge, his stay, his shield, his song, and his joy, there will be no fear that Jesus' name will cease to be heard. We can never give up that name. We let the Unitarian take the gospel without a godhead in it; we let him deny Jesus Christ; but as long as Christians, true Christians, live, as long as we taste that the Lord is gracious, have manifestations of his love, sights of his face, whispers of his mercy, assurances of his affection, promises of his grace, hopes of his blessing, we cannot cease to honor his name. But if all these were gone—if we were to cease to sing his praise, would Jesus Christ's name he forgotten then? No; the stones would sing, the hills would be an orchestra, the mountains would skip like rams, and the little lulls like lambs; for is he not their creator? And if these lips, and the lips of all mortals were dumb at once, there are creatures enough in this wide world besides. Why, the sun would lead the chorus; the moon would play upon her silver harp, and sweetly sing to her music; stars would dance in their measured courses; the shoreless depths of ether would become the home of songs; and the void immensity would burst out into one great shout, "Thou art the glorious Son of God; great is thy majesty, and infinite thy power." Can Christ's name be forgotten? No; it is painted on the skies; it is written on the floods; the winds whisper it; the tempests howl it; the seas chant it; the stars shine it; the beasts low it; the thunders proclaim it; earth shouts it; heaven echoes it. But if that were gone—if this great universe should all subside in God, just as a moment's foam subsides into the wave that bears it and is lost forever—would his name be forgotten then? No. Turn your eyes up yonder; see heaven's *terra firma*. "Who are these that are arrayed in white, and whence came they?" "These are they that came out of great tribulation; they have washed their robes, and made them white in the blood of the Lamb; therefore they are before the throne of God, and praise him day and night in his temple." And if these were gone; if the last harp of the glorified had been touched with the last fingers: if the last praise of the saints had ceased; if the last hallelujah had echoed through the then deserted vaults of heaven, for they would be gloomy then; if the last immortal had been buried in his grave, if graves there might be for immortals—would his praise cease then? No, by heaven! no; for yonder stand the angels; they too sing his glory; to him the cherubim and seraphim do cry without ceasing, when they mention his name, in that thrice holy chorus, "Holy, holy, holy, Lord God of armies." But if these were perished—if angels had been swept away, if the wing of seraph never flapped the ether, if the voice of the cherub never sung his flaming sonnet, if the living creatures ceased their everlasting chorus, if the measured symphonies of glory were extinct in silence, would his name then be lost? Ah! no; for as God upon the throne he sits, the everlasting One, the Father, Son, and Holy Ghost. And if the universe were all annihilated, still would his name be heard, for the Father would hear it, and the Spirit would hear it, and, deeply graven on immortal marble in the rocks of ages, it would stand—Jesus the Son of God, co-equal with his Father. "His name shall endure forever."

JESUS rose, and as the Lord our Savior rose, so all his followers must rise. Die I must—this body must be a carnival for worms; it must be eaten by those tiny cannibals; peradventure it shall be scattered from one portion of the earth to another; the constituent particles of this my frame will enter into . plants, from plants pass into animals, and thus be carried into far distant realms; but, at the blast of the archangel's trumpet, every separate atom of my body shall find its fellow; like the bones lying in the valley of vision, though separated from one another, the moment God shall speak, the bone will creep to its bone; then the flesh shall come upon it; the four winds of heaven shall blow, and the breath shall return. So let me die, let beasts devour me, let fire turn this body into gas and vapor, all its particles shall yet again be restored; this very selfsame actual body shall start up from its grave, glorified and made like Christ's body, yet still the same body, for God hath said it. Christ's same body rose; so shall mine. O my soul, dost thou now dread to die? Thou wilt lose thy partner body a little while, but thou wilt be married again in heaven; soul and body shall again be united before the throne of God. The grave—what is it? It is the bath in which the Christian puts the clothes of his body to have them washed and cleansed. Death—what is it? It is the waiting-room where we robe ourselves for immortality; it is the place where the body, like Esther, bathes itself in spices that it may be fit for the embrace of its Lord.

REGENERATION and resurrection are sometimes used as it were in common, in the New Testament, although the distinction we usually make is, that regeneration applies to the soul, and resurrection to the body. Now when a man is born of the Spirit, it is not by a gradual refining of his corrupt inclinations, but by a powerful quickening of the Holy Ghost. Just so when the dead are raised: it shall not be by a process of nature, but by an instantaneous putting forth of the mighty power of God. Still, I tell you that there shall be a similarity in the result. The body that lies shrouded in its narrow bed shall awake at the call of Jesus unspeakably refreshed. It was exhausted; and as nature could no longer sustain the vital functions, it fell an easy prey to corruption; yet it shall arise without weariness, or pain, or sickness, or deformity. The former things that occasioned death shall have passed away. Instead of the pale corpse shall he the raised body, with the bloom of immortality on the cheek, and the divine glow of deathless vigor in the heart, fitted to greet the Sun of Righteousness as he ushers in a cloudless, bright, eternal day.

SEEST thou yonder thief hanging upon the cross? Behold the fiends at the foot thereof, with open mouths; charming themselves with the sweet thought, that another soul shall give them meat in hell. Behold the death-bird fluttering his wings o'er the poor wretch's head; vengeance passes by and stamps him for her own; deep on his breast is written "a condemned sinner;" on his brow is the clammy sweat, expressed from him by agony and death. Look in his heart; it is filthy with the crust of years of sin; the smoke of lust is hanging within in black festoons of darkness; his whole heart is hell condensed. Now, look at him. He is dying. One foot seems to be in hell; the other hangs tottering in life—only kept by a nail. There is a power in Jesus' eye. That thief looks: he whispers, "Lord, remember me." Turn your eye again there. Do you see that thief? Where is the clammy sweat? It is there. Where is that horrid anguish? It is *not* there. Positively there is a smile upon his lips. The fiends of hell, where are they? There are none; but a bright seraph is present, with his wings out spread, and his hands ready to snatch that soul, now a precious jewel, and bear it aloft to the palace of the great King. Look within his heart; it is white with purity. Look at his breast; it is not written "condemned," but "justified." Look in the book of life: his name is graven there. Look on Jesus' heart: there on one of the precious stones he bears that poor thief's name. Yea, once more, look! seest thou that bright one among the glorified, clearer than the sun, and fair as the moon? That is the thief! That is the power of Jesus; and that power shall endure forever.

THERE on that deathbed lies a saint; no gloom is on his brow, no terror on his face; weakly but placidly he smiles; he groans, perhaps, but yet he sings. He sighs now and then, but oftener he shouts. Stand by him. "My brother, what makes thee look in death's face with such joy?" "Jesus," he whispers. "What makes thee so placid and calm? "Hie name of Jesus." See, he forgets everything! Ask him a question; he cannot answer it—he does not understand you. Still he smiles. His wife comes, inquiring, "Do you know my name?" He answers, "No." His dearest friend requests him to remember his intimacy. "I know you not," he says. Whisper in his ear, "Do you know the name of Jesus?" and his eyes flash glory, and his face beams heaven, and his lips speak sonnets, and his heart bursts with eternity; for he hears the name of Jesus, and that name shall endure forever. He who landed one in heaven will land me there. Come on, death. I will mention Christ's name there. O grave! this shall be my glory, the name of Jesus! Hell-dog! this shall be thy death—for the sting of death is extracted—Christ our Lord. "His name shall endure forever."

OH! there is nothing that can so advantage you, nothing can so prosper you, so assist you, so make you walk towards heaven rapidly, so keep your head upwards towards the sky, and your eyes radiant with glory, like the imitation of Jesus Christ. It is when, by the power of the Holy Spirit, you are enabled to walk with Jesus in his very foot steps, and tread in his ways, you are most happy and you are most known to be the sons of God. For your sake, my brethren, I say, be like Christ.

THE death of the saints is precious in the sight of the Lord. On their account we have cause rather to rejoice than to weep. And why? Because we have a hope—we hope that they are safely housed in heaven. Yes, we have the fond and firm persuasion that already their redeemed spirits have flown up to the eternal throne. We do believe that they are at this moment joining in the hallelujahs of paradise, feasting on the fruits of the tree of life, and walking by the side of the "river, the streams whereof make glad the heavenly city of our God." We know they are supremely blessed; we think of them as glorified spirits above, who are present with the Lord Jesus.

O CHRISTIAN! because Christ sticks close, the devil will stick close too; he will be at you and with you; the dog of hell will never cease his howlings, till you reach the other side of Jordan; no place in this world is out of bowshot of that great enemy; till you have crossed the stream, his arrows *can* reach you, and they will. If Christ gave himself for you, the devil will do all he can to destroy you; if Christ has been long-suffering to you, Satan will be persevering, in hopes that Christ may forget you; he will strive after you, and strive until he shall see you safely landed in heaven.

POOR sinner, do take heart. The shepherds have been after thee many a day, but they could not find thee; remember God knows, as we know not, where thou art. If thou art in the deepest pit in the forest, his almighty eye can see to the bottom. Aye, and in one of the favored moments of the day of salvation—that time accepted—he will send home a promise so sweetly that all thy fetters shall break off in an instant—thy night shall be scattered—thy dawn begin; and he will give thee the oil of joy for mourning and the garment of praise for the spirit of heaviness. Believe now, and thou shalt be comforted now; for the time of faith is the time of comfort.

THOUGH all weapons are alike approved by the warrior in his thirst for blood, there seems something more cowardly in the attack of the archer than in that of the swordsman. The swordsman plants himself near you, foot to foot, and lets you defend yourself, and deal your blows against him; but the archer stands at a distance, hides himself in ambuscade, and, without your knowing it, the arrow comes whizzing through the air, and perhaps penetrates your heart. Just so are the enemies of God's people. They very seldom come foot to foot with us; they will not show their faces before us; they hate the light, they love darkness; they dare not come and openly accuse us to our face, for then we could reply; but they shoot the bow from a distance, so that we cannot answer them; cowardly and dastardly as they are, they forge their arrow heads, and aim them, winged with hell-birds' feathers, at the hearts of God's people.

THIS is no common grave; it is not an excavation dug out by the spade for a pauper, in which to hide the last remains of his miserable and over wearied bones. It is a princely tomb; it was made of marble, cut in the side of a hill. Stand here, believer, and ask why Jesus had such a costly sepulcher. He had no elegant garments; he wore a coat without seam, woven from the top throughout, with out an atom of embroidery. He owned no sumptuous palace, for he had not where to lay his head. His sandals were not rich with gold, or studded with brilliants. He was poor. Why, then, does he lie in a noble grave? We answer, for this reason: Christ was unhonored till he had finished his sufferings; Christ's body suffered contumely, shame, spitting, buffeting, and reproach, until he had completed his great work; he was trampled under foot, he was "despised and rejected of men; a man of sorrows, and acquainted with grief;" but the moment he had finished his undertaking, God said, "No more shall that body be disgraced; if it is to sleep, let it slumber in an honorable grave; if it is rest, let nobles bury it; let Joseph the councilor, and Nicodemus, the man of Sanhedrin, be present at the funeral; let the body be embalmed with precious spices, let it have honor; it has had enough of contumely, and shame, and reproach, and buffeting; let it now be treated with respect." Christian, dost thou discern the meaning? Jesus, after he had finished his work, slept in a costly grave; for now his Father loved and honored him, since his work was done.

IF you want truth to go round the world you must hire an express train to pull it; but if you want a lie to go round the world, it will fly: it is as light as a feather, and a breath will carry it. It is well said in the old Proverb, "A lie will go round the world while truth is pulling its boots on." Nevertheless, it does not injure us; for if light as a feather, it travels as fast, its effect is just about as tremendous as the effect of down, when it is blown against the walls of a castle; it produces no damage what ever, on account of its lightness and littleness. Fear not, Christian. Let slander fly, let envy send forth its forked tongue, let it hiss at you, your bow shall abide in strength. Oh! shielded warrior, remain quiet, fear no ill; but, like the eagle in its lofty eyrie, look thou down upon the fowlers in the plain, turn thy bold eye upon them and say, "Shoot ye may, but your shots will not reach half way to the pinnacle where I stand. Waste your powder upon me if ye will; I am beyond your reach." Then clap your wings, mount to heaven, and there laugh them to scorn, for ye have made your refuge God, and shall find a most secure abode.

IF any of you desire to be saved by works, remember one sin will spoil your righteousness; one dust of this earth's dross will spoil the beauty of that perfect righteousness which God requires at your hands. If ye would be saved by works, ye must be as holy as the angels, ye must be as pure and as immaculate as Jesus; for the law requires perfection, and nothing short of it; and God, with unflinching vengeance, will smite every man low who cannot bring him a perfect obedience. If I cannot, when I come before his throne, plead a perfect righteousness as being mine, God will say, "you have not fulfilled the demands of my law; depart, accursed one! You have sinned, and you must die."

HERE are the Roman Catholics. They are the successors of the apostles! But, I think, if Peter and Paul were to come and see their successors, they would think there was a mighty difference between themselves and them. By way of parable, suppose the Virgin Mary, Peter, and Paul, should come one Sunday, and go to a cathedral. Well, when they entered, the Virgin heard them singing something to her honor, and praise, and glory; she jogged Peter, and said—"What are these people after? They are worshiping me. My son said to me, 'Woman, what have I to do with thee?' He never worshiped me," she said; "let us turn out of this." They stopped a little longer, and they heard one of them say that the Apostle Peter was the head of the church; and his successor, the Pope, was therefore the head. Peter jogged the Virgin Mary, and said—"What a lie that is; I was never head of the church at all. Did I not fall into sin? I the head of the church! A pretty head I was." Soon afterwards, Paul heard them preaching justification by works. "Come out," said he; "there is no gospel here. I preached justification by faith without works, and they are preaching justification by works." And so, upon that, all three of them went out. By and by, they came to a place where they heard them singing—"Glory, honor, praise and power, be unto the Lamb that sitteth on the throne;" and then they heard them speak of those who were "kept by the power of God through faith unto salvation." "Ah," said Peter, "this is the place; and here I will stay." Those are the successors of the apostles who are like the apostles.

CHRIST had no transgressions of his own; he took ours upon his head; he never committed a wrong, but he took all my sin, and all yours, if ye are believers; concerning all his people, it is true, he bore their griefs and carried their sorrows in his own body on the tree; therefore, as they were others' sins, so he rested in another's grave; as they were sins imputed, so that grave was only imputedly his. It was not his sepulcher; it was the tomb of Joseph.

IT is childish to doubt; it is manhood's glory to trust. Plant your foot upon the immovable Rock of Ages; lift your eye to heaven; scorn the world; never play craven; bend your fist in the world's face, and bid defiance to it and hell, and you are a man, and noble. But crouch, and cringe, and dread, and doubt, and you have lost your Christian dignity, and are no longer what you should be.

LET me imagine a man entering heaven without a change of heart. He comes within the gates. He hears a sonnet. He starts! It is to the praise of his *enemy*. He sees a throne, and on it sits one who is glorious; but it is his *enemy*. He walks streets of gold, but those streets belong to his *enemy*. He sees hosts of angels, but those hosts are the servants of his *enemy*. He is in an *enemy's* house; for he is at *enmity* with God. He could not join the song, for he would not know the tune. There he would stand, silent, motionless, till Christ would say, with a voice louder than ten thousand thunders, "What dost thou here? Enemies at a marriage banquet? Enemies in the children's house? Enemies in heaven? Get thee gone? 'Depart, ye cursed, into everlasting fire in hell!'"

THERE have been some who have been noble men, but have carried their courage to excess; they have thus been caricatures of Christ, and not portraits of him. We must amalgamate with our boldness the *loveliness* of Jesus' disposition. Let courage be the brass, let love be the gold. Let us mix the two together, so shall we produce a rich Corinthian metal, fit to be manufactured into the beautiful gate of the temple.

OUR lost friends are lost forever; we recollect that there is no shadow of a hope for them; when the iron gate of hell is once closed upon them, it shall never he unbarred again, to give them free exit; when once shut up within those walls of sweltering flame which girdle the fiery gulf, there is no possibility of flight; we recollect that they have "forever "stamped upon their chains, "forever "carved in deep lines of despair upon their hearts. It is the hell of hell, that everything there lasts forever. Here, time wears away our griefs, and blunts the keen edge of our sorrow; but there time never mitigates the woe; hell grows more hellish, as eternity marches on with its mighty paces. The abyss be comes more dense and fiery—the sufferers grow more ghastly and wretched, as years, if there be such sad variety in that fixed state, roll their ever lasting rounds. Here the sympathy of loving kindred, in the midst of sickness or suffering, can alleviate our pain; but there, the tortured ghosts are sport for fiends, and the mutual upbraidings and reproaches of fellow-sinners give fresh stings to torment too dread to be endured. Here, too, when nature's last palliative shall fail, to die may be a happy release; a man can count the weary hours till death shall give him rest: but, oh! remember, there is no death in hell; death, which is a monster on earth, would be an angel in hell. If death could go there, all the damned would fall down and worship him; every tongue would sing, and every heart would praise; each cavern then would echo with a shout of triumph till all was still, and silence brood where terrors reigned. But no, the terrible reality is this—"Their worm dieth not, and the fire is not quenched."

THE artist, when he paints, knows right well that he shall not be able to excel Apelles; but that does not discourage him; he uses his brush with all the greater pains, that he may at least in some humble measure resemble the great master. So the sculptor, though persuaded that he will not rival Praxiteles, will hew out the marble still, and seek to be as near the model as possible. Thus so the Christian man; though he feels he never can mount to the heights of complete excellence and perceives that he never can on earth become the exact image of Christ, still holds it up before him, and measures his own deficiencies by the distance be tween himself and Jesus. This will he do; forgetting all he has attained, he will press forward, crying, *Excelsior!* going upwards still, desiring to be conformed more and more to the image of Christ Jesus.

MAN cannot please God without bringing to himself a great amount of happiness; for, if any man pleases God, it is because God accepts him as his son, gives him the blessings of adoption, pours upon him the bounties of his grace, makes him a blessed man in this life, and insures him a crown of everlasting life, which he shall wear, and which shall shine with unfading luster, when the wreaths of earth's glory have all been melted away; while, on the other hands, if a man does not please God, he inevitably brings upon himself sorrow and suffering in this life; he puts a worm and a rottenness in the core of all his joys; he fills his death-pillow with thorns, and he supplies the eternal fire with fagots of flame which shall forever consume him.

THE holiest men, the most free from *impurity*, have always felt it most. He whose garments are the whitest, will best perceive the spots upon them. He whose crown shineth the brightest, will know when he hath lost a jewel. He who giveth the most light to the world, will always be able to discover his own darkness. The angels of heaven veil their faces; and the angels of God on earth, his chosen people, must always veil their faces with humility, when they think of what they were.

TAKE the cold iron, and attempt to weld it if you can into a certain shape. How fruitless the effort! Lay it on the anvil, seize the blacksmith's hammer with all your might, let blow after blow fall upon it, and you shall have done nothing. Twist it, turn it, use all your implements, but you shall not be able to fashion it as you would. But put it in the fire, let it be softened and made malleable, then lay it on the anvil, and each stroke shall have a mighty effect, so that you may fashion it into any form you may desire. So take your heart, not cold as it is, not stony as it is by nature, but put it into the furnace; there let it be molten, and after that it can be turned like wax to the seal, and fashioned into the image of Jesus Christ.

MIGHTIER than giants are men of the race of heaven; should they once arouse themselves to battle they could laugh at the spear and the habergeon. But they are a patient generation, enduring ills without resenting them, suffering scorn without reviling the scoffer. Their triumph is to come when their enemies shall receive the vengeance due; then shall it be seen by an assembled world that the "little flock" were men of high estate, and the "offscouring of all things" were verily men of real strength and dignity.

THE Word is able to convert just as extensively as God the Spirit pleases to apply it; and I can see no reason why, if converts come in by ones and twos now, there should not be a time when hundreds and thousands shall come to God. The same sermon which God blesses to ten, if he pleased, he could bless to an hundred. I know not but that in the latter days, when Christ shall come, and shall begin to take the kingdom to himself, every minister of God shall be as successful as Peter on the day of Pentecost. I am sure the Holy Spirit is able to make the Word successful; and the reason why we do not prosper, is, that we have not the Holy Spirit attending us with might and energy, as they had then.

IF by the power of the Spirit ye become followers of Jesus, ye shall enter glory. For at heaven's gate there sits an angel, who admits no one who has not the same features as our adorable Lord. There comes a man with a crown upon his head. "Yes," he says, "thou hast a crown, it is true, but crowns are not the medium of access here." Another approaches, dressed in robes of state and the gown of learning. "Yes," says the angel, "it may be good, but gowns and learning are not the marks that shall admit you here." Another advances, fair, beautiful, and comely. "Yes," saith the angel, "that might please on earth, but beauty is not wanted here." There cometh another, who is heralded by fame, and prefaced by the blast of the clamor of mankind; but the angel saith, "It is well with man, but thou hast no right to enter here." Then there appears another; poor he may have been; illiterate he may have been; but the angel, as he looks at him, smiles and says, "It is Christ again; a second edition of Jesus Christ is there. Come in, come in. Eternal glory thou shalt win. Thou art like Christ; in heaven thou shalt sit, because thou art like him." Oh, to be like Christ is to enter heaven; but to be unlike Christ is to descend to hell.

IF there is one virtue which most commends Christians, it is that of kindness: it is to love the people of God, to love the Church, to love the world, to love all. But how many have we in our churches of crab-tree Christians, who have mixed such a vast amount of vinegar and such a tremendous quantity of gall in their constitutions, that they can scarcely speak one good word to you. They imagine it impossible to defend religion except by passionate ebullitions; they cannot speak for their dishonored Master without being angry with their opponent; and if anything is awry, whether it be in the house, the church, or anywhere else, they conceive it to be their duty to set their faces like flint, and to defy everybody. They are like isolated icebergs, no one cares to go near them. They float about on the sea of forgetfulness, until at last they are melted and gone; and though, good souls, we shall be happy enough to meet them in heaven, we are precious glad to get rid of them from the earth. They were always so unamiable in disposition, that we would rather live an eternity with them in heaven than five minutes on earth. Be ye not thus. Imitate Christ in your loving spirits; speak kindly, act kindly, and do kindly, that men may say of you, "He has been with Jesus."

THOSE who have not to work hard, think they will love heaven as a place of service. That is very true. But to the working man, to the man who toils with his brain or with his hands, it must ever be a sweet thought that there is a land where we shall rest. Soon, this voice will never be strained again; soon, these lungs will never have to exert themselves beyond their power; soon, this brain shall not be racked for thought; but I shall sit at the banquet-table of God; yea, I shall recline on the bosom of Abraham, and be at ease forever. Oh! weary sons and daughters of Adam, you will not have to drive the ploughshare into the unthankful soil in heaven, you will not need to rise to daily toils before the sun hath risen, and labor still when the sun hath long ago gone to his rest; but ye shall be still, ye shall be quiet, ye shall rest yourselves, for all are rich in heaven, all are happy there, all are peaceful. Toil, trouble, travail, and labor, are words that cannot be spelled in heaven; they have no such things there, for they always rest.

OH! if you could have seen Paul preach, you would not have gone away as you do from some of us, with half a conviction that we do not mean what we say. His eyes preached a sermon without his lips, and his lips preached it, not in a cold and frigid manner, but every word fell with an over whelming power upon the hearts of his hearers. He preached with power, because he was in downright earnest. You had a conviction, when you saw him, that he was a man who felt he had a work to do, and must do it, and could not contain himself unless he did do it. He was the kind of preacher whom you would expect to see walk down the pulpit-stairs straight into his coffin, and then stand before his God, ready for his last account.

CHRIST'S sepulcher was cut in a rock. It was not cut in mold that might be worn away by the water, or might crumble and fall into decay. The sepulcher stands, I believe, entire to this day; if it does not naturally, it does spiritually. The same sepulcher which took the sins of Paul shall take my iniquities into his bosom; for if I ever lose my guilt, it must roll off my shoulders into the sepulcher. It was cut in a rock, so that if a sinner were saved a thousand years ago, I too can be delivered, for it is a rocky sepulcher where sin was buried—if was a rocky sepulcher of marble where my crimes were laid forever—buried never to have a resurrection.

IT will not save me to know that Christ is a Savior; but it will save me *to trust* him to be *my* Savior. I shall not be delivered from the wrath to come, by believing that his atonement is sufficient; but I shall be saved, by making that atonement my trust, my refuge, and my all. The pith, the essence, of faith lies in this—a casting oneself on the promise. It is not the life-buoy on board the ship that saves the man when he is drowning, nor is it his belief that it is an excellent and successful invention. No! he must have it around his loins, or his hand upon it, or else he will sink.

A MAN who has not faith proves that he cannot stoop; for he has not faith, for this reason, because he is too proud to believe. He declares, he will not yet yield his intellect, he will not become a child, and believe meekly what God tells him to believe. He is too proud, and he cannot enter heaven, because the door of heaven is so low that no one can enter in by it unless they will bow their heads. There never was a man who could walk into salvation erect. We must go to Christ on our bended knees; for, though he is a door big enough for the greatest sinner to come in, he is a door so low that men must stoop if they would be saved. Therefore it is, that faith is necessary, because a want of faith is certain evidence of absence of humility.

THERE be some men that are born into this world master-spirits, who walk about it as giants, wrapped in mantles of light and glory. I refer to the poets, men who stand aloft like Colossi, mightier than we, seeming to be descended from celestial spheres. There be others of acute intellect, who, searching into mysteries of science, discover things that have been hidden from the creation of the world; men of keen research, and mighty erudition; and yet, of each of these—poet, philosopher, metaphysician, and great discoverer—it shall be said, "The carnal mind is enmity against God!" Ye may train him up, ye may make his intellect almost angelic, ye may strengthen his soul until he shall take what are riddles to us, and unravel them with his Augers in a moment; ye may make him so mighty, that he can grasp the iron secrets of the eternal hills and grind them to atoms in his fist; ye may give him an eye so keen, that he can penetrate the arcana of rocks and mountains; ye may add a soul so potent, that he may slay the giant Sphinx, that had for ages troubled the mightiest men of learning; yet, when ye have done all, his mind shall be a depraved one, and his carnal heart shall still be in opposition to God.

———————————

I READ in God's word that the angel shall plant one foot upon the earth, and the other upon the sea, and shall swear by him that liveth and was dead, that *time* shall be no longer. But if a soul could die in a thousand years, it would die in *time*; if a million of years could elapse, and then the soul could be extinguished, there would be such a thing as *time*; for, talk to me of years, and there is *time*. But, sirs, when that angel has spoken the word, "Time shall be no longer," things will then be eternal; the spirit shall proceed in its ceaseless revolution of weal or woe, never to be stayed, for there is no time to stop it; the fact of its stopping would imply time; but everything shall be eternal, for time shall cease to be. It well becomes you, then, to consider where ye are and what ye are. Oh! stand and tremble on the narrow neck of land between the two unbounded seas, for God in heaven alone can tell how soon thou mayest be launched upon the eternal future. May God grant that, when that last hour may come, we may be prepared for it! Like the thief, unheard, unseen, it steals through night's dark shade. Perhaps, as here I stand, and rudely speak of these dark, hidden things, soon may the hand be stretched, and dumb the mouth that lisps the faltering strain. Oh, thou that dwellest in heaven, thou power supreme, thou everlasting King, let not that hour intrude upon me in an ill-spent season; but may it find me rapt in meditation high, hymning my great Creator.

O CHURCH of God! believe thyself invincible, and thou art invincible; but stay to tremble and fear, and thou art undone. Lift up thy head and say, "I am God's daughter; I am Christ's bride." Do not stop to prove it, but affirm it; march through the land, and kings and princes shall bow down be fore thee, because thou hast taken thine ancient prowess and assumed thine ancient glory.

OH! hast thou ever thought how many souls sink to hell every hour? Did the dreary thought that the death-knell of a soul is tolled by every tick of yonder clock, ever strike thee? Hast thou never thought that myriads of thy fellow creatures are in hell now, and that myriads more are hastening thither? and yet dost thou sleep? What! physician, wilt thou, sleep when men are dying? Sailor, wilt thou sleep when the wreck is out at sea, and the life-boat is waiting for hands to man it? Christian, wilt thou tarry while souls are being lost? I do not say that thou canst save them—God alone can do that—but thou mayest be the instrument; and wouldst thou lose the opportunity of winning another jewel for thy crown in heaven? wouldst thou sleep while work is being done?

MENTAL power may fill a chapel; but spiritual power fills the church. Mental power may gather a congregation; spiritual power will save souls. We want spiritual power. Oh! we know some before whom we shrink into nothing as to talent, but who have no spiritual power, and when they speak they have not the Holy Spirit with them; but we know others, simple-hearted, worthy men, who speak their country dialect, and who stand up to preach in their country place, and the Spirit of God clothes every word with power; hearts are broken, souls are saved, and sinners are horn again. Spirit of the living God! we want thee. Thou art the life, the soul; thou art the source of thy people's success; without thee they can do nothing, with thee they can do everything.

SOME say that children learn sin by imitation. But no: take a child away, place it under the most pious influences, let the very air it breathes he purified by piety; let it constantly drink in draughts of holiness; let it hear nothing but the voice of prayer and praise; let its ear be always kept in tune by notes of sacred song; and that child, notwithstanding, may still become one of the grossest of transgressors; and though placed apparently on the very road to heaven, it shall, if not directed by divine grace, march downwards to the pit. The young crocodile, I have heard, when broken from the shell, will in a moment begin to put itself in a posture of attack, opening its mouth as if it had been taught and trained. We know that young lions, when tamed and domesticated, still will have the wild nature of their fellows of the forest, and were liberty given them, would prey as fiercely as others. So with the child; you may bind him with the green withes of education, you may do what you will with him, since you cannot change his heart, that carnal mind shall still be at enmity against God; and notwithstanding intellect, talent, and all you may give to boot, it shall be of the same sinful complexion as every other child, if not as apparently evil; for "the carnal mind is enmity against God."

IN hell, there is no hope. They have not even the hope of dying—the hope of being annihilated. They are forever—forever—forever—lost!

On every chain in hell, there is written "forever." In the fires, there blazes out the words "forever." Up above their heads, they read "forever." Their eyes are galled, and their hearts are pained with the thought that it is "forever." Oh! if I could tell you tonight that hell would one day be burned out, and that those who were lost might be saved, there would be a jubilee in hell at the very thought of it. But it cannot be—it is "*forever*" they are "cast into utter darkness."

DID you ever think of the value of a soul? Ah! ye have not heard the howls and yells of hell; ye have not heard the mighty songs and hosannas of the glorified; ye have no notion of what eternity is, or else ye would know the value of a soul.

SLEEPY Christian, let me shout in thine ears: thou art sleeping while souls are being lost, sleeping while men are being damned, sleeping while hell is being peopled, sleeping while Christ is being dishonored, sleeping while the devil is grinning at thy sleepy face, sleeping while demons are dancing round thy slumbering carcass, and telling it in hell that a Christian is asleep. You will never catch the devil asleep; let not the devil catch you asleep. Watch, and be sober, that ye may be always up to do your duty.

WE who constitute a part of the Israel of God, were once the slaves of sin and Satan: we served with hard bondage and rigor whilst in our natural state; no bondage was ever more terrible than ours; we indeed made bricks without straw, and labored in the very fire; but by the strong hand of God we have been delivered. We have come forth from the prison-house; with joy we behold ourselves emancipated—the Lord's free men. The iron yoke is taken from our necks; we no longer serve our lusts, and pay obedience to the tyrant's sin. With a high hand and an outstretched arm, our God has led us forth from the place of our captivity, and joyfully we pursue our way through the wilderness.

WHAT with the wild beasts of Rome, what with the antichrist of Mohammed, what with the thou sands of idolatries and false gods, what with infidelity in all its myriad shapes, many are the enemies of God, and mighty are the hosts of hell. Lo, you see them gathered together this day; horseman upon horseman, chariot upon chariot, gathered together against the Most High. I see the trembling church, fearing to be overthrown; I mark her leaders bending their knees in solemn prayer, and crying, "Lord, save thy people, and bless thy heritage." But mine eye looks through the future with telescopic glance, and I see the happy period of the latter days, when Christ shall reign triumphant. I shall ask them where is Babel? where is Rome? where is Mohammed? and the answer shall come—where? Why they have sunk into the depths; they have sunk to the bottom as a stone. Down there the horrid fire devours them, for the sea of glass is mingled with the fire of judgment. Today I see a battlefield: the whole earth is torn by the hoofs of horses; there is the rumble of cannon and the roll of drum. "To arms! to arms!" both hosts are shouting. But you wait awhile, and you shall walk across this plain of battle, and say, "Seest thou that colossal system of error dead? There lies another, all frozen, in ghastly death, in motionless stupor. There lieth infidelity; there sleepeth secularism and the secularist; there he those who defied God. I see all this vast host of rebels lying scattered upon the earth. "Sing unto the Lord, for he hath triumphed gloriously; Jehovah has gotten unto himself the victory, and the last of his enemies are destroyed." Then shall he the time when shall be sung "the song of Moses and of the Lamb."

CHRIST in a man, the gospel in the soul, is the power of God, and the wisdom of God. We will picture the Christian from his beginning to his end. We will give a short map of his history. He begins there, in that prison house, with huge iron bars, which he cannot file; in that dark damp cell, where pestilence and death are bred. There, in poverty and nakedness, without a pitcher to put to his thirsty lips, without a mouthful even of dry crust to satisfy his hunger, that is where he begins—in the prison chamber of conviction, powerless, lost and ruined. Between the bars I thrust my hand to him, and gave to him in God's name the name of Christ to plead. Look at him; he has been filing away at these bars many and many a day, without their yielding an inch; but now he has got the name of Christ upon his lips; he puts his hand upon the bars, and one of them is gone, and another, and another; and he makes a happy escape, crying, "I am free, I am free, I am free! Christ has been the power of God to me, in bringing me out of my trouble." No sooner is he free, however, than a thousand doubts meet him. He comes soon into the furnace of trouble; he is thrust into the innermost prison, and his feet are made fast in the stocks. God has put his hand upon him. He is in deep trouble; at midnight he begins to sing of Christ; and lo! the walls begin to totter, and the foundation of the prison to shake; and the man's chains are taken off, and he comes out free; for Christ hath delivered him from trouble. Here is a hill to climb on the road to heaven. Wearily he pants up the side of that hill, and thinks he must die, ere he can reach the summit. The name of Jesus is whispered in his ear; he leaps to his feet and pursues his way, with fresh courage, until the summit is gained, when he cries, "Jesus Christ is the strength of my song: he also hath become my salvation." See him again. He is on a sudden beset by many enemies; how shall he resist them? With this true sword, this true Jerusalem blade, Christ and him crucified. With this he keeps the devil at arm's length; with this he fights against temptation, against lust, against spiritual wickedness in high places, and with this he resists. Now, he has come to his last struggle; the river Death rolls black and sullen before him; dark shapes rise upward from the flood, and howl and fright him. How shall he cross the stream? How shall he find a landing-place on the other side? Dread thoughts perplex him for a moment; he is alarmed; but he remember Jesus died; and catching up that watchword he ventures to the flood. Before his feet the Jordan flies apace; like Israel of old, he walks through, dry shod, singing as he goes to heaven, "Christ is with me, Christ is with me, passing through the stream! Victory, victory, victory, to him that loveth me!"

REMEMBER, thy sins are like sowing for a harvest. What a harvest is that which thou hast sown for thy poor soul! Thou hast sown the wind, thou shalt reap the whirlwind; thou hast sown iniquity, thou shalt reap damnation. But what hast thou done against the gospel? Remember, how many times this year thou hast heard it preached. Why, since thy birth, there have been wagon loads of sermons wasted on thee. Thy parents prayed for thee in thy youth; thy friends instructed thee till thou didst come to manhood. Since then how many a tear has been wept by the minister for thee! How many an earnest appeal has been shot into thine heart! But thou hast rent out the arrow. Ministers have been concerned to save thee, and thou hast never been concerned about thyself. What hast thou done against Christ? Remember, Christ has been a good Christ to sinners here; but as there is nothing that burns so well as that soft substance oil, so there is nothing that will be so furious as that gentle-hearted Savior, when he comes to be your judge. Fiercer than a lion on his prey is rejected love. Despise Christ on the cross, and it will be a terrible thing to be judged by Christ on his throne.

BELOVED, can you conceive how much Christ will love you when you are in heaven? Have you ever tried to fathom that bottomless sea of affection in which you shall swim, when you shall bathe yourself in seas of heavenly rest? Did you ever think of the love which Christ will manifest to you, when he shall present you without spot, or blemish, or any such thing, before his Father's throne? Well, pause and remember, that he loves you at this hour as much as he will love you then; for he will be the same forever as he is today, and he is the same to day as he will be forever. This one thing I know: if Jesus' heart is set on me he will not love me one atom better when this head wears a crown, and when this hand shall with joyous fingers touch the strings of golden harps, than he does now, amidst all my sin, and care and woe. I believe that saying which is written—"As the Father hath loved me, even so have I loved you;" and a higher degree of love we cannot imagine. The Father loves his Son infinitely, and even so today, believer, doth the Son of God love thee. Every bowel yearns over thee; all his heart flows out to thee. All his life is thine; all his person is thine. He cannot love thee more; he will not love thee less. "The same yesterday, today, and forever."

———————

AFTER passing the Red Sea, the song of Moses was sung by the side of a sea, which was glassy, and still; for a little season the floods had been disturbed, divided, separated, congealed, but afterwards when Israel had passed the flood, they became as ever, for the enemy had sunken to the bottom like a stone, and the sea returned to its strength when the morning appeared. Is there ever a time, then, when this great sea of Providence, which now stands parted to give a passage to God's saints, shall become a level surface? Is, there a day when the now divided dispensations of God, which are kept from following out their legitimate tendency to do justice upon sin —when the two seas of justice shall commingle, and the one sea of God's providence shall be "a sea of glass mingled with fire?" Yes, the day is drawing nigh when God's enemies shall no longer make it necessary for God's providence to be apparently disturbed to save his people, when the great designs of God shall be accomplished, and therefore when the walls of water shall roll together, whilst in their in most depths the everlasting burning fire shall consume the wicked. Oh! the sea shall be calm upon the surface: the sea upon which God's people shall walk shall seem to be a sea that is clear, without a weed, without an impurity; whilst down in its hollow bosom, far beyond all mortal ken, shall be the horrid depths where the wicked must forever dwell in the fire which is mingled with the glass.

———————

FROM the fiery days of the stakes of Smithfield even until now, the world's black heart has hated the church, and the world's cruel hand and laughing lip have been forever against us. The host of the mighty are pursuing us, and are thirsty for our blood, and anxious to cut us off from the earth. Such is our position unto this hour, and such must it be until we are landed on the other side of Jordan, and until our Maker comes to reign on the earth.

CHRIST is the same; upon his brow there is ne'er a furrow; his locks are grey with reverence, but not with age; his feet stand as firm as when they trod the everlasting mountains in the years before the world was made—his eyes as piercing as when, for the first time, he looked upon a newborn world. Christ's person never changes. Should he come on earth to visit us again, as sure he will, we should find him the same Jesus; as loving, as approachable, as generous, as kind, and though arrayed in nobler garments than he wore when first he visited earth, though no more the Man of Sorrows and griefs acquaintance, yet he would be the same person, unchanged by all his glories, his triumphs, and his joys. We bless Christ that amid his heavenly splendors his person is just the same, and his nature unaffected. "Jesus Christ the same yesterday, and today, and forever."

GOD'S first and greatest object is his own glory. There was a time, before all time, when there was no day but the Ancient of days, when God dwelt alone in the magnificence of his sublime solitude. Whether he should create, or not create, was a question depending upon the answer to another question—Would it be to his honor or not? He determined that he would glorify himself by creating; but, in creating, beyond all doubt, his motive was his glory. And since that time, he hath ever ruled the earth, and even blessed it with the same object in his infinite mind—his own glory and honor. Lesser motive for God to have, were less than divine; it is the highest position to which you or I could attain, to live for God; and the very highest virtue of God is for him to magnify himself in all his greatness as the Infinite and the Eternal. Whatever, then, God permits or does, he doth with this one motive, his own glory. And even salvation, costly though it was, and infinitely a benefaction to us, had for its first object, and for its grand result, the exaltation of the Being and of the attributes of the Supreme Ruler.

WHENEVER God has blessed the Church, he has secured himself the glory of the blessing, though they have had the profit of it. Sometimes he has been pleased to redeem his people by might; but then he has so used the might and power that all the glory hath come to him, and his head alone hath worn the crown. Did he smite Egypt, and lead forth his people, with a strong hand and an out stretched arm; the glory was not to the rod of Moses, but to the Almighty power which made the rod so potent. Did he lead his people through the wilderness, and defend them from their enemies? Still, did he, by teaching the people their dependence, upon him preserve to himself all the glory? So that not Moses or Aaron amongst the priests or prophets could share the honor with him. And tell me, if ye will, of slaughtered Anak, and the destruction of the tribes of Canaan; tell me of Israel possessing the promised land; tell me of Philistines routed, and laid heaps on heaps; of Midianites made to fall on each other; tell me of kings and princes who fled apace and fell, until the ground was white, like the snow in Salmon. I will say of every one of these triumphs, "sing ye *to the Lord,* for *he* hath triumphed gloriously;" and I will say at the end of every victory, "Crown *him*, crown *him*, for *he* hath done it; and let *his* name be exalted and extolled, world without end."

DID you ever hear of a nation under British rule being converted to God? Mr. Moffat and our great friend Dr. Livingston have been laboring in Africa with great success, and many have been converted. Did you ever hear of Caffir tribes protected by England, ever being converted? It is only a people that have been left to themselves, and preached to by men as men, that have been brought to God. For my part, I conceive, that when an enterprise begins in martyrdom, it is none the less likely to succeed; but when conquerors begin to preach the gospel to those they have conquered, it will not succeed; God will teach us that it is not by might. All swords that have ever flashed from scabbards have not aided Christ a single grain. The religion of the Islamists might be sustained by cimitars, but Christians' religion must be sustained by love. The great crime of war can never promote the religion of peace. The battle, and the garment rolled in blood, are not a fitting prelude to "peace on earth; goodwill to men." And I do firmly hold, that the slaughter of men, that bayonets, and swords, and guns, have never yet been, and never can be, promoters of the gospel. The gospel will proceed without them, but never through them. "Not by might." Now don't be befooled again, if you hear of the English conquering in China, don't go down on your knees and thank God for it, and say, it's such a heavenly thing for the spread of the gospel—it just is not. Experience teaches you that; and if you look upon the map you will find I have stated the truth, that where our arms have been victorious, the gospel has been hindered rather than not; so that where South Sea Islanders have bowed their knees and cast their idols to the bats, British Hindoos have kept their idols; and where Bechuanas and Bushmen have turned unto the Lord, British Caffirs have not been converted; not perhaps because they were British, but because the very fact of the missionary being a Briton, put him above them, and weakened their influence. Hush thy trump, O war; put away thy gaudy trappings and thy bloodstained drapery; if thou thinkest that the cannon with the cross upon it is really sanctified, and if thou imaginest that thy banner hath become holy, thou dreamest of a lie. God wanteth not thee to help his cause. "It is not by armies, nor by power, but by my Spirit, saith the Lord."

WE have delighted in our happier moments, in days that have rolled away, to think of him that loved us when we had no being; we have often sung with rapture of him that loved us when we loved not him.

> "Jesus sought me when a stranger,
> Wandering from the fold of God;
> He to save my soul from danger
> Interposed his precious blood."

We have looked back, too, upon the years of our troubles and our trials; and we can bear our solemn though humble witness, that he has been true to us in all our exigencies, and has never failed us once. Come, then, let us comfort ourselves with this thought —that though today he may distress us with a sense of sin, yet his heart is just the same to us as ever. Christ may wear masks that look black to his people, but his face is always the same; Christ may some times take a rod in his hand instead of a golden scepter; but the name of his saints is as much engraved upon the hand that grasps the rod as upon the palm that clasps the scepter.

GOD will not acquit the wicked, *because he is good*. The Judge must condemn the murderer, because he loves his nation. The kindness of a king demands the punishment of those who are guilty. It is not wrathful in the legislature to make severe laws against great sinners; it is but love towards the rest that sin should be restrained. You great flood-gates, which keep back the torrent of sin, are painted black, and look right horrible; like horrid dungeon gates, they afright my spirit; but are they proofs that God is not good? No; if ye could open wide those gates, and let the deluge of sin flow on us, then would you cry, "O God, O God! shut the gates of punishment again, let law again be established, set up the pillars, and swing the gates upon their hinges; shut again the gates of punishment, that this world may not again be utterly destroyed by men who have be come worse than brutes." It needs for very goodness sake that sin should be punished. Mercy, with her weeping eyes (for she hath wept for sinners), when she finds they will not repent, looks more terribly stern in her loveliness than Justice in all his majesty; she drops the white flag from her hand, and saith—"No; I called, and they refused; I stretched out my hand, and no man regarded; let them die, let them die;"*and that terrible word from the lip of Mercy's self is harsher thunder than the very damnation of Justice. Oh, yes, the goodness of God demands that men should perish, if they will sin.

O MY heart, I bid thee now put thy treasure where thou canst never lose it. Put it in Christ; put all thine affections in his person, all thy hope in his glory, all thy trust in his efficacious blood, all thy joy in his presence, and then thou wilt have put thyself and put thine all where thou canst never lose any thing, because it is secure.

Remember, O my heart, that the time is coming when all things must fade, and when thou must part with all. Death's gloomy night must soon put out thy sunshine; the dark flood must soon roll between thee and all thou hast. Then put thine heart with him who will never leave thee; trust thyself with him who will go with thee through the black and surging current of death's stream, and who will walk with thee up the steep hills of heaven and make thee sit together with him in heavenly places forever. Go, tell thy secrets to that friend that sticketh closer than a brother. My heart, I charge thee, trust all thy concerns with him who never can be taken from thee, who will never leave thee, and who will never let thee leave him, even "Jesus Christ the same yesterday, and today, and forever."

CHRIST JESUS, whom we adore, thou art as young as ever! We came into this world with the ignorance of infancy; we grow up searching, studying, and learning with the diligence of youth; we attain to some little knowledge in our riper years; and then in our old age we totter back to the imbecility of our childhood. But oh, our Master! thou didst perfectly foreknow all mortal or eternal things from before the foundations of the world, and thou knowest all things now, and forever thou shalt be the same in thine omniscience. We are one day strong, and the next day weak—one day resolved, and the next day wavering—one hour constant, and the next hour as unstable as water. We are one moment holy, kept by the power of God; we are the next moment sinning, led astray by our own lusts; but our Master is forever the same; pure, and never spotted; firm, and never changing—everlastingly Omnipotent, unchangeably Omniscient. From him no attribute doth pass away; to him no parallax, no tropic, ever comes; without variableness or shadow of a turning, he abideth fast and firm.

SOMETIMES tears are base things; the offspring of a cowardly spirit. Some men weep when they should knit their brows, and many a woman weepeth when she should resign herself to the will of God. Many of those briny drops are but an expression of child-like weakness. It were well if we could wipe such tears away, and face a frowning world with a constant countenance. But ofttimes tears are the index of strength. There are periods when they are the noblest thing in the world. The tears of penitents are precious; a cup of them were worth a king's ransom. It is no sign of weakness when a man weeps for sin; it shows that he hath strength of mind; nay, more, that he hath strength imparted by God, which enables him to forswear his lusts and overcome his passions, and to turn unto God with full purpose of heart. And there are other tears, too, which are the evidences not of weakness, but of might—the tears of tender sympathy are the children of strong affection, and they are strong like their pa rents. He that loveth much must weep much; much love and much sorrow must go together in this vale of tears. The unfeeling heart, the unloving spirit may pass from earth's portal to its utmost hound almost without a sigh except for itself; but he that loveth hath digged as many wells of tears as he has chosen objects of affection; for by as many as our friends are multiplied, by so many must our griefs be multiplied too, if we have love enough to share in their griefs and to bear their burden for them. The largest hearted man will miss many sorrows that a smaller one will feel, but he will have to endure many sorrows the poor narrow-minded spirit never knoweth.

UNDERSTANDING can never get to that peace which the Christian hath attained. The philosopher may teach us much; he can never give us rules whereby to reach the peace that Christians have in their conscience. Diogenes may tell us to do without everything, and may live in his tub, and then think himself happier than Alexander, and that he enjoys peace; but we look upon the poor creature after all, and though we may be astonished at his courage, yet we are obliged to despise his folly. We do not believe that even when he had dispensed with everything, he possessed a quiet of mind, a total and entire peace, such as the true believer can enjoy. We find the greatest philosophers of old laying down maxims for life, which they thought would certainly promote happiness. We find that they were not always able to practice them themselves, and many of their disciples, when they labored hard to put them in execution, found themselves encumbered with impossible rules to accomplish impossible objects. But the Christian man does with faith what a man can never do himself.

THERE is one expression in the song of Moses which ought to be, and I believe is, when set to music, very frequently repeated. It is that part of the song, as recorded in the Psalms, where it is declared that the whole host of Pharoah were utterly destroyed, and there was not one of them left. When that great song was sung by the side of the Red Sea, there was, no doubt, a special emphasis laid upon that expression, "not one." I think I hear the hosts of Israel. "When the words were known by them, they began and they proceeded thus—"There is not one of them left;" and then in various parts the words were repeated, "Not one, not one." And then the women with their sweet voices sang, "Not one, not one." I believe that at the last, a part of our triumph will be the fact, that there is not one left. "We shall look abroad throughout the earth, and see it all a level sea; and not one foe pursuing us— "not one, not one!" Raise thyself never so high, O thou deceiver, thou canst not live; for not one shall escape. Lift thy head never so proudly, O despot, thou canst not live; for not one shall escape. O heir of heaven, not one sin shall cross the Jordan after thee; not one shall pass the Red Sea to overtake thee; but this shall be the summit of thy triumph—"Not one, not one! not one of them is left."

ALL things have changed. We believe that not only in appearance but in reality, the world is growing old. The sun itself must soon grow dim with age; the folding up of the worn-out vesture has commenced; the changing of the heavens and the earth has certainly begun. They shall perish; they all shall wax old as doth a garment: but forever blessed be him who is the same, and of whose years there is no end. The satisfaction that the mariner feels, when after having been tossed about for many a day, he puts his foot upon the solid shore, is just the satisfaction of a Christian when, amidst all the changes of this troublous life, he plants the foot of his faith upon such a text as this—"The same yesterday, and today, and forever." The same stability that the anchor gives the ship, when it hath at last got the grip of some immovable rock, that same stability doth our hope give to our spirits, when, like an anchor, it fixes itself in a truth so glorious as this—"Jesus Christ the same yesterday, and today, and forever."

IT would seem as if some men had been sent into this world for the very purpose of being the world's weepers. God's great house is thoroughly furnished with everything; everything that can express the thoughts and the emotions of the inhabitants God hath made. I find in nature plants to be everlasting weepers. There by the lonely brook, where the maiden cast away her life, the willow weeps forever; and there in the graveyard, where men lie slumbering till the trumpet of the archangel shall awaken them, stands the dull cypress, mourning in its somber garments. Now, as it is with nature, so it is with the race of man. Mankind have bravery and boldness; they must have their heroes to express their courage. Mankind have some love to their fellow creatures; they must have their fine philanthropists to live out mankind's philanthropy. Men have their sorrows; they must have their weepers; they must have men of sorrows, who have it for their avocation and their business, to weep, from the cradle to the grave; to be ever weeping, not so much for themselves as for the woes of others.

DEAR friends, the last song in this world, the song of triumph, shall be full of God, and of no one else. Here you praise the instrument; today you look on this man and on that, and you say, "Thank God for this minister, and for this man!" Today you say, "Blessed be God for Luther, who shook the Vatican, and thank

God for Whitfield, who stirred up a slumbering church;" but in that day you shall not sing of Luther, nor of Whitfield, nor of any of the mighty ones of God's hosts; forgotten shall their names be for a season, even as the stars refuse to shine when the sun himself appeareth. The song shall be unto Jehovah, and Jehovah only; we shall not have a word to say for preachers nor bishops, not a syllable to say for good men and true; but the whole song from first to last shall be, "Unto him that loved us, and hath washed us from our sins in his own blood, unto him be glory forever and ever. Amen."

YOU know, beloved, that after all, the greatest works that have been done have been done by the ones. The hundreds do not often do much; the companies never do; it is the units, just the single individuals, that after all are the power and the might. Take any parish in England where there is a well-regulated society for doing good—it is some young woman or some young man who is the very life of it. Take any Church, there are multitudes in it, but it is some two or three that do the work. Look on the Reformation; there might be many reformers, but there was but one Luther; there might be many teachers, but there was but one Calvin. Look ye upon the preachers of the last age, the mighty preachers who stirred up the churches; there were many coadjutors with them; but after all, it was not Whitfield's friends, nor Wesley's friends, but the men themselves that did it. Individual effort is, after all, the grand thing. A man alone can do more than a man with fifty men at his heels to fetter him. Committees are very seldom of much use; and bodies and societies sometimes are loss of strength instead of gain. It is said, that if Noah's Ark had had to be built by a company, they would not have laid the keel yet; and it is perhaps true. There is scarcely anything done by a body; it almost always fails; because what is many men's business is just nobody's business at all. Just the same with religion, the grand things must be done by the ones, the great works of God must be accomplished by single men. Look back through old history. Who delivered Israel from the Philistines? It was a solitary Samson. Who was it gathered the people together to rout the Midianites? It was one Gideon, who cried, "The sword of the Lord and of Gideon." Who was he that smote the enemy? It was one Shamgar, with his ox goad, or it was an Egon, who with his dagger, put an end to his country's tyrant. Separate men—Davids with their slings and stones, have done more than armies will accomplish.

OH! ye that lean wearily on your staff, the support of your old age, have ye not sins still clinging to your garments? Are your lives as white as the snowy hair that crowns your head? Do you not still feel that transgression besmears the skirts of your robe, and mars its spotlessness? How often are you now plunged into the ditch till your own clothes do abhor you. Cast your eyes over the sixty, the seventy, the eighty years, during which God hath spared your lives; and can ye for a moment think it possible, that ye can number up your innumerable transgressions, or compute the weight of the crimes which you have committed? O ye stars of heaven! the astronomer may measure your distance and tell your height, but O ye sins of man kind! ye surpass all thought. O ye lofty mountains! the home of the tempest, the birthplace of the storm! man may climb your summits and stand wonderingly upon your snows; but ye hills of sin! ye tower higher than our thoughts; ye chasms of transgressions! ye are deeper than our imagination dares to dive. Do you accuse me of slandering human nature? It is because you know it not. If God had once manifested your heart to yourself, you would bear me witness, that so far from exaggerating, my poor words fail to describe the desperateness of our evil. Oh! if we could each of us look into our hearts today—if our eyes could be turned within, so as to see the iniquity that is graven as with the point of the diamond upon our stony hearts, we should then say to the minister, that however he may depict the desperateness of guilt, yet can he not by any means surpass it. How great then, beloved, must be the ransom of Christ, when he saved us from all these sins! The men for whom Jesus died, however great their sin, when they believe, are justified from all their transgressions. Though they may have indulged in every vice and every lust which Satan could suggest, and which human nature could perform, yet once believing, all their guilt is washed away. Year after year may have coated them with blackness, till their sin hath become of double dye; but in one moment of faith, one triumphant moment of confidence in Christ, the great redemption takes away the guilt of numerous years. Nay, more, if it were possible for all the sins that men have done, in thought, or word, or deed, since worlds were made, or time began, to meet on one poor head—the great redemption is all-sufficient to take all these sins away, and wash the sinner whiter than the driven snow.

YOU see yonder ship. After a long voyage, it has neared the haven, but is much injured; the sails are rent to ribbons, and it is in such a forlorn condition that it cannot come up to the harbor: a steamtug is pulling it in with the greatest possible difficulty. That is like the righteous being "scarcely saved." But do you see that other ship? It has made a prosperous voyage; and now, laden to the water's edge, with the sails all up and with the white canvas filled with the wind, it rides into the harbor joyously and nobly. That is an "abundant entrance;" and if you and I are helped by God's Spirit to add to our faith, virtue, and so on, we shall have at the last an "abundant entrance into the kingdom of our Lord Jesus Christ.'

MOSES not only rejoiced for what had been done, but for the future consequences of it. He says—"The people of Canaan, whom we are about to attack, will now be seized with sudden fear; by the greatness of thy arm they shall be as still as a stone." Oh! I think I hear them singing that too, sweetly and softly—"as still as a stone." How would the words come full, like gentle thunder heard in the distance—"as still as a stone!" And when we shall get on the other side the flood, see the triumph over our enemies, and behold our Master reigning, this will form a part of our song—that they must henceforth be "as still as a stone." There will be a hell, but it will not be a hell of roaring devils, as it now is. They shall be "as still as a stone." There will be legions of fallen angels, but they shall no longer have courage to attack us or to defy God: they shall be "as still as a stone." Oh! how grand will that sound, when the hosts of God's redeemed, looking down on the demons chained, bound, silenced, struck dumb with terror, shall sing exultingly over, them! They must be as still as a stone; and there they must lie, and bite their iron bands. The fierce despiser of Christ can no more spit in his face; the proud tyrant can no more lift his hands to oppress the saints; even Satan can no more attempt to destroy. They shall be "as still as a stone."

OH! who shall measure the heights of the Savior's all-sufficiency? First, tell how high is sin, and, then, remember that as Noah's flood prevailed over the tops of earth's mountains, so the flood of Christ's redemption prevails over the tops of the mountains of our sins. In heaven's courts there are today men that once were murderers, and thieves, and drunkards, and whoremongers, and blasphemers, and persecutors; but they have been washed—they have been sanctified. Ask them whence the brightness of their robes hath come, and where their purity hath been achieved, and they, with united breath, tell you that they have washed their robes, and made them white in the blood of the Lamb.

OH! how did heaven wonder! how did the stars stand still with astonishment! and how did the angels stay their songs a moment, when for the first time, God showed how he might be just, and yet be gracious! Oh! I think I see heaven astonished, and silence in the courts of God for the space of an hour, when the Almighty said, "Sinner, I must and will punish thee on account of sin! But I love thee; the bowels of my love yearn over thee. How can I make thee as Admah? How shall I set thee as Zeboim? My justice says 'smite,' but my love stays my hand, and says, 'spare, spare the sinner!' Oh! sinner, my heart hath devised it; my Son, the pure and perfect, shall stand in thy stead, and be accounted guilty, and thou, the guilty, shall stand in my Son's stead and be accounted righteous!" It would make us leap upon our feet in astonishment if we did but understand this thoroughly—the wonderful mystery of the transposition of Christ and the sinner.

CHRIST longed for the cross, because he looked for it as the goal of all his exertions. He could never say "It is finished" on his throne: but on his cross he did cry it. He preferred the sufferings of Cal vary to the honors of the multitude who crowded round about him; for, preach as he might, and bless them as he might, and heal them as he might, still was his work undone. He was straitened; he had a baptism to be baptized with, and how was he straitened till it was accomplished. "But," he said, "now I pant for my cross, for it is the topstone of my labor. I long for my sufferings, because they shall be the completion of my great work of grace." It is the end that bringeth the honor; it is the victory that crowneth the warrior rather than the battle. And so Christ longed for this, his death, that he might see the completion of his labor.

SOMETIMES, right solemnly, the sacred mysteries of eternal wrath must he preached, but far oftener let us preach the wondrous love of God. There are more souls won by wooing than by threatening. It is not hell, but Christ, we desire to preach, O sinners, we are not afraid to tell you of your doom, but we do not choose to be forever dwelling on that doleful theme. We rather love to tell you of Christ, and him crucified. We want to have our preaching rather full of the frankincense of the merits of Christ than of the smoke, and fire, and terrors of Mount Sinai, we are not come unto Mount Sinai, but unto Mount Zion —where milder words declare the will of God, and rivers of salvation are abundantly flowing.

COME, my soul, art thou at peace with God? Hast thou seen thy pardon signed and sealed with the Redeemer's blood? Come, answer this, my heart; hast thou cast thy sins upon the head of Christ, and hast thou seen them all washed away in the crimson streams of blood? Canst thou feel that now there is a lasting peace between thyself and God, so that come what may, God shall not be angry with thee—shall not condemn thee—shall not consume thee in his wrath, nor crush thee in his hot displeasure? If it be so, then, my heart, thou canst scarcely need to stop and ask the second question— Is my conscience at peace? For, if my heart condemn me not, God is greater than my heart, and doth know all things; if my conscience bears witness with me, that I am a partaker of the precious grace of salvation, then happy am I! I am one of those to whom God hath given the peace which passeth all understanding. Now, why is this called "the peace of God?" We suppose it is because it comes from God—because it was planned by God—because God gave his Son to make the peace— because God gives his Spirit to give the peace in the conscience—because, indeed, it is God himself in the soul, reconciled to man, whose is the peace. And while it is true that this man shall have the peace— even the Man-Christ, yet we know it is because he was the God-Christ that he was our peace. And hence we may clearly perceive how Godhead is mixed up with the peace which we enjoy with our Maker, and with our conscience.

FULL many a time has a preacher rendered Scripture dark by his explanations, instead of making it brighter. Many a preacher has been like a painted window, shutting out the light, instead of admitting it.

HAST thou never fled to Christ for refuge? Dost thou not believe in the Redeemer? Hast thou never confided thy soul to his hands? Then hear me; in God's name, hear me just a moment. My friend, I would not stand in thy position for an hour, for all the stars twice spelt in gold! For what is thy position? Thou hast sinned, and God will not acquit thee; he will punish thee. He is letting thee live; thou art reprieved. Poor is the life of one that is reprieved without a pardon! Thy reprieve will soon run out; thine hour-glass is emptying every day. I see on some of you death has put his cold hand, and frozen your hair to whiteness. Ye need your staff, it is the only barrier between you and the grave now; and you are, all of you, old and young, standing on a narrow neck of land, between two boundless seas—that neck of land, that isthmus of life, narrowing every moment, and you are yet unpardoned. There is a city to be sacked, and you are in it—soldiers are at the gates; the command is given that every man in the city is to be slaughtered save he who can give the password. "Sleep on, sleep on; the attack is not today; sleep on, sleep on." "But it is tomorrow, sir." "Aye, sleep on, sleep on; it is not till tomorrow ; sleep on, procrastinate, procrastinate." "Hark! I hear a rumbling at the gates; the battering ram is at them; the gates are tottering." "Sleep on, sleep on; the soldiers are not yet at your doors; sleep on, sleep on; ask for no mercy yet; sleep on, sleep on!" "Aye, but I hear the shrill clarion sound; they are in the streets. Hark, to the shrieks of men and women! They are slaughtering them; they fall, they fall, they fall!" "Sleep on; they are not yet at *your* door." "But hark! they are at the gate; with heavy tramp I hear the soldiers marching up the stairs!" "Nay, sleep on, sleep on; they are not yet in your room." "Why, they are there; they have burst open the door that parted you from them, and there they stand!" "No, sleep on, sleep on; the sword is not yet at your throat; sleep on, sleep on!" It *is* at your throat; you start with horror. Sleep on, sleep on! But you are gone! "Demon, why didst thou tell me to slumber! It would have been wise in me to have escaped the city when first the gates were shaken. Why did I not ask for the password before the troops came? Why, by all that is wise, why did I not rush into the streets, and cry the password when the soldiers were there? Why stood I till the knife was at my throat? Aye, demon that thou art, be cursed; but I am cursed with thee forever!" You know the application; it is a parable you can all expound; ye need not that I should tell you that death is after you, that justice must devour you, that Christ crucified is the only password that can save you; and yet you have not learned it—that with some of you death is nearing, nearing, nearing, and that with all of you he is close at hand! I need not expound how Satan is the demon, how in hell you shall curse him and curse yourselves because you procrastinated—how that seeing God was slow to anger you were slow to repentance—how, because he was great in power, and kept back his anger, therefore you kept back your steps from seeking him; and here you are what you are!

WORKS of art require some education in the beholder, before they can be thoroughly appreciated. We do not expect that the uninstructed should at once perceive the varied excellences of a painting from some master hand; we do not imagine that the superlative glories of the harmonies of the Princes of Song will enrapture the ears of clownish listeners. There must be something in the man himself, before he can understand the wonders either of nature or of art. Certainly this is true of character. By reason of failures in our character and faults in our life, we are not capable of understanding all the separate beauties, and the united perfection of the character of Christ, or of God, his Father. "Were we ourselves as pure as the angels in heaven, were we what our race once was in the garden of Eden, immaculate and perfect, it is quite certain that we should have a far better and nobler idea of the character of God than we can by possibility attain unto in our fallen state. But you cannot fail to notice, that men, through the alienation of their natures, are continually misrepresenting God, because they cannot appreciate his perfection. Does God at one time withhold his hand from wrath? Lo, they say that God hath ceased to judge the world, and looks upon it with listless, phlegmatic indifference. Does he at another time punish the world for sin? They say he is severe and cruel. Men *will* misunderstand him, because they are imperfect themselves, and are not capable of admiring the character of God.

THE *cross of Christ is Christ's glory.* Man seeks to win his glory by the slaughter of others— Christ by the slaughter of himself: men seek to get crowns of gold—he sought a crown of thorns: men think that glory lieth in being exalted over others— Christ thought that his glory did lie in becoming "a worm and no man," a scoff and reproach amongst all that beheld him. He stooped when he conquered; and he counted that the glory lay as much in the stooping as in the conquest.

IF kingdoms should go to rack the Christian need not tremble. Just for a minute imagine a scene like this. Suppose for the next three days the sun should not rise; suppose the moon should be turned into a clot of blood, and shine no more upon the world; imagine that a darkness that might be felt, brooded over all men; imagine next that all the world did tremble in an earthquake till every tower and house and hut fell down: imagine next that the sea forgot its place and leaped upon the earth, and that the mountains ceased to stand, and, began to tremble from their pedestals; conceive after that a blazing comet streamed across the sky—that the thunder bellowed incessantly—that the lightnings without a moment's pause followed one the other; conceive then that thou didst behold divers terrible sights, fiendish ghosts and grim spirits; imagine next, that a trumpet, waxing exceeding loud, did blow; that there were heard the shrieks of men dying and perishing; imagine, that in the midst of all this confusion there was to be found a saint. My friend, "Jesus Christ the same yesterday, today, and forever," would keep . him as secure amidst all these horrors as we are to day. Oh! rejoice! I have pictured the worst that can come. *Then* you would be secure. Come what may then, you are safe, while Jesus Christ is the same.

COMING to Christ is just the one essential thing He that cometh not to Christ, do what he may, or think what he may, is yet in "the gall of bitterness and in the bonds of iniquity." Coming to Christ is the very first effect of regeneration. No sooner is the soul quickened than it at once discovers its lost estate, is horrified thereat, looks out for a refuge, and believing Christ to be a suitable one, flies to him and reposes in him. Where there is not this coming to Christ, it is certain that there is as yet no quickening; where there is no quickening, the soul is dead in trespasses and sins, and being dead it cannot enter into the kingdom of heaven.

SINNER, unconverted sinner, thou hast often tried to save thyself; but thou hast often failed. Thou hast, by thine own power and might, sought to curb thy evil passions and licentious desires; with thee, I lament that all thine efforts have been unsuccessful. And I warn thee, it will be unsuccessful, for thou never canst by thine own might save thy self; with all the strength thou hast, thou never canst regenerate thine own soul; thou canst never cause thyself to be born again. And though the new birth is absolutely necessary, it is absolutely impossible to thee, unless God the Spirit shall do it.

WHEN man fell in the garden, manhood fell entirely; there was not one single pillar in the temple of manhood that stood erect. It is true, conscience was not destroyed. The pillar was not shattered; it fell, and it fell in one piece, and there it lies along, the mightiest remnant of God's once perfect work in man. But that conscience is fallen, I am sure. Look at men. Who among them is the possessor of a "good conscience toward God," but the regenerated man? Do you imagine that if men's consciences always spoke loudly and clearly to them, they would live in the daily commission of acts, which are as opposed to the right as darkness to light? No, beloved; conscience can tell me that I am a sinner, but conscience cannot make me *feel* that I am one. Conscience may tell me that such and such a thing is wrong, but how wrong it is conscience itself does not know. Did any man's conscience, unenlightened by the Spirit, ever tell him that his sins deserved damnation? Or if conscience did do that, did it ever lead any man to feel an abhorrence of sin as sin? In fact, did conscience ever bring a man to such a self-renunciation, that he did totally abhor himself and all his works and come to Christ? No, conscience, although it is not dead, is ruined, its power is impaired, it hath not that clearness of eye and that strength of hand, and that thunder of voice, which it had before the fall; but hath ceased to a great degree, to exert its supremacy in the town of Mansoul. Then, beloved, it becomes necessary for this very reason, because conscience is depraved, that the Holy Spirit should step in, to show us our need of a Savior, and draw us to the Lord Jesus Christ!

PRAYER is the certain forerunner of salvation. Sinner, thou canst not pray and perish; prayer and perishing are two things that never go together. I ask you not what your prayer is; it may be a groan, it may be a tear, a worldless prayer, or a prayer in broken English, ungrammatical and harsh to the ear: but if it be a prayer from the inmost heart, thou shalt be saved; or else this promise is a lie. As surely as thou prayest, whoever thou mayest be, whatever thy past life, whatever the transgressions in which thou hast indulged, though they be the foulest which pol lute mankind, yet if from thine heart thou has learned to pray—

> Prayer is the breath of God in man,
> Returning whence it came"—

And thou canst not perish with God's breath in thee. 'Whosoever shall call upon the name of the Lord shall be saved!"

"FEAR not, thou worm Jacob, and ye men of Israel; I will help thee." Come, bring your fears out tonight, and serve them in the worst way you can. Hang them here upon the scaffold. Come now, and blow them away at the great guns of the promises, let them be destroyed forever. They are renegade mutineers; let them be cut off, let them be utterly destroyed, and let us go and sing, "Therefore will we not fear, though the earth be removed, and though the mountains be carried into the midst of the sea; though the waters thereof roar and be troubled, though the mountains shake with the swelling thereof." "I *will* help *thee*," saith the Redeemer.

LEARN to look upon God as being as severe in his justice as if he were not loving, and yet as loving as if he were not severe. His love does not diminish his justice, nor does his justice, in the least degree, make warfare upon his love. The two things are sweetly linked together in the atonement of Christ. But, mark, we can never understand the fullness of the atonement till we have first grasped the Scriptural truth of God's immense justice. There was never an ill word spoken, nor an ill thought conceived, nor an evil deed done, for which God will not have punishment from some one or another. He will either have satisfaction from you, or else from Christ. If you have no atonement to bring through Christ, you must forever lie paying the debt which you never can pay, in eternal misery; for as surely as God is God, he will sooner lose his Godhead than suffer one sin to go unpunished, or one particle of rebellion unrevenged.

WHAT would her Majesty think of her soldiers, if they should swear they were loyal and true, and were to say—"Your Majesty, we prefer not to wear these regimentals; let us wear the dress of civilians! We are right honest men and upright; but do not care to stand in your ranks, acknowledged as your soldiers; we had rather slink into the enemy's camp, and into your camps too, and not wear anything that would mark us as being your soldiers!" Ah! some of you do the same with Christ. You are going to be secret Christians, are you, and slink into the devil's camp, and into Christ's camp, but acknowledged by none? Well, ye must take the chance of it, if ye will be so; but I should not like to risk it. It is a solemn threatening, "of him will I be ashamed when I come in the glory of my Father, and all his holy angels with me!" It is a solemn thing, I say, when Christ says, "Except a man take up his cross and follow me, he cannot be my disciple."

THE common habit with the harlot or the profligate, is to drive
them out of society as a curse. It is not right, it is not Christian-
like. We are bound to love even sinners, and not to drive them
from the land of hope, but seek to reclaim even these. Is a man a
rogue, a thief, or a liar? I cannot love his roguery, or I should be a
rogue myself. I cannot love his lying, or I should be untrue; but I
am bound to love *him* still, and even though I am wronged by him,
yet I must not harbor one vindictive feeling, but as I would desire
God to forgive me, so I must forgive him. And if he so sins against
the law of the land, that he is to be punished (and rightly so), I am
to love him in the punishment; for I am not to condemn him to
imprisonment vindictively, but I am to do it for his good, that he
may be led to repent through the punishment; I am to give him such
a measure of punishment as shall be adequate, not as an atonement
for his crime, but to teach him the evil of it, and induce him to
forsake it. But let me condemn him with a tear in my eye, because
I love him still. And let me, when he is thrust into prison, take
care that all his keepers attend to him with kindness, and although
there be a necessity for sternness and severity in prison discipline,
let it not go too far, lest it merge into cruelty, and become wanton,
instead of useful. I am bound to love him, though he be sunken in
vice and degraded. The law knows of no exception. It claims my
love for him. I must love him. I am not hound to take him to my
house; I am not bound to treat him as one of my family. There may
be some acts of kindness which would be imprudent, seeing that
by doing them I might ruin others and reward vice. I am bound to
set my *face* against him, as I am just, but I feel I ought not to set my
heart against him, for he is my brother-man, and though the devil
has besmeared his face, and spits his venom in his mouth, so that
when he speaks he speaks in oaths, and when he walks, his feet are
swift to shed blood, yet he is a man, and as a man he is my brother,
and as a brother I am bound to love him, and if by stooping I can
lift him up to something like moral dignity, I am wrong if I do not
do it, for I am bound to love him as I love myself.

THERE are a class of men who are a great deal nobler than the herd of simpletons who allow the sublimities of the Godhead to be concealed by their carking care for mere sensual good. There are some who do not forget that there is a God; no, they are astronomers, and they turn their eyes to heaven, and they view the stars, and they marvel at the majesty of the Creator. Or they dig into the bowels of the earth, and they are astonished at the magnificence of God's works of yore. Or they examine the animal, and marvel at the wisdom of God in the construction of its anatomy. They, whenever they think of God, think of him with the deepest awe, with the profoundest reverence. You never hear them curse or swear: you will find that their souls are possessed of a deep awe of the great Creator. But ah! my friends, this is not enough: this is not obedience to the command. God does not say thou shalt wonder at him, thou shalt have awe of him. He asks more than that: he says, "Thou shalt love me!"

SUPPOSE a liar says that it is not in his power to speak the truth, that he has been a liar so long, that he cannot leave it off; is that an excuse for him? Suppose a man who has long indulged in lust should tell you that he finds his lusts have so girt about him like a great iron net that he cannot get rid of them, would you take that as an excuse? Truly it is none at all. If a drunkard has become so foully a drunkard, that he finds it impossible to pass a public-house without stepping in, do you therefore excuse him? No, because his inability to reform lies in his nature, which he has no desire to restrain or conquer. The thing that is done, and the thing that causes the thing that is done, being both from the root of sin, are two evils which cannot excuse each other. What though the Ethiopian cannot change his skin, nor the leopard his spots? It is because you have learned to do evil that you cannot now learn to do well; and instead, therefore, of letting you sit down to excuse yourselves, let me put a thunderbolt beneath the seat of your sloth, that you may be startled by it and aroused. Remember that to sit still is to be damned to all eternity!

LET not your exertions end in tears, mere weeping will do nothing without action. Get on your feet; ye that have voices and might, go forth and preach the gospel, preach it in every street and lane of this huge city; ye that have wealth, go forth and spend it for the poor, and sick, and needy, and dying, the uneducated, the unenlightened; ye that have time, go forth and spend it in deeds of goodness; ye that have power in prayer go forth and pray; ye that can handle the pen, go forth and write down iniquity—every one to his post, every one of you to your gun in this day of battle; now for God and for his truth; for God and for the right; let every one of us who knows the Lord seek to fight under his banner!

DREAMS, the disordered fabrics of a wild imagination; the totterings often of the fair pillars of a grand conception; how can they be the means of salvation? You know Rowland Hill's good answer; I must quote it in default of a better. When a woman pleaded that she was saved because she dreamed, he said, "Well, my good woman, it is very nice to have good dreams when you are asleep; but I want to see how you act when you are awake; for if your conduct is not consistent in religion when you are awake, I will not give a snap of the finger for your dreams." Ah, I do marvel that ever any person should go to such a depth of ignorance as to tell me the stories that I have heard myself about dreams. Poor dear creatures, when they were sound asleep they saw the gates of heaven opened, and a white angel came and washed their sins away, and then they saw that they were pardoned; and since then they have never had a doubt or a fear. It is time that you should begin to doubt, then; very good time that you should; for if that is all the hope you have, it is a poor one remember it is, "Whosoever calls upon the name of God," not whosoever dreams about him. Dreams may do good. Sometimes people have been frightened out of their senses in them; and they were better out of their senses than they were in, for they did more mischief when they were in their senses than they did when they were out; and the dreams did good in that sense. Some people, too, have been alarmed by dreams; but to trust to them is to trust to a shadow, to build your hopes on bubbles, scarcely needing a puff of wind to burst them into nothingness. Oh! remember, you want no vision, no marvelous appearance. If you have had a vision or a dream, you need not despise it; it may have benefited you; but do not trust to it. But if you have had none, remember it is not the mere calling upon God's name to which the promise is appended.

THROUGH the fall, and through our own sin, the nature of man has become so debased, and depraved, and corrupt, that it is impossible for him to come to Christ without the assistance of God the Holy Spirit. Now, in trying to exhibit how the nature of man thus renders him unable to come to Christ, you must allow me just to take this figure. You see a sheep; how willingly it feeds upon the herbage! You never knew a sheep sigh after carrion; It could not live on lion's food. Now bring me a wolf; and you ask me whether a wolf cannot eat grass, whether it cannot be just as docile and just as domesticated as the sheep. I answer No; because its nature is contrary thereunto. You say, "Well, it has ears and legs; can it not hear the shepherd's voice, and follow him whithersoever he leadeth it?" I answer, certainly, there is no physical cause why it cannot do so, but its nature forbids, and therefore I say it *cannot* do so. Can it not be tamed? cannot its ferocity be removed? Probably it may so far be subdued that it may become apparently tame, but there will always be a marked distinction between it and the sheep, because there is a distinction in nature. Now, the reason why man cannot come to Christ, is not because he cannot come, so far as his body or his mere power of mind is concerned, but because his nature is so corrupt that he has neither the will nor the power to come to Christ, unless drawn by the Spirit. But let me give you a better illustration. You see a mother with a babe in her arms. You put a knife into her hand and tell her to stab that babe to the heart. She replies, and very truthfully, "I cannot." Now, so far as her bodily power is concerned, she can, if she pleases; there is the knife, and there is the child. The child cannot resist, and she has quite sufficient strength in her hand immediately to stab it to its heart. But she is quite correct when she says she cannot do it. As a mere act of the mind, it is quite possible she might think of such a thing as killing the child, and yet she says she cannot think of such a thing; and she does not say falsely, for her nature as a mother forbids her doing a thing from which her soul revolts. Simply because she is that child's parent she feels she cannot kill it. It is even so with a sinner. Coming to Christ is so obnoxious to human nature that, although, so far as physical and mental forces are concerned (and these have but a very narrow sphere in salvation) men could come if they would: it is strictly correct to say that they cannot and will not unless the Father who hath sent Christ doth draw them.

YOU who have never meditated on Jesus Christ— what do you think shall become of you when your bitterness shall be in your month? "When you taste death, how do you hope to destroy its ill flavor? Yet "that last, that bitter cup which mortal man can taste," is but a dire presentiment. "When you have to drink that gall in hell forever—when the cup of torments which Jesus did not drain for you will have to be drained by yourself—what will you do then? The Christian can go to heaven, because Christ has drunk destruction dry for him; but the ungodly and unconverted man will have to drink the dregs of the wine of Gomorrah. What will you do then? The first drops are bad enough, when you sip here the drops of remorse on account of sin; but that future cup in hell—that terrific mixture which God deals out to the lost in the pit—what will you do when you have to drink that? when your meditation will be, that you rejected Jesus, that you despised his Gospel, that you scoffed at his word? 'What will you do in that dread extremity?

IF this night, ere you rest, you could say that with God, as well as all the world, you are at peace, you may go out tomorrow, and whatever your business, I am not afraid for you. You are more than a match for all the temptations to false doctrine, to false living, or to false speech that may meet you. For he that has peace with God is armed *cap-à-pié*; he is covered from head to foot in a panoply. The arrow may fly against it, but it cannot pierce it, for peace with God is a mail so strong that the broad sword of Satan itself may be broken in twain ere it can pierce the flesh. Oh! take care that you are at peace with God; for, if you are not, you ride forth to tomorrow 's fight unarmed, naked; and God help the man that is unarmed when he has to fight with hell and earth. Oh, be not foolish, but "put on the whole armor of God," and then be confident, for you need not fear.

THE whole world was drowned except those happy ones who were found in the ark. The mightiest beast and the tiniest insect, the stately elephant and the loathsome reptile, the fleet horse and the creeping snail, the graceful antelope and the ugly toad—every living substance that was upon the face of the ground was involved in one common doom, save those only who were preserved alive in the ark. The noblest animals, endowed with the finest instincts, were all drowned, despite their powers of swimming (if they were not fish), save those only who were sheltered in the ark. The strongest winged fowls that ever cut the air were all wearied in their flight and fell into the water, save those only who were housed in the ark. The proudest tenants of the forest, those who ranged fearlessly in the broad light of day, or those who prowled stealthily under the cover of night, the strongest, the mightiest, all were swallowed up in the vast abyss, save those only who were commanded by God to hide themselves within the shelter of the ark. Even so, there is only one way of salvation for all men living under heaven. There is only one name whereby they can be saved. 'Wouldst thou be saved, rich man? There is no way but that whereby the poverty-stricken pauper is also to be saved. Wouldst thou be delivered, thou man of intelligence? Thou shalt be saved in the same way as the most ignorant. There is none other name under heaven given among men whereby we must be saved, but Jesus Christ and him crucified. There were not two arks, but one ark: so there are not two Saviors, but one Savior. There was no other means of salvation except the ark: so there is no plan of deliverance except by Jesus Christ, the Savior of sinners. In vain you climb the lofty top of Sinai: fifteen cubits upwards shall the waters prevail. In vain you climb to the highest pinnacles of your self-conceit and your worldly merit: ye shall be drowned—drowned beyond the hope of salvation; for "other foundations can no man lay than that which is laid—Jesus Christ and him crucified."

———————

THE first thing the Holy Spirit does when he comes into a man's heart is this: he finds him with a very good opinion of himself: and there is nothing which prevents a man coming to Christ like a good opinion of himself. Why, says man, "I don't want to come to Christ. I have as good a righteousness as anybody can desire. I feel I can walk into heaven on my own rights." The Holy Spirit lays bare his heart, lets him see the loathsome cancer that is there eating away his life, uncovers to him all the blackness and defilement of that sink of hell, the human heart, and then the man stands aghast. "I never thought I was like this. Oh! those sins I thought were little, have swelled out to an immense stature. What I thought was a mole hill, has grown into a mountain; it was but the hyssop on the wall before, but now it has become a cedar of Lebanon. Oh," saith the man within himself, "I will try and reform; I will do good deeds enough to wash these black deeds out." Then comes the Holy Spirit and shows him that he cannot do this, takes away all his fancied power and strength, so that the man falls down on his knees in agony and cries, "Oh! once I thought I could save myself by my good works, but now I find that—

> 'Could my tears forever flow,
> Could my zeal no respite know,
> All for sin could not atone,
> Thou must save and thou alone.'"

Then the heart sinks, and the man is ready to despair. And saith he, "I never can be saved. Nothing can save me." Then comes the

Holy Spirit, and shows the sinner the cross of Christ, gives him eyes anointed with heavenly eye-salve, and says, "Look to yonder cross, that man died to save sinners; you feel that you are a sinner; he died to save you." And he enables the heart to believe, and to come to Christ. And when it comes to Christ, by this sweet drawing of the Spirit, it finds "a peace with God which passeth all understanding, which keeps his heart and mind through Jesus Christ our Lord." Now, you will plainly perceive that all this may be done without any compulsion. Man is as much drawn willingly, as if he were not drawn at all; and he comes to Christ with full consent, with as full a consent as if no secret influence had ever been exercised in his heart. But that influence must be exercised, or else there never has been and there never will be, any man who either can or will come to the Lord Jesus Christ.

A VAUNT, Satan! While I am at peace with God, I am a match for all thy temptations. Thou offerest me silver; I have gold. Thou bringest before me the riches of the earth; I have something more substantial than these. Avaunt, tempter of human kind! Avaunt, thou fiend! Your temptations and blandishments are lost on one who has peace with God. This peace, too, will keep the heart undivided. He who has peace with God will set his whole heart on God. "Oh!" says he, "why should I go to seek anything else on earth, now that I have found my rest in God? As the bird by wandering, so should I be if I went elsewhere. I have found a fountain; why should I go and drink at the broken cistern that will hold no water? I lean on the arm of my beloved; why should I rest on the arm of another? I know that religion is a thing worth my following; why should I leave the pure snows of Lebanon to follow something else? I know and feel that religion is rich when it brings forth to me a hundred-fold the fruits of peace; why should I go and sow elsewhere? I will be like the maiden Ruth, I will stop in the fields of Boaz. Here I will ever stay and never wander."

THE wrath of man shall praise God. I believe the last song of
the redeemed, when they shall ultimately triumph, will celebrate in
heavenly stanzas the wrath of man overcome by God. Sometimes
after great battles, monuments are raised to the memory of the fight;
and of what are they composed? They are composed of weapons of
death and of instruments of war which have been taken from the
enemy. Now, to use that illustration as I think it may be properly
used, the day is coming when fury, and wrath, and hatred, and strife,
shall all be woven into a song; and the weapons of our enemies, when
taken from them, shall serve to make monuments to the praise of
God. Rail on, rail on, blasphemer! Smite on, smite on, tyrant! Lift
thy heavy hand, O despot; crush the truth, which thou canst not
crush; knock from his head the crown—the crown that is far above
thy reach—poor puny impotent mortal as thou art! Go on, go on! But
all thou doest shall but increase his glories. For aught we care, we bid
you still proceed with all your wrath and malice. Though it shall be
worse for you, it shall be more glorious for our Master; the greater
your preparations for war, the more splendid shall be his triumphal
chariot, when he shall ride through the streets of heaven in pompous
array. The more mighty your preparations for battle, the more rich
the spoil which he shall divide with the strong. O Christian, fear
not the foe! Remember the harder his blows, the sweeter thy song;
the greater his wrath, the more splendid thy triumph; the more he
rages, the more shall Christ be honored in the day of his appearing.

IT is better to be cheated sometimes ourselves than that we
should cheat others; and it is cheating others to suspect those on
whose characters there resteth no suspicion. We acknowledge such
morality among men, but we act not so towards God; we believe any
liar sooner than we believe him.

I WILL *help* thee. That is very little for me to do, to *help* thee.

Consider what I have done already. What! not help thee? "Why, I bought thee with my blood. What! not help thee? I have died for thee; and if I have done the greater, will I not do the less? *Help* thee, my beloved! It is the least thing I will ever do for thee. I have done more, and I will do more. Before the day-star first began to shine I chose thee. "I will *help* thee." I made the covenant for thee, and exercised all the wisdom of my eternal mind in the scheming of the plan of salvation. "I will *help* thee." I became a man for thee; I doffed my diadem, and laid aside my robe; I laid the purple of the universe aside to become a man for thee. If I did this, I will *help* thee. I gave my life, my soul, for thee; I slumbered in the grave, I descended into Hades, all for thee; I will *help* thee. It will cost me nothing. Redeeming thee cost me much, but I have all and abound. In helping thee, I am giving thee what I have bought for thee already. It is no new thing. I can do it easily. "Help thee?" Thou needst never fear that. If thou needest a thousand times as much help as thou dost need, I would give it thee; but it is little that thou dost require compared with what I have to give. 'Tis great for thee to need, but it is nothing for me to bestow. "*Help* thee?" Fear not. If there were an ant at the door of thy granary asking for help, it would not ruin thee to give him a handful of thy wheat; and thou art nothing but a tiny insect at the door of my all-sufficiency. All that thou couldst ever eat, all that thou couldst ever take, if thou wert to take on to all eternity, would no more diminish my all-sufficiency, than the drinking of the fish would diminish the sea. No; "I will *help* thee." If I have died for thee, I will not leave thee.

THE Samaritan, when he saw the wounded man on the road to Jericho, felt that he was in his neighborhood, and that therefore he was his neighbor, and he was bound to love him. "Love thy neighbor." Perhaps he is in riches, and thou art poor, and thou livest in thy little cot side-by-side with his lordly mansion. Thou seest his estates, thou markest his fine linen, and his sumptuous raiment. God has given him these gifts, and if he has not given them to thee, covet not his wealth, and think no hard thoughts concerning him. There will ever be differences in the circumstances of man, so let it be. Be content with thy own lot, if thou canst not better it, but do not look upon thy neighbor, and wish that he were poor as thyself, and do not aid or abet any who would rid him of his wealth, to make thee hastily rich. Love him, and then thou canst not envy him. Mayhap, on the other hand, thou art rich, and near thee reside the poor. Do not scorn to call them neighbors. Do not scorn to own that thou art bound to love even them. The world calls them thy inferiors. In what are they inferior? They are thine equals really, though not so in station. "God hath made of one blood all people that dwell on the face of the earth." Thou art by no means better than they. They are men, and what art thou more than that? They may be men in rags, but men in rags are men; and if thou be a man arrayed in scarlet, thou art no more than a man. Take heed that thou love thy neighbor, even though he be in rags, and scorn him not, though sunken in the depths of poverty.

NEITHER Paul, nor an angel from heaven, nor Apollos, nor Cephas can help you in salvation. It is not of man, neither by men, and neither pope nor archbishop, nor bishop, nor priest, nor minister, nor any one hath any grace to give to others. We must each of us go ourselves to the fountain-head, pleading this promise—"Whosoever calleth in the name of the Lord Jesus, shall be saved." If I were shut up in the mines of Siberia, where I could never hear the gospel, if I did call upon the name of Christ, the road is just as straight without the minister as with him, and the path to heaven is just as clear from the wilds of Africa, and from the dens of the prison-house and the dungeon, as it is from the sanctuary of God. Nevertheless, for edification, all Christians love the ministry, though not of salvation; though neither in priest nor preacher do they trust, yet the word of God is sweet to them, and "beautiful on the mountains are the feet of them that bring glad tidings of peace."

CAN ye think what must have been the greatness of the atonement which was the substitution for all this agony which God would have cast upon us, if he had not poured it upon Christ? Look! look! look with solemn eye through the shades that part us from the world of spirits, and see that house of misery which men call hell! Ye cannot endure the spectacle. Remember that in that place there are spirits forever paying their debt to divine justice; but though some of them have been for these four thou sand years sweltering in the flame, they are no nearer a discharge than when they began; and when ten thousand times ten thousand years shall have rolled away, they will no more have made satisfaction to God for their guilt than they have done up till now. And now can you grasp the thought of the greatness of your Savior's mediation when he paid your debt, and paid it all at once; so that there now remaineth not one farthing of debt owing from Christ's people to their God, except a debt of love. To justice the believer oweth nothing; though he owed origin ally so much that eternity would not have been long enough to suffice for the paying of it, yet, in one moment Christ did pay it all, so that the man who believeth is entirely justified from all guilt, and set free from all punishment, through what Jesus hath done. Think ye, then, how great his atonement if he hath done all this.

WE never read that Noah called up Shem, Ham, and Japheth to work at the pumps, nor yet that they had any, for there was not a bit of leakage about the ark. No doubt there were storms that year; but we do not hear that the ship was ever in danger of being wrecked. The rocks, it is true, were too low down to touch her bottom; for fifteen cubits upwards did the waters prevail, and the mountains were covered. Rising twenty-seven feet above the loftiest mountains, she had no quicksands to fear; they were too deep below her keel. But of course she was exposed to the winds; sometimes the hurricane might have rattled against her, and driven her along. Doubtless, at another time, the hail beat on her top, and the lightnings scarred the brow of night; but the ark sailed on, not one was cast out from her, nor were her sailors wearied with constant pumping to keep out the water, or frequent repairs to keep her secure. Though the world was inundated and ruined, that one ark sailed triumphantly above the waters. The ark was safe, and all who were in her were safe too.

THOUGH there were many rooms in the ark, *there was only one door.* It is said, "And the door of the ark shalt thou set in the side thereof." And so, there is only one door into the ark of our salvation, and that is Christ. There are not two Christs preached, one in one chapel, and another in another. "If any man preach any other doctrine than that ye have received, let him be accursed." There is but one Gospel. We take in the righteous out of all sections, but we do not take in all sections. We pick out the godly from amongst them all, for we believe there is a remnant according to the election of grace in the vilest of them. But, still, there is only one door, and "he that cometh not in by the door, but climbeth up some other way, the same is a thief and a robber." There was only one door to the ark.

SINNER, thy deepest woes have been felt by someone, even more keenly than thou feelest them now. Thou sayest, "I sink in deep mire where there is no standing." There have been some that have sunk far deeper than thou hast sunk. Thou art up to thy ankles; I have known some to have been up to the loins, and there have been some that have been covered over their very heads, so that they could say, "All thy waves and thy billows have gone over me." Your distresses are very painful, but they are not singular; others have had to endure the same. Be comforted, it is not a desert island; others have been there too; and if they have passed through this, and won the crown, thou shalt pass through it, and inherit yet the glory of the believer on the breast of Christ.

MY God, I could not drink from thy well, if thou hadst not put there the earthen pitcher of my Savior; but with him living waters from thy sacred well I draw. Heaven! thou art too bright; I could not bear thy insufferable light, if I had not this shade with which I cover thee; but through it, as through a mist, I do behold the halo of thy glory, undiminished in its effulgence, but somewhat diminished in their potency which would be my destruction.

BEGIN with science of Christ crucified, and you will begin with the sun, you will see every other science moving around it in complete harmony. The greatest mind in the world will be evolved by beginning at the right end. The old saying is, "Go from nature up to nature's God;" but it is hard working up hill. The best thing is to go from nature's God down to nature; and if you once get to nature's God, and believe Him, and love Him, it is surprising how easy it is to hear music in the waves, and songs in the wild whisperings of the winds; to see God everywhere, in the stones, in the rocks, in the rippling brooks, and hear him everywhere in the lowing of cattle, in the rolling of thunders, and in the fury of tempests. Get Christ first, put him in the right place, and you will find him to be the wisdom of God in your own experience.

THE devil, who has been a liar from the beginning, we will credit; but if our God promises any thing, we say, "Surely this is too good to be true," and we doubt the fulfillment, because it is not brought to pass exactly at the time and in the way we anticipate. Let us never harbor such suspicions of our God. If we say in our haste, "All men are liars," let us preserve this one truth, "God cannot lie."

IN nature, after evening time there cometh night. The sun hath had its hours of journeying; the fiery steeds are weary; they must rest. Lo, they descend the azure steeps and plunge their burning fetlocks in the western sea, while night in her black chariot follows at their heels. God, however, over steps the rule of nature. He is pleased to send to his people times when the eye of reason expects to see no more day, but fears that the glorious landscape of God's mercies will be shrouded in the darkness of his forgetfulness. But instead thereof, God overleapeth nature, and declares that at evening time, instead of darkness there shall be light.

GOD is "slow to anger." When mercy cometh into the world, she driveth winged steeds; the axles of her chariot-wheels are glowing, hot with speed; but when wrath cometh, it walketh with tardy footsteps; it is not in haste to slay, it is not swift to condemn. God's rod of mercy is ever in his hands outstretched; God's sword of justice is in its scabbard: not rusted in it—it can be easily with drawn—but held there by the hand that presses it back into its sheath, crying, "Sleep, O sword, sleep; for I will have mercy upon sinners, and will forgive their transgressions." God hath many orators in heaven; some of them speak with swift words. Gabriel, when he cometh down to tell glad tidings, speaketh swiftly: angelic hosts, when they descend from glory, fly with wings of lightning, when they proclaim, "Peace on earth, good will towards men;" but the dark angel of wrath is a slow orator; with many a pause between, where melting pity joins her languid notes, he speaks; and when but half his oration is completed he often stays, and withdraws himself from his rostrum, giving way to pardon and to mercy; he having but addressed the people that they might be driven to repentance, and so might receive peace from the scepter of God's love.

THERE is another man. He does not lack any thing, but still he feels that some great loss may injure him considerably. Go and write this down in thy cash-book. If thou hast made out thy cash-account truly, put this down: "The Lord is my shepherd, I shall not want;" put that down for something better than pounds, shillings and pence, something better than gold and silver. "The Lord is my shepherd, I shall not want." "Ah!" says the cold, calculating man, "your promise is not worth having, sir." No; it would not, if it were my promise. But fortunately it is not. It is God's promise.

THE Lord is his shepherd, he shall not want. What a glorious inheritance! Walk up and down it, Christians; lie down upon it, it will do for thy pillow; it will be soft as down for thee to lie upon. "Hie Lord is my shepherd, I shall not want." Climb up that creaking staircase to the top of thy house, lie down on thy hard mattress, wrap thyself round with a blanket, look out for the winter when hard times are coming, and say, "What shall I do?" But, then, just hum over to thyself these words, "The Lord is my shepherd, I shall not want." That will be like the hush of a lullaby to your poor soul, and you will soon sink to slumber.

THE *ark had sundry stories in it*. They were not all of one height. There were lower, second, and third stories. Now, this is a figure of the different kinds of Christians who are carried to heaven. There is my poor mourning brother, who lives in the bottom story; he is always singing, "Lord what a wretched land is this!" He lives just near the keel, on the bare ribs of the ark. He is never very happy. A little light reaches him from the window at times; but generally he is so far from the light that he walks in darkness, and sees very little indeed. His state is that of constant groaning; he likes to hear it said, "Through much tribulation you will enter the kingdom of heaven;" if you paint the Christian life as a very gloomy one, he will like your picture, for his is gloomy indeed; he is always poring over texts such as these, "Oh, wretched man that I am," or that other, "They that pass through the valley of Beca make it a well; the rain also filleth the pools." He is down in the lower story of the ark. But never mind; he is in the ark, though he has little faith, and very much doubt. "With lower, second, and third stories shalt thou make it." There is one of our brethren up a little higher, and he is saying, "I cannot exactly say I am safe; yet I have a hope that my head will be kept above the billows, though it goes hard with me at times. Now and then, too, the Lord bestows 'some drops of heaven' upon me. Sometimes I am like the mountains of Hermon, where 'the Lord commanded the blessing, even life forevermore.' He is in the second story. Well, but he is no safer than the other one. He that is in the second story is no safer, though he is happier than the man on the ground floor. All are safe, so long as they are in the ark. For my part, I like the uppermost story best. I had rather live up there, where I can sing, "O God, my heart is fixed, I will sing and give praise, even with my glory." I love the place where the saints are always admonishing and encouraging one another with psalms, and hymns, and spiritual songs. I confess that I am obliged to go down to the lower story sometimes; but I like running up the ladder to the third deck, whenever I can. But I am no more safe when I am in the top story than I am when I am in the bottom. The same wave that would split the ship and drown me, were I in the lowest story, would drown me if I were in the highest. However high some of us, and however low others of us may be, the same vessel bears us all, for we are one crew in one boat, and there is no dividing us. Come, then, my poor desponding hearer, is that your place, somewhere down at the bottom of the hold, along with the ballast? Are you always in trials and troubles? Ah! well, fear not, so long as you are in the ark. Do not be afraid, Christ is your strength and righteousness. A wave comes against the side of the ship, but it does not hurt the ship, it only drives the wedges in tighter. The master is at the helm—will not that assure your heart? It has floated over so many billows—will not that increase your confidence? It must, indeed, be a strong billow that will sink it now; there never shall be such an one. And where, think you, is the power that could destroy the souls who are sheltered in the ark of our salvation? Who can lay anything to the charge of God's elect, since Christ hath died, and God the Father hath justified us? Happy assurance! We are all safe, so sure as we are in the covenant. The ark floated triumphantly on amidst all the dangers without, and when it finally rested on Mount Ararat, and God spake to Noah again, saying, "Go forth of the ark, thou, and thy wife, and thy sons, and thy sons' wives with thee. Bring forth with thee every living thing;" then the inventory was complete, all were safely landed. So, too, will Christ present the perfect number of all his people to the Father in the last day; not one shall perish. The ark of our salvation shall bring all its living freight into the haven of everlasting rest.

THERE are some persons whose eyes are so weak that the light seems to be injurious to them, especially the red rays of the sun, and a glass has been invented, which rejects the rays that are injurious, and allows only those to pass which are softened and modified to the weakness of the eye. It seems as if the Lord Jesus were some such a glass as this. The grace of God the Trinity, shining through the man Christ Jesus, becomes a mellow, soft light, so that mortal eye can bear it.

WHEREVER the church is, there is God. God is pleased, in his mercy and condescension, to stoop from the highest heavens to dwell in this lower heaven—the heaven of his church. It is here, among the household of faith, he deigns—let me say it with sacred reverence—to unbend himself, and hold familiar intercourse with those round about him whom he hath adopted into his family. He may be a consuming fire abroad, but when he comes into his own house he is all mercy, mildness, and love. Abroad he does great works of power; but at home in his own house he does great works of grace.

YOU are not dying now; but you will be dying soon. None of you have taken a lease of your life; it is impossible for you to guarantee to yourself existence for another hour. And if you are Godless and Christless, ye have all in your veins the venom of that death unutterable which will make your departure doleful beyond expression! Men are dying every day around us; at this very hour there are thousands departing into the world of spirits. In upper chambers, where mourning relatives are pouring floods of tears upon their burning brows; far away on the wild sea, where the sea-gull utters the only scream over the ship-wrecked mariner; down, deep, deep, deep, in the lowest valley, and high upon the loftiest hills, men are dying now, and dying in agonies. Ah, and ye must die also! and will ye march on heedlessly; will ye go on step after step, singing merrily all the way, and dreaming not of that which is to come! Oh, will ye he like the silly bullock that goeth easily to the slaughter, or will ye be like the lamb that licks the butcher's knife! Mad, mad O man, that thou shouldst go to eternal wrath and to the chambers of fell destruction, and yet no sigh comes from thy heart; no groan is uttered by thy lips! Thou diest every day, but groanest never, till the last day of thy death, which is the beginning of thy misery. Yes, the condition of the mass of men is just like the condition of the children of Israel when they were bitten by the serpents.

THE Savior seems to calm his glory, to tone it down to our poor feeble frame. His name put into this wine of heaven, does not diminish in the least degree its sparkling and its exhilarating power; but it takes out of it that deep strength which might up set an angel's brain, if he could drink to his full. It takes away the profundity of mystery, which would make the deep old wine of the kingdom intoxicating rather than cheering.

IT is singular that other men think they shall live forever, but men convinced of sin, who seek a Savior, are afraid they shall not live another moment. You have known the time when you dared not shut your eyes for fear you should not open them again on earth; when you dreaded the shadows of the night lest they should darken forever the light of the sun, and you should dwell in outer darkness throughout eternity. You have mourned as each day has entered, and you have wept as it has depart ed, because you fancied that your next step might precipitate you into your eternal doom. I have known what it is to tread the earth and fear lest every tuft of grass should but cover a door to hell; trembling, lest every particle, and every atom, and every stone, should be so at league with God against me as to destroy me.

WHEN God's power doth restrain himself, then it is power indeed, the power to curb power, the power that binds omnipotence is omnipotence surpassed. God is great in power, and therefore doth he keep in his anger. A man who has a strong mind can bear to be insulted, can bear offenses, because he is strong. The weak mind snaps and snarls at the little; the strong mind bears it like a rock; it moveth not though a thousand breakers dash upon it, and cast their pitiful malice in the spray upon its summit. God marketh his enemies, and yet he moveth not; he standeth still, and letteth them curse him, yet he is not wrathful? If he were less of a God than he is, if he were less mighty than we know him to be, he would long ere this have sent forth the whole of his thunders, and emptied the magazines of heaven; he would long ere this have blasted the earth with the wondrous mines he hath prepared in its lower surface; the flame that burneth there would have consumed us, and we should have been utterly destroyed. We bless God that the greatness of his power is just our protection; he is slow to anger because he is great in power.

THERE was never a soul yet, that sincerely sought the Savior, who perished before he found him. No; the gates of death shall never shut on thee till the gates of grace have opened for thee; till Christ has washed thy sins, away thou shalt never be baptized in Jordan's flood. Thy life is secure, for this is God's constant plan—he keeps his own elect alive till the day of his grace, and then he takes them to himself. And inasmuch as thou knowest thy need of a Savior, thou art one of his, and thou shalt never die until thou hast found him.

THE pillars of the earth were placed in their everlasting sockets by the omnipotent right hand of Christ; the curtains of the heavens were drawn upon their rings of starry light by him who was from ever lasting the all-glorious Son of God. The orbs that float aloft in ether, those ponderous planets, and those mighty stars, were placed in their positions, or sent rolling through space by the eternal strength of him who is "the first and the last." "the Prince of the kings of the earth." Christ is the power of God, for he is the Creator of all things, and by him all things exist.

MANY men believe in the existence of a God, but they do not love that belief. They know there is a God, but they greatly wish there were none. Some would be very pleased, ye would set the bells a-ringing if you believed there were no God. Why, if there were no God, then you might live just as you liked; if there were no God, then you might run riot and have no fear of future consequences. It would be to you the greatest joy that could be, if you heard that the eternal God had ceased to be. But the Christian never wishes any such a thing as that. The thought that there is a God is the sun shine of his existence. His intellect bows before tho Most High; not like a slave who bends his body because he must, but like the angel who prostrates himself because he loves to adore his Maker. His intellect is as fond of God as his imagination. "Oh!" he saith, "my God, I bless thee that thou art; for thou art my highest treasure, my richest and my rarest delight. I love thee with all my intellect; I have neither thought, nor judgment, nor conviction, nor reason, which I do not lay at thy feet, and consecrate to thine honor.

METHINKS, when God launched the sun from his 1FJL hand and sent him on his course, he said, "Prove me now;" see, O sun, if I do not uphold thee till thou hast done thy work and finished thy career; rejoice thou mayest, "as a strong man to run a race," but while thou fulfillest thy circuits, and nothing is hid from thy heat, thou shalt prove my glory and shed light upon my handiwork. When the Almighty whirled the earth in space, methinks he said, "Prove me now," O earth, see if I do not perpetuate thy seasons, and give thee "seed-time and harvest, cold and heat, summer and winter, day and night," refreshing thee with incessant providence. And to each creature he made, I can almost think the Almighty said, "Prove me now." Tiny gnat, thou art about to dance in the sunshine; thou shalt prove my goodness. Huge leviathan, thou shalt stir up the deep and make it frothy; go forth, and prove my power. Ye creatures, whom I have endowed with various instincts, wait on me; I will give you your meat in due season. And you, ye mighty thunders and ye swift lightnings, go, teach the world reverence and show forth my omnipotence.

I HAVE often remarked that when men have been adopting a patent process of building up a church, by the revivalist sermons of some thundering, crazy-brained preachers, after the first excitement has subsided that church has become sickly and fallen into a very sad and grievous state. Those revivalists have often been like locusts in our churches, devouring every green thing; and the revivals they have stimulated have well-nigh brought us to destruction. God will not have men usurp his prerogative in the building; and though they may with their own hand speedily pile up a mighty structure, yet, like the baseless fabric of a vision, it soon disappears and is it gone. In his building he suffers no man to use trowels or hammer: he will use men for trowels and hammers, but he will not allow them to make use of themselves or of others. His own hands shall perform it.

WHEN the light of God's grace comes into your heart, it is something like the opening of the windows of an old cellar that has been shut up for many days. Down in that cellar, which has not been opened for many months, are all kinds of loathsome creatures, and a few sickly plants blanched by the darkness. The walls are dark and damp by the trail of reptiles; it is a horrid filthy place in which no one would willingly enter. You may walk there in the dark very securely, and except now and then for the touch of some slimy creature, you would not believe the place was so bad and filthy. Open those shutters, clean a pane of glass, let a little light in, and now see how a thousand noxious things have made this place their habitation. Sure, 'twas not the light that made this place so horrible, but it was the light that showed how horrible it was before. So let God's grace just open a window and let the light into a man's soul, and he will stand astonished to see at what a distance he is from God.

CHRIST JESUS cast into the river of God, makes all the streams more sweet; and when the believer sees God in the person of the Savior, he then sees the God whom he can love, and to whom with boldness he can approach.

SHOULD ever so great a misfortune come upon us, if we can trace it to the providence of God, we bear it cheerfully; but if we have inflicted it upon ourselves, then how fearful is it! And let every man remember that if he perish after having heard the gospel, he will be his own murderer. Sinner thou wilt drive the dagger into thine heart thyself. If thou despisest the gospel, thou art preparing fuel for thine own bed of flames, thou art hammering out the chain for thine own everlasting binding; and when damned, thy mournful reflection will be this— I have damned myself, I cast myself into this pit; for I rejected the gospel; I despised the message; I trod under foot the Son of Man; I would have none of his rebukes; I despised his sabbaths; I would not hearken to his exhortations, and now I perish by mine own hand, the miserable suicide of my own soul."

REMEMBER, all you want to know to get to heaven is, the two things that begin with "S"—Sin and Savior. Do you feel your sin? Christ is your Savior; trust to him, pray to him; and as you are here now, and I am talking to you, you will one day be in heaven. I will tell you two prayers to pray. First, pray this prayer—"Lord show me myself." That is an easy one for you. Lord, show me myself? show me my heart; show me my guilt; show me my danger; Lord, show me myself? And when you have prayed that prayer, and God has answered it (and remember, he hears prayer), when he has answered it, and shown you yourself here is another prayer for you—"Lord, show me *thyself.* Show me thy work, thy love, thy mercy, thy cross, thy grace." Pray that; and those are about the only prayers you want to pray, to get to heaven with—"Lord, show me myself;" "Lord, show me thyself." You do not want to know much, then. You need not spell, to get to heaven; you need not be able to speak English, to get to heaven; the ignorant and rude are welcome to the cross of Christ and salvation.

GOD "will not acquit the wicked;" how prove I this? I prove it thus. Never once has he pardoned an unpunished sin; not in all the years of the Most High, not in all the days of his right hand, has he once blotted out sin without punishment. What! say you, were not those in heaven pardoned? Are there not many transgressors pardoned, and do they not escape without punishment? Has he not said, "I have blotted out thy transgressions like a cloud, and like a thick cloud thine iniquities?" Yes, true, most true, and yet my assertion is true also—not one of all those sins that have been pardoned were pardoned without punishment. Do you ask me why and how such a thing as that can be the truth? I point you to you dreadful sight on Calvary; the punishment which fell not on the forgiven sinner fell there. The cloud of justice was charged with fiery hail; the sinner deserved it; it fell on him; but, for all that, it fell and spent its fury; it fell there, in that great reservoir of misery; it fell into the Savior's heart. The plagues, which need should light on our ingratitude, did not fall on us, but they fell some where; and who was it that was plagued? Tell me, Gethsemane; tell me, O Calvary's summit, who was plagued? The doleful answer comes, "*Eli, Eli, lama sabachthani?*" "My God, my God, why hast thou forsaken me?" It is Jesus suffering all the plagues of sin. Sin is still punished, though the sinner is delivered.

SEE what vitality the gospel has. Plunge her under the wave, and she rises, the purer from her washing; thrust her in the fire and she comes out the more bright for her burning; cut her in sunder, and each piece shall make another church; behead her, and like the hydra of old, she shall have a hundred heads for every one you cut away. She cannot die, she must live; for she has the power of God within her.

IN the ark, *rooms* were made. Those who lived in one room did not stand or sit with those who lived in another; but they were all in the same ark. So I have sometimes thought, there are our Wesleyan friends, some of them love the Lord; I have no doubt they that do are in the ark, though they do not occupy the same apartment as we do. There are our Baptist friends, those who love the Lord; we welcome into our room. Then there are our Independent friends, those that love the Lord; they are in another room. And our Presbyterian and Episcopalian brethren—in all these various sections are some who are called of God and brought into the ark, though they are in different rooms. But, beloved, they are all in *one* ark. There are not two Gospels. As long as I can find a man that holds the same Gospel, it does not matter what order of church government he adopts if he be in Christ Jesus—it is of little consequence what room he is in so long as he is in the ark. If he belongs to those of whom it is written, "By grace are ye saved, through faith, and that not of yourselves, it is the gift of God," I will call him my brother. We cannot all expect to be in one room. The elephants did not live with the tigers, and the lions did not lie down with the sheep. There were different rooms for different classes of creatures; and it is a good thing there are different denominations, for I am sure some of us would not get on very comfortably with certain other denominations. We should want more liberty than we could get in the Church of England; we should want more freedom than we could get with the Presbyterians; we should want more soundness of doctrine than we could get with the Wesleyans; and we should want a little more brotherly love, perhaps, than we could get with some of the strict Baptists. We should not entirely agree with them all; and happy is he who can sometimes put his head into one room and sometimes into another, and can say to all that love the Lord Jesus Christ, "Grace be with you all so long as you are in the ark."

IT is a singular thing that *there was only one window in the ark.* That one window may fitly represent *the ministry of the Holy Ghost.* There is only one light which lighteneth every man who cometh into the world, if he be lightened at all. Christ is the light, and it is the Holy Spirit of truth by whom Christ is revealed. Thus we discern sin, righteousness, and judgment. No other conviction is of any real value. As we are brought under the teachings of the Spirit, we do perceive our guilt and misery, and our redemption and refuge in Christ. No other means exist. There is only one window to the ark. "Why," says one, "there are some of us who see light through one minister and some through another." True, my friend; but still there is only one window. Ministers are only like panes of glass, and you can obtain no light through them but by the operations of the same Spirit that worketh in them. And even then the different panes of glass give different shades of light. There you have your fine polished preacher; he is a bit of stained glass, not very transparent, made to keep the light out rather than to let it in. There is another pane; he is a square cut diamond; he seems an old-fashioned preacher, but still he is a bit of good glass, and lets the light through. Another one is cut after a more refined style; but still he is plain and simple, and the light shines through him. But there is only one light, and only one window. He who revealeth to us the light of the knowledge of the glory of God in the face of Jesus Christ is the Holy Spirit.

IF we listen to the rippling of the freshet at the mountain side, to the tumbling of the avalanche, to the lowing of the cattle, to the singing of the birds, to every voice and sound of nature, we shall hear this answer to the question, "God is our maker; he hath made us, and not we ourselves."

ON the morning, when the ark door was opened, you might have seen in the sky a pair of eagles, a pair of sparrows, a pair of vultures, a pair of ravens, a pair of humming-birds, a pair of all kinds of birds that ever cut the azure, that ever floated on wing, or whispered their song to the evening gales. In they came. But if you had watched down on the earth, you would have seen come creeping along a pair of snails, a pair of snakes, and a pair of worms. There ran along a pair of mice; there came a pair of lizards, and in there flew a pair of locusts. There were pairs of creeping creatures, as well as pairs of flying creatures. Do you see what I mean by that? There are some of you that can fly so high in know ledge, that I should never be able to scan your great and extensive wisdom; and others of you so ignorant, that you can hardly read your Bibles. Never mind; the eagle must come down to the door, and you must go up to it. There is only one entrance for you all; and as God saved the birds that flew, so he saved the reptiles that crawled. Are you a poor, ignorant, crawling creature, that never was noticed—without intellect, without repute, without fame, without honor? Come along, crawling one! God will not exclude you. I have often wondered how the poor snail crawled in; but I dare say he started many a year before. And some of you have started for years, and still you keep crawling on. Ah! then, come along with thee, poor snail! If I could just pick thee up, and help thee on a yard or two, I would he glad to do if. It is strange how long you have been nigh to the ark, but not yet entered in; how long you have been near the portals of the church, but never joined it.

I DO not think any one of the children of God proves all of God, but that they are all proving different parts of his one grand character, so that when the whole history of Providence shall he writ ten, and the lives of all the saints shall he recorded, the title of the book will he, "Proofs of God." There will be one compendious proof, that he is God and changeth not; that With him there "is no variableness, neither shadow of turning."

NO easy path has the gospel had. The good bark of the Church has had to plough her way through seas of blood, and those who have manned her have been bespattered with the bloody spray; yea, they have had to man her and keep her in motion, by laying down their lives unto the death.

BUT do ye want further proof that God will not acquit the wicked? Need I lead you through a long list of terrible wonders that God has wrought— the wonders of his vengeance? Shall I show you blighted Eden? Shall I let you see a world all drowned—sea monsters whelping and stabling in the palaces of kings? Shall I let you hear the last shriek of the last drowning man as he falls into the flood and dies, washed by that huge wave from the hill top? Shall I let you see death riding upon the summit of a crested billow, upon a sea that knows no shore, and triumphing because his work is done; his quiver empty, for all men are slain, save where life floats in the midst of death in yonder ark? Need I let you see Sodom, with its terrified inhabitants, when the volcano of almighty wrath spouted fiery hail upon it? Shall I show you the earth opening its mouth to swallow up Korah, Dathan and Abiram? Need I take you to the plagues of Egypt? Shall I again repeat the death shriek of Pharaoh, and the drowning of his host? Surely, ye need not to be told of cities that are in ruins, or of nations that have been cut off in a day; ye need not to be told how God has smitten the earth from one side to the other, when he has been wroth, and how he has melted mountains in his hot displeasure. Nay, we have proofs enough in history, proofs enough in Scripture, that "he will not at all acquit the wicked." If ye wanted the best proof, however, ye should borrow the black wings of a miserable imagination, and fly beyond the world, through the dark realm of chaos, on, far on, where those battlements of fire are gleaming with a horrid light—if through them, with a spirit's safety, ye would fly, and would behold the worm that never dies, the pit that knows no bottom, and could you there see the fire unquenchable, and listen to the shrieks and wails of men that are banished forever from God—if, sirs, it were possible for you to hear the sullen groans, and hollow moans, and shrieks of tortured ghosts, then would you come back to this world, amazed and petrified with horror, and you would say, "Indeed, he will not acquit the wicked."

WE endure ten times as much anxiety in this world as we need, because we confide not in divine promise half as much as we might.

If we were to live more on God's promise, and less on creature feelings, we should be happier men and we men, all of us. If we were to get hold of a promise, and say, "There, let me abide by this; though the world says it is not true, I will believe it." Could we live alway in faith on the promises, the shafts of the enemy could never reach us.

FEAR hath kept many a child of God from doing his duty, from making a bold profession; hath brought bondage into his spirit. Fear misused, thou art the Christian's greatest curse, and thou art the sinner's ruin. Thou art a sly serpent, creeping amongst the thorns of sin, and when thou art allowed to twist thyself around manhood, thou dost crush it in thy folds, and poison it with thy venom. Nothing can be worse than this sinful fear; it hath slaughtered its myriads and sent thousands to hell. But it yet may seem a paradox; fear, when rightly employed, is the very brightest state of Christianity, and is used to express all piety, comprehended in one emotion. "The fear of God "is the constant description which the Scripture gives of true religion.

REMEMBER that the time you have for self-examination is, after all, very short. Soon thou wilt know the great secret. I perhaps may not say words rough enough to rend off the mask which thou hast now upon thee, but there is one called Death who will stand no complement. You may masquerade it out today in the dress of the saint, but death will soon strip you, and you must stand before the judgment-seat after death has discovered you in all your nakedness, be that naked innocence or naked guilt. Remember, too, though you may deceive yourself, you will not deceive your God. You may have light weights, and the beam of the scale in which you weigh yourself may not be honest, and may not therefore tell the truth; but when God shall try you he will make no allowances; when the everlasting Jehovah grasps the balances of justice and puts his law into one scale, ah, sinner, how wilt thou tremble when he shall put thee into the other; for unless Christ be thy Christ thou wilt be found light weight—thou wilt be weighed in the balances and found wanting, and be cast away forever.

MEN who are passionate and swift in anger give a word and a blow; sometimes the blow first and the word afterwards. Oftentimes kings, when subjects have rebelled against them, have crushed them first, and then reasoned with them afterwards; they have given no time of threatening, no period of repentance; they have allowed no space for turning to their allegiance; they have at once crushed them in their hot displeasure, making a full end of them. Not so God: he will not cut down the tree that doth much cumber the ground, until he hath digged about it, and dunged it; he will not at once slay the man whose character is the most vile; until he has first hewn him by the prophets he will not hew him by judgments; he will warn the sinner ere he condemn him; he will send his prophets, "rising up early and late," giving him "line upon line, and precept upon precept, here a little and there a little." He will not smite the city without warning; Sodom shall not perish, until Lot hath been within her. The world shall not be drowned, until eight prophets hath been preaching in it, and Noah, the eighth, cometh to prophesy of the coming of the Lord. He will not smite Nineveh till he hath sent a Jonah. He will not crush Babylon till his prophets have cried through its streets. He will not slay a man until he hath given many warnings, by sicknesses, by the pulpit, by providence, and by consequences.

LOOK back on the paths of your pilgrimage. Some of you can count as many Ebenezers as there are milestones from here to York; Ebenezers piled up, with oil poured on the top of them; places where you have said, "Hitherto the Lord hath helped me." Look through the pages of your diary, and you will see time after time, when your perils and exigencies were such as no earthly skill could relieve, and you felt constrained to witness what others among you have never felt—you felt that there is a God, that there is a Providence—"a God who compasseth your path," and "is acquainted with all your ways."

EACH of God's saints is sent into the world to prove some part of the divine character. Per haps I may be one of those who shall live in the valley of ease, having much rest, and hearing sweet birds of promise singing in my ears. The air is calm and balmy, the sheep are feeding round about me, and all is still and quiet. Well, then. I shall prove the love of God in sweet communings. Or, perhaps, I may be called to stand where the thunder clouds brew, where the lightnings play, and tempestuous winds are howling on the mountain top. Well, then, I am born to prove the power and majesty of our God; amid dangers he will inspire me with courage; amid toils he will make me strong. Perhaps it shall be mine to preserve an unblemished character, and so prove the power of sanctifying grace in not being allowed to backslide from my professed dedication to God. I shall then be a proof of the omnipotent power of grace, which alone can save from the power as well as the guilt of sin. The diverse cases of all the Lord's family are intended to illustrate different parts of his ways; and in heaven I do think one part of our blessed employ will be to read the great book of the experience of all the saints, and gather from that book the whole of the divine character as having been proved and illustrated. Each Christian man is a manifestation and display of some position or other of God; a different part may belong to each of us, but when the whole shall be combined, when all the rays of evidence shall be brought, as it were, into one great sun, and shine forth with meridian splendor, we shall see in Christian experience a beautiful revelation of our God.

IF I once wandered on you mountain top, and Jesus climbed up and caught me, and put me on his shoulders, and carried me home, I cannot and dare not doubt that he is my shepherd. If I had belonged to some other sheep-owner he would not have sought me. And from the fact that he did seek, I learn that he must be my shepherd. Did I think any man convinced me of sin, or that any human power had converted me, I should fear I was that man's sheep and that he was my shepherd. Could I trace my deliverance to the hand of a creature, I should think that some creature might be my shepherd; but since he who has been reclaimed of God must and will confess that God alone has done it, and will ascribe to his free grace, and to that alone, his deliverance from sin, such a one will feel persuaded that the Lord must be his shepherd, because he brought him, he delivered him, he snatched him out of the jaw of the lion and out of the paw of the bear.

GIVE me ten thousand pounds, and one reverse of fortune may scatter it all away; but let me have a spiritual hold of this divine assurance— "The Lord is my shepherd, I shall not want"— then I am all right—I am set up for life. I cannot break with such stock as this in hand. I never can be a bankrupt, for I hold this security—"The Lord is my shepherd, I shall not want." Do not give me ready money now; give a checkbook, and let me draw what I like. This is what God does with the believer. He does not immediately transfer his inheritance to him, but lets him draw what he needs out of the riches of his fullness in Christ Jesus.

O BELOVED! Surely it lacks but little teaching in the school of grace to make out that we ourselves are fools. True wisdom is sure to set folly in a strong light. I have heard of a young man who went to college; and when he had been there one year, his parent said to him, "What do you know? Do you know more than when you went?" "Oh! yes," said he, "I do." Then he went the second year, and was asked the same question—"Do you know more than when you went?" "Oh! no," said he, "I know a great deal less." "Well," said the father, "you are getting on." Then he went the third year, and was asked the same question—"What do you know now?" "Oh!" said he, "I don't think I know anything." "That is right," said the father, "you have now learned to profit, since you say you know nothing." He who is convinced that he knows nothing of himself as he ought to know, gives up steering his ship, and lets God put his hand on the rudder. He lays aside his own wisdom, and cries, "Oh God! my little wisdom is cast at thy feet; my little judgment is given to thee."

DO NOT get despising the little ones because they have not had so many trials as you have. You great *standard* men, do not get cutting the children of God in pieces because they have not been in such fights as you have. The master leads the sheep where he pleases, and be sure he will lead them rightly, and as long as they can say the word "my," do not trouble yourselves where they learned it—if they can say from their hearts, "The Lord is my shepherd, I shall not want."

SPIRITUAL mercies are good things, and not only good things, but the best things, so that you may well ask for them; for if no good things will be withholden, much more will none of the best things.

WARS, confusions, and tumults, are but the wherewith God will purge the diseased body of this earth from its innumerable ills. They are but a terrible tornado with which God shall sweep away the pestilence and fever that lurk in the moral atmosphere; they are but the great hammers with which he breaks in pieces the gates of brass, to make a way for his people; they are but the threshing wains, with which he doth thresh the mountains and beat them small, and make the hills as chaff, that Israel may rejoice in the Lord, and that the sons of Jacob may triumph in their God. As it hath been in the beginning, so it shall be even unto the end. The noise and the tumult of war in India shall produce good; the blood of our sisters shall be avenged, not by the sword, but by the gospel. On India's blood-red gods, the arm of the Lord shall yet be felt; the might of him that sits upon the throne shall be acknowledged by the very men, who, first in the fray, have blasphemed the God of Israel. Let us not fear, let us not tremble; the end of all things cometh at last, and that end shall certainly be the desired one, and all the wrath of man shall not frustrate the designs of God. The past troubles assure us for the present, and console us for the future. "Come behold the works of the Lord, what desolations he hath made in the earth."

OH, WHEN you get to heaven, ye children of God, will ye praise any but your Master? Calvinists, today you love John Calvin; will you praise him there? Lutheran, today thou dost love the memory of that stern reformer; wilt thou sing the song of Luther in heaven? Follower of Wesley, thou hast a reverence for that evangelist; wilt thou in heaven have a note for John Wesley? None, none, none! Giving up all names and all honors of men, the strain shall rise in undivided and unjarring unison "unto him that loved us, that washed us from our sins in his blood, unto him be glory forever and ever."

IT seems that everything Christ-like must have a history like that of Christ. His beginnings were small—the manger and the stable. So with the beginnings of that society which we love, and which we believe to be the very incarnation of the Spirit of Christ. Its beginnings also were small; but its latter end shall doubtless greatly increase—for, hath not the end of Christ become exceedingly glorious? He hath ascended up on high; he sitteth at the right hand of God, our Father, and doubtless this agency which God now employeth for the conversion of the world, shall have its ascension, and God shall greatly magnify it. But as. Christ was called to suffer, so must everything Christ-like suffer with him. The Christian who is the most like his Master will understand the most of the meaning of that term, "fellowship with him in his sufferings;" and inasmuch as the Missionary Society is like Christ, and hath Christ's heart and Christ's aim, it also must suffer like Jesus. This year we have been made to sip of that cup. The blood of our martyrs has been shed; our confessors have witnessed to the faith of the Lord Jesus; at the hands of bloodthirsty and cruel men they have met their fate, and again the seed of the church has been sown in the blood of the martyred saint.

I BEG you read the page of history, and mark the various catastrophes which have happened to this world; and I appeal to you, as persons who have understanding, and who can trace the Lord's hand in these matters—have not all these things worked together for good? and hitherto, have not the revolutions, the destruction of empires, and the fall of dynasties, been eminent helps to the progress of the gospel? Far be it from us to lay the blood of men at God's door. Let us not for one moment be guilty of any thought that the sin and the iniquity which have brought war into the world is of God; but, at the same time, as firm believers in the doctrine of predestination, and as firmly holding the great truth of a Divine providence, we must hold that God is the author of the darkness as well as of the light—that he creates the providential evil as well as the good—that while he sendeth the shower from on high, he also is the father of the devastating storm. Oh! I say, then, come and see the Lord's hand in "Aceldama, the field of blood." Come ye, and behold the Lord's hand in every shake of the pillars of the constitutions of the monarchies of earth. See the Lord's hand in the rumbling of every tower and the tumbling down of every pinnacle which had aspired to heaven. For he hath done it—he hath done it! God is present everywhere.

I HAVE a fond belief that the day is coming, when Nelson, on the top of his monument, shall be upset, and Mr. Whitfield set there, or the apostle Paul. I believe that Napier, who stands in the square there, will lose his station. We shall say about these men, "They were very respectable men in the days of our forefathers, who did not know better than to kill one another, but we do not care for them now!" Up goes John Wesley, where stood Napier! Away goes someone else, who was an earnest preacher of the gospel, to occupy the place high over the gate where another warrior rides upon his horse. All these things, the trickery of an ignorant age, the gewgaws of a people who loved blood shed despite their profession of religion, must yet be broken up for old iron and old brass; every statue that stands in London shall yet be sold, and the price thereof cast at the apostles' feet, that they may make distribution as every man hath need. Wars must cease, and every place where war reigneth and hath now its glory, must yet pass away, and fade and wither. We give all honor to these men now, for these are the days of our ignorance, and God in some degree winketh at us; but when the gospel spreads we shall then find, that when every heart is full of it, it will be impossible for us to tolerate the very name of war; for when God has broken the bow, and burned the chariot, we shall break the image and dash the sculpture into a thousand atoms. We shall think, when the trade is done, the men that did it may well be forgotten.

THAT maniac nonsense about God doing his own work and our sitting still and doing nothing, ought to have been buried long ago. I know not how to characterize it: it has done us immense damage. We know that God has accomplished his own work; but he always has worked and always will work with means.

YOU know that in Solomon's temple there was no sound of hammer heard; for the stones were made ready in the quarries, and brought all shaped and marked so that the masons might know the exact spot in which they were to be placed; so that no sound of iron was needed. All the planks and timbers were carried to their right places, and all the catches with which they were to be linked together were prepared, so that there might not be even the driving of a nail—everything was ready beforehand. It is the same with us. When we get to heaven, there will be no sanctifying us there, no squaring us with affliction, no hammering us with the rod, no making us meet there. We must be made meet here; and blessed be his name, all that Christ will do beforehand. When we get there, we shall not need angels to put this member of the Church in one place, and that member in another; Christ who brought the stones from the quarry and made them ready, shall himself place the people in their inheritance in paradise. For he has himself said, "I go to prepare a place for you, and if I go away, I will come again and I will receive you unto myself." Christ shall be his own usher; he shall receive his people himself; he shall stand at the gates of heaven himself to take his own people, and to put them in their alloted heritage in the land of the blessed.

I REMEMBER Edward Irving once preached a sermon to a vast congregation, upon, missions; I think he preached for four hours; and the object of the sermon was to prove that we were all wrong— that we ought to send out our missionaries without purse or scrip, giving them nothing! Edward never volunteered to go himself! If he had done so, we might have endorsed his opinion. But he stayed at home, and did not go. Now, we are no believers in that. If a man loves the ministry, if he can only preach Christ's gospel in poverty, God bless him in his poverty; if he has to be a tent-maker, like Paul, and to work for his own living, and to go forth without purse or scrip! But *as a church* we cannot have that. "No, no," we say, "brother, if you are going to a foreign land, and you give your life and health, and if you renounce the comforts of your family, we cannot let you go without anything. The least we can do is to provide for your needs." And one says, "There! though you go without purse or scrip, you cannot get across the sea except you have a ship; I will pay your passage-money." Another says, "You cannot preach to these people without learning the language; and while you are learning the language you must eat and drink. It is quite impossible that you can live by faith, unless you have something that you can nourish your body with: here are the funds to support you, that you may give all your time to the preaching of the Word." Ah! if we did but love Christ better, my brothers and sisters, if we lived nearer to the cross, if we knew more of the value of his blood, if we wept like him over Jerusalem, if we felt more what it was for souls to perish, and what it was for men to be saved—if we did but rejoice with Christ in the prospect of his seeing the travail of his soul, and being abundantly satisfied—if we did but delight more in the divine decree, that the kingdoms of this world *shall* be given to Christ, I am sure we should all of us find more ways and more means for the sending forth of the gospel of Christ.

IF you would find God, he dwelleth on every hilltop, and in every valley; God is everywhere in creation; but if you want a special display of him, if you would know what is the secret place of the tabernacle of the Most High, the inner chamber of divinity, you must go where you find the church of true believers, for it is here he makes his continual residence known— in the hearts of the humble and contrite, who tremble at his word.

———————

CHRIST has made the plan of his Church. You and I have made a great many plans for the building up of that Church. The Presbyterian makes his plans extremely precise. He will put an elder in every corner, and the Presbytery is the great ground-work—the pillar and the ground of the truth; and right is he in so doing to an extent. The Episcopalian builds his temple too. He will have a bishop at the door-post, and he will have a priest to shut the gate. He will have everything built according to the model that was seen by Cranmer in the mount, if he ever was there at all. And those of us who are of a severer discipline, and have a simpler style, must have Christ's Church always built in the congregational order: every congregation distinct and separate, and governed by its own bishop, and deacons, and elders. But mark, Christ does not attend to our points of church-government, for there is one part of Christ's Church that is Episcopalian, and looks as if a bishop of the Church of England had ordered it; another part is Presbyterian; another Baptist; another Congregational; and yet all these styles of architecture somehow, fused into one by the Great Architect, make that goodly structure which is called "the temple of Christ, the Church of the living God, the pillar and ground of truth."

———————

HAPPY the day when every war-horse shall be retired from battle, when every spear shall become a pruning-hook, and every sword shall be made to till the soil which once it stained with blood. It is of that my text prophesies, and my text naturally brings me to that, as the great climax of the gospel dispensation. This will be the last triumph of Christ; before death itself shall be dead; death's great jackal, war, must die also, and then shall there be peace on earth, and the angel shall say, "I have gone up and down through the earth, and the earth sitteth still and is at rest; I heard no tumult of war nor noise of battle." This is what we hope for. Let us fight on with diligence and earnestness.

HEAVEN singeth evermore. Before the throne of God, angels and redeemed saints extol his name. And this world is singing too; sometimes with the loud noise of the rolling thunder, of the boiling sea, of the dashing cataract, and of the lowing cattle; and often with that still, solemn harmony, which floweth from the vast creation, when in its silence it praiseth God. Such is the song which gushes in silence from the mountain lifting its head to the sky, covering its face sometimes with the wings of mist, and at other times unveiling its snow-white brow before its Maker, and reflecting back bis sunshine, gratefully thanking him for the light with which it has been made to glisten, and for the gladness of winch it is the solitary spectator, as in its grandeur it looks down upon the laughing valleys. The tune to which heaven and earth are set, is the same. In heaven they sing, "The Lord be exalted; let his name be magnified forever." And the earth singeth the same: "Great art thou in thy works, O Lord! and unto thee be glory."

JESUS CHRIST excels Solomon, for he provides all the materials. He hews them himself; he rough casts them first, and then afterwards polishes them till he makes them ready to transport them to the hill of God, whereon his temple is to be built. I was thinking what a pretty figure was that floating of the trees of Lebanon after being sawn into planks and made ready to be fixed as pillars of the temple—what a fine emblem of death! Is it not just be with us? Here we grow, and are at length cut down, and made ready to become pillars of the temple. Across the stream of death, we are ferried by a loving hand, and brought to the port of Jerusalem, where we are safely landed, to go no more out forever, but to abide as eternal pillars in the temple of our Lord. Now, you know, the Tyrians floated these rafts; but no stranger, no foreigner shall float us across the stream of death. It is remarkable that Jesus Christ always uses expressions with regard to his people, which impute their death to him alone. You will recollect the expression in the Revelation— "Thrust in thy sickle, and reap: for the time is come for thee to reap; for the harvest of the earth is ripe." But when he begins to reap, not the vintage, which represents the wicked that were to be crushed, but the harvest which represents the godly; then it is said, "He that sat upon the throne thrust in the sickle." He did not leave it to his angels, he did it himself. It is so with the bringing of those planks, and the moving of those stones. I say no king of Tyre and Sidon shall do it; Jesus Christ, who on the death of death and hell's destruction, himself shall pilot us across the stream, and land us safe on Canaan's side. "He shall build the temple of the Lord."

AFFLICTIONS cannot sanctify us, except as they are used by Christ, as his mallet and his chisel. Our joys and our efforts cannot make us ready for heaven, apart from the hand of Jesus who fashioneth our hearts aright, and prepareth us to be partakers of the inheritance of the saints in light.

THE man who comes between two belligerents, and bears the stroke himself—the man who will lie down on the earth, and plead with others that they would cease from warfare—these are the blessed. How rarely are they set on high. They are generally set aside, as people who cannot be blessed, even though it seem that they try to make others so. Here is the world turned upside down. The warrior with his garment stained in blood, is put into the ignoble earth, to die and rot; but the peace-maker is lifted up, and God's crown of blessing is put round about his head, and men one day shall see it, and struck with admiration they shall lament their own folly, that they exalted the blood-red sword of the warrior, but that they did rend the modest mantle of the man who did make peace among mankind.

BRING me here a Hottentot, or a man from Kamschatka, a wild savage who has never listened to the Word. That man may have every sin in the catalog of guilt except one; but that one I am sure he has not. He has not the sin of rejecting the gospel when it is preached to him. But you, when you hear the gospel, have an opportunity of committing a fresh sin; and if you have rejected it, you have added a fresh iniquity to all those others that hang about your neck.

I SUPPOSE there is scarce a kingdom of the world where you do not see God's handiwork in crushing his enemies. It is to the shame of the idolater that he worships a God that his fathers knew not. Although there he some hoary systems of iniquity; in most cases the system is still new—new compared with the giant mountains, the first-horn of nature—new compared with those old idolatries that have long since died away in the clouds of forgetfulness. It seems to me to he a very pleasing theme for us to speak of these desolations that God has made. For mark this—again we say it—as it was in the beginning, it is now, and forever shall he. The false gods shall yet yield their sway; the temples shall yet be unroofed; their houses shall be burned with fire, and their names shall be left for a reproach; their dignity shall not be honored, neither shall homage be given unto their name.

AH! what a host of thoughts cluster around the dying-bed of a child whom we have taught. Next to the father and the mother, I should think the Sabbath-school teacher will take the most interest in the dying one. You will recollect, "There lies withering the flower which my hand hath watered; there is an immortal soul about to pass the portals of eternity, whom I have taught."

WHAT a dreadful thing it must be to be an unfaithful preacher on a dying-bed. (Oh that I may be saved from that!) To be upon one's bed when life is over; to have had great opportunities, mighty congregations, and to have been so diligent about something else as to have neglected to preach the full and free gospel of our Lord Jesus Christ! methinks as I laid in my bed a-dying, I should see specters and grim things in the room. One would come and stare upon me and say, "Ah! you are dying. Remember how many times I sat in the front of the gallery, and listened to you, but you never once told me to escape from the wrath to come; you were talking to me about something I did not under stand; but the simple matter of the gospel you never preached to me, and I died in doubt and trembling. And now you are coming to me to the hell which I have inherited because you were unfaithful." And when in your grey and dying age we see the generations which have grown up around our pulpits, we shall think of them all. We shall think of the time when as striplings we first began to preach; we shall recollect the youths that then crowded, then the men, and then the grey heads that passed away. And methinks as they come on in grim procession, they will everyone leave a fresh curse upon our conscience because we were unfaithful. The death-bed of a man who has murdered his fellows, of some grim tyrant who has let the bloodhounds of war loose upon man kind, must be an awful thing. When the soldier, and the soldier's widow, and the murdered man of peace rise up before him; when the smoke of devastated countries seems to blow into his eyes and make them sore and red; when the blood of men hangs on his conscience like a great red pall; when bloody murder, the grim chamberlain, draws red curtains round his bed, and when he begins to approach the last end where the murderer must inherit his dreary doom, it must be a fearful time indeed. But, methinks to have murdered souls must be more awful still—to have distributed poison to children instead of bread, to have given them stones when they asked us for right food, to have taught them error when we ought to have taught them the truth as it is in Jesus, or to have spoken to them with cold listlessness when earnestness was needed.

AS long as there is a particle of selfishness remaining in us, it will mar our sweet enjoyment of Christ; and until we get a complete riddance of it, our joy will never be unmixed with grief.

We must dig at the roots of our selfishness to find the worm which eats our happiness.

TWO men go up to the temple to pray, the one a believer, the other an unbeliever. He that is an unbeliever may have the gifts of oratory, the mightiest fluency of speech, but his prayer is an abomination unto God, whilst the feeblest utterance of the true believer is received with smiles by him that sits upon the throne. Two persons go to the Master's table—the one loveth the ordinance in its outward sign, and reverenceth it with superstition, but he knows not Christ; the other believes in Jesus, and knows how to eat his flesh and drink his blood as a worthy partaker in that divine ordinance; God is honored in the one, the ordinance is dishonored in the other.

IT seems to me, that every Sunday-school teacher has a right to put "Reverend "before his name as much as I have, or if not, if he discharges his trust he certainly is a "Right Honorable." He teaches his congregation and preaches to his class. I may preach to more, and he to less, but still he is doing the same work, though in a smaller sphere. I am sure I can sympathize with Mr. Carey, when he said of his son Felix, who left the missionary work to be come an ambassador, "Felix has drivelled into an ambassador;" meaning to say, that he was once a great person as a missionary, but that he had afterwards accepted a comparatively insignificant office. So I think we may say of the Sabbath-school teacher, if he gives up his work because he cannot attend to it, on account of his enlarged business, he drivels into a rich merchant. If he forsakes his teaching because he finds there is so much else to do, he drivels into something less than he was before; with one exception, if he is obliged to give up to attend to his own family, and makes that family his Sabbath-school class, there is no drivelling there; he stands in the same position as he did before.

HAVE you not noticed how magnificently peace winneth its reprisals at the hands of war? Look through this country. Methinks if the angel of peace should go with us, as we journey through it, and stop at the various ancient towns, where there are dismantled castles, and high mounds from which every vestige of a building has long been swept, the angel would look us in the face, and say, "I have done all this: war scattered my peaceful subjects, burned down my cottages, ravaged my temples, and laid my mansions with the dust. But I have attacked war in his own strongholds and I have routed him. Walk through his halls. Can you hear now the footfalls of the warrior? Where now the sound of the clarion and the drum?" The sheep is feeding from the cannon's mouth, and the bird builds his nest where once the warrior did hang his helmet. As rare curiosities we dig up the swords and spears of our forefathers, and little do we consider that in this we are doing tribute to peace. For peace is the conqueror. It hath been a long duel, and much blood hath been shed; but peace hath been the victor. "War, after all, has but spasmodic triumphs; and again it sinks—it dies; but peace ever reigneth. If she be driven from one part of the earth, yet she dwelleth in another; and while war, with busy hand, is piling up here a wall, and there a rampart, and there a tower, peace—with her gentle finger, is covering o'er the castle with the moss and the ivy, and casting the stone from the top, and letting it lie level with the earth.

A HEEDLESS spirit is a curse to the soul; a rash, presumptuous conversation will eat as doth a canker. "Too-bold" was never Too-wise nor Too-loving. Careful walking is one of the best securities of safe and happy standing. It is solemn cause for doubting when we are indifferent in our behavior to our best Friend.

OH! thou that fearest for the ark of the Lord; thou that tremblest at the firmness with which falsehood keeps its throne: look thou on these desolations and be of good cheer; God hath done mighty things, and we will do them yet again. One can never pass, even in our own country, a ruined abbey, or a destroyed priory, or an old broken down cathedral, without a sweet satisfaction. They are fair ruins, all the fairer because they are ruined, because their inhabitants are forgot ten, because the monk no longer prowls our streets, because the nun, though she is here and there to be found, yet is no more honored, because the apostate church to which they belong has ceased to have power among us, as once it had.

EVERY stone that is in the temple, Jesus Christ ordained should be put where it is; even those stones that are most contemptible and unseen, were put in their places by him. There is not one board of cedar, one piece of burnished pinnacle, that was not foreseen and pre-arranged in that eternal covenant of grace which was the great plan that Christ, the Almighty Architect, did draw for the building of the temple to his praise.

SUPPOSE someone entering heaven were to say to the redeemed, "Suspend your songs for a moment! Ye have been praising Christ, lo, these six thousand years; many of you have without cessation praised him now these many centuries! Stop your song a moment; pause and give your songs to someone else for an instant." Oh, can you conceive the scorn with which the myriad eyes of the redeemed would smite the tempter? "Stop from praising him! No, never. Time may stop, for it shall be no more; the world may stop, for its revolutions must cease; the universe may stop its cycles and the movings of its world, but for us to stop our songs—never, never!"—and it shall be said, "Hallelujah, hallelujah, hallelujah, the Lord God Omnipotent reigneth!"

LAUGH at religion now! scoff at Christ now! now that the angels are gathering for the judgment; now that the trumpet sounds exceedingly loud and long; now that the heavens are red with fire, that the great furnace of hell overleaps its boundary, and is about to encircle thee in its flame; now despise religion! Ah! no. I see thee. Now thy stiff knees are bending, now thy bold forehead for the first time is covered with hot sweat of trembling, now thine eyes that once were full of scorn are full of tears; thou dost look on him whom thou didst despise, and thou art weeping for thy sin. O sinner, it will be too late then; there is no cutting of the stone after it gets to Jerusalem. Where thou fallest there thou liest. Where judgment finds thee, there eternity shall leave thee. Time shall be no more when judgment comes, and when time is no more, change is impossible! In eternity there can be no change, no deliverance, no signing of acquittal. Once lost, lost forever; once damned, damned to all eternity.

CHRIST must be his own architect. He will bring out different points of truth in different ways. Why, I believe that different denominations are sent on purpose to set out different truths. There are some of our brethren a little too high, they bring out better than any other people the grand old truths of sovereign grace. There are some, on the other hand, a little too low; they bring out with great clearness the great and truthful doctrines of man's responsibility. So that two truths that might have been neglected, either the one or the other, if only one form of Christianity existed, are both brought out, both made resplendent, by the different denominations of God's people, who are alike chosen of God, and precious to him.

THE man whose soul is saturated with grateful affection to his crucified Lord will weep when the enemy seems to get an advantage; he will water his couch with tears when he sees a declining church; he will lift up his voice like a trumpet to arouse the slumbering, and with his own hand will labor day and night to build up the breaches of Zion; and should his efforts be successful, with what joyous gratitude will he lift up his heart unto the King of Israel, extolling him as much—yea, more—for mercies given to the Church than for bounties conferred upon himself.

LOVE to Christ smooths the path of duty, and wings the feet to travel it: it is the bow which impels the arrow of obedience; it is the mainspring moving the wheels of duty; it is the strong arm tugging the oar of diligence. Love is the marrow of the bones of fidelity, the blood in the veins of piety, the sinew of spiritual strength—yea, the life of sincere devotion. He that hath love can no more be motionless than the aspen in the gale, the sere leaf in the hurricane, or the spray in the tempest. As well may hearts cease to beat, as love to labor. Love is instinct with activity, it cannot be idle; it is full of energy, it cannot content itself with littles; it is the well-spring of heroism, and great deeds are the gushings of its fountain; it is a giant— it heapeth mountains upon mountains, and thinks the pile but little; it is a mighty mystery, for it changes bitter into sweet; it calls death life, and life death, and it makes pain less painful than enjoyment. Love has a clear eye, but it can see only one thing—it is blind to every interest but that of its Lord; it seeth things in the light of his glory, and weigheth actions in the scales of his honor; it counts royalty but drudgery if it cannot reign for Christ, but it delights in servitude as much as in honor, if it can thereby advance the Master's kingdom; its end sweetens all its means; its object lightens its toil, and removes its weariness. Love, with refreshing influence, girds up the loins of the pilgrim, so that he forgets fatigue; it casts a shadow for the way faring man, so that he feels not the burning heat; and it puts the bottle to the lip of thirst.

WE are *willing* to serve God when we love his Son: there may be obstacles, but no unwillingness. We would be holy even as God is holy, and perfect even as our Father which is in heaven is perfect.

MAY God make us ever careful that, by his Holy Spirit's aid, we may be able to live unto him as those that are alive from the dead; and since in many things we fall short of his perfect will, let us humble ourselves, and devoutly seek the molding of his hand to renew us day by day. We ought ever to desire a perfect life as the result of full consecration, even though we shall often groan that "it is not yet attained." Our prayer should be—

> "Take my soul and body's powers;
> Take my memory, mind, and will;
> All my goods, and all my hours;
> All I know, and all I feel;
> All I think, or speak, or do;
> Take my heart—but make it new."

WE love Jesus when we are advanced in the divine life, from a participation with him in the great work of his incarnation. We long to see our fellow-men turned from darkness to light, and we love him as the sun of righteousness, who can alone illuminate them. We hate sin, and therefore we rejoice in him as manifested to take away sin. We pant for holier and happier times, and therefore we adore him as the coming Ruler of all lands, who will bring a millennium with him in the day of his appearing.

WHEN Jesus Christ came to build his temple, he found no mountain on which to build it; he had no mountain in our nature, he had to find a mountain in his own, and the mountain upon which he has built his Church is the mountain of his own unchangeable affection, his own strong love, his own omnipotent grace and infallible truthfulness. It is this that constitutes the mountain upon which the Church is built, and on this the foundation hath been digged, and the great stones laid in the trenches with oaths and promises and blood to make them stand secure, even though earth should rock and all creation suffer decay.

AS the affectionate wife obeys because she loves her husband, so does the redeemed soul delight in keeping the commands of Jesus, although compelled by no force but that of love. This divine principle will render every duty pleasant; yea, when the labor is in itself irksome, this heavenly grace will quicken us in its performance by reminding us that it is honorable to suffer for our Lord.

HEAVEN is a state of entire acquiescence in the will of God, and perfect sympathy with his purposes.

I REMEMBER a story of one, who remarked to a minister, what a wonderful thing it was to see so many people weeping. "Nay," said he, "I will tell you something more wonderful still, that so many will forget all they wept about when they get outside the door." And you will do this. Still, when you have done it, you will recollect that you have not been without the strivings of God's Spirit. You will remember that God has, this morning, as it were, put a hurdle across your road, digged a ditch in your way, and put up a hand-post, and said, "take warning! beware, beware, beware! you are rushing madly into the ways of iniquity!" And I have come before you this morning, and in God's name I have said, "Stop, stop, stop, thus saith the Lord 'consider your ways, why will ye die? Turn ye, turn ye, why will ye die, O house of Israel?" And now, if ye will put this from you, it must be even so; if you will put out these sparks, if you will quench this first burning torch, it must be so! On your own head be your blood; at your own door lay your iniquities.

GOOD men are more tender over the reputation of Christ than over their own good name; for they are willing to lose the world's favorable opinion rather than that Christ should be dishonored.

BELIEVE and live," is preached every day in your hearing. Many of you tins ten, twenty, thirty, forty, or fifty years have been hearing the gospel, and you dare not say, "I did not know what the gospel was." From your earliest childhood many of you have listened to it. The name of Jesus was mingled with the hush of lullaby. You drank in a holy gospel with your mother's milk, and yet despite all that, you have never sought Christ. "Knowledge is power," men say. Alas! Knowledge, when not used, is wrath, *wrath*, WRATH to the uttermost, against the man who knows, and yet doth not that which he knoweth to be right.

OH! how has our blood boiled when the name of Jesus has been the theme of scornful jest! how have we been ready to invoke the fire of Elias upon the guilty blasphemers! or when our more carnal heat has subsided, how have we wept, even to the sobbing of a child, at the reproach cast upon his most hallowed name! Many a time we have been ready to burst with anguish when we have been speechless before the scoffer, because the Lord had shut us up, that we could not come forth; but at other seasons, with courage more than we had considered to be within the range of our capability, we have boldly reproved the wicked, and sent them back abashed.

WE, who are saved by grace, have room enough in our Redeemer's character for eternal love and wonder. His characters are so varied, and all of them so precious, that we may still gaze and adore. The Shepherd folding the lambs in his bosom, the Breaker dashing into pieces the opposing gates of brass, the Captain routing all his foes, the Brother born for adversity, and a thousand other delightful pictures of Jesus, are all calculated to stir the affections of the thoughtful Christian.

IF a sense of unity in aim be capable of binding hosts of men into one compact body, beating with one heart, and moving with the same step—then it is easy to believe that the heavenly object in which the saints and their Savior are both united, is strong enough to form a lasting bond of love between them.

HE that is not afraid of sinning has good need to be afraid of damning. Truth hates error, holiness abhorreth guilt, and grace cannot but detest sin. If we do not desire to be cautious to avoid offending our Lord, we may rest confident that we have no part in him, for true love to Christ will rather die than wound him.

WE remember to have heard a preacher at a funeral most beautifully betting forth this parable: "A certain nobleman had a spacious garden, which he left to the care of a faithful servant, whose delight it was to train the creepers along the trellis, to water the seeds in the time of drought, to support the stalks of the tender plants, and to do every work which could render the garden a Paradise of flowers. One morning he rose with joy, expecting to tend his beloved flowers, and hoping to find his favorites increased in beauty. To his surprise, he found one of his choicest beauties rent from its stem, and, looking around him, he missed from every bed the pride of his garden, the most precious of his blooming flowers. Full of grief and anger, he hurried to his fellow-servants, and demanded who had thus robbed him of his treasures. They had not done it, and he did not charge them with it; but he found no solace for his grief till one of them remarked: 'My lord was walking in the garden this morning, and I saw him pluck the flowers and carry them away.' Then truly he found he had no cause for his trouble. He felt it was well that his master had been pleased to take his own, and he went away, smiling at his loss, because his lord had taken them. So," said the preacher, turning to the mourners, "you have lost one whom you regarded with much tender affection. The bonds of endearment have not availed for her retention upon earth. I know your wounded feelings when, instead of the lovely form which was the embodiment of all that is excellent and amiable, you behold nothing but ashes and corruption. But remember, my beloved, the Lord hath done it. He hath removed the tender mother, the affectionate wife, the inestimable friend. I say again, remember your own Lord has done it; therefore do not murmur, or yield yourselves to an excess of grief." There was much force as well as beauty in the simple allegory: it were well if all the Lord's family had grace to practice its heavenly lesson, in all times of bereavement and affliction.

OH newborn soul, trembling with anxiety, if thou hast not yet beheld the fair face of thy beloved, if thou canst not as yet delight in the majesty of his offices, and the wonders of his person, let thy soul be fully alive to the richness of his grace, and the preciousness of his blood. These thou hast in thy possession—the pledges of thine interest in him; love him then for these, and in due time he will discover unto thee fresh wonders and glories, so that thou shalt be able to exclaim, "The half has not been told me." Let Calvary and Gethsemane endear thy Savior to thee, though as yet thou hast not seen the brightness of Tabor, or heard the eloquence of Olivet. Take the lower room if thou canst not reach another, for *the lowest room is in the house,* and its tables shall not be naked. But study to look into thy Redeemer's heart, that thou mayst become more closely knit unto him. Remember there is a singular love in the bowels of our Lord Jesus to his people, so superlatively excellent, that nothing can compare with it. No husband, no wife, nor tender-hearted mother can compete with him in affection, for his love passeth the love of women. Nothing will contribute more to make thee see Jesus Christ as admirable and lovely than a right apprehension of his love to thee; this is the constraining, ravishing, engaging, and overwhelming consideration which will infallibly steep thee in a sea of love to him.

THIS feeling of fear lest we should "slip with our feet," is a precious feature of true spiritual life. It is much to be regretted that it is so lightly prized by many, in comparison with the more martial virtues; for, despite its apparent insignificance, it is one of the choicest fruits of the Spirit, and its absence is one of the most deplorable evidences of spiritual decay.

"WE love him because he first loved us." Here is the starting point of love's race. This is the rippling rill which afterwards swells into a river, the torch with which the pile of piety is kindled. The emancipated spirit loves the Savior for the freedom which he has conferred upon it; it beholds the agony with which the priceless gift was purchased, and it adores the bleeding sufferer for the pains which he so generously endured.

IT is worth while to be a man, despite all the sorrows of mortality, if we may have grace to talk in the fashion of a full-assured believer when he rejoices in the plenitude of his possessions and grate fully returns his love as his only possible acknowledgment. Listen to him while he talks in the following strain: "*My* Beloved is mine, and I am his. The grant is clear and my claim is firm. Who shall despoil me of it when God hath put me in possession, and doth own me as the lawful heritor? *My* Lord hath himself assured me that he is mine, and hath bid me call his father, *my* father. I know of a surety that the whole Trinity are *mine*. 'I will be *thy* God' is my sweet assurance. O my soul, arise and take possession; inherit thy blessedness, and cast up thy richess; enter into *thy* rest, and tell how the Lord hath dealt bountifully with thee. I will praise thee, O *my* God; *my* king, I subject my soul unto thee. O, *my* Glory, in thee will I boast all the day; O *my* Rock, on thee will I build all my confidence. O staff of my life and strength of my heart, the life of my joy and joy of my life, I will sit and sing under thy shadow, yea, I will sing a song of loves touching *my* Well-beloved." This is a precious experience, happy is the man who enjoys it.

IN some circles it is believed that in the event of another reign of persecution, there are very few in our churches who would endure the fiery trial: nothing, we think, is more unfounded. It is our firm opinion that the feeblest saint in our midst would receive grace for the struggle, and come off more than a conqueror. God's children are the same now as ever. Real piety will as well endure the fire in one century as another. There is the same love to impel the martyrdom, the same grace to sustain the sufferer, the same promises to cheer his heart, and the same crown to adorn his head. "We believe that those followers of Jesus who may perhaps one day be called to the stake, will die as readily as any who have gone before. Love is still as strong as death, and grace is still made perfect in weakness. *We* may be weak in grace, but *grace* is not weak.

OUR favorite master of quaint conceits (Herbert) has singularly said in his poem entitled "Unkindness"—

"My friend may spit upon my curious floor."

True, most true, our Beloved may do as he pleases in our house, even should he break its ornaments and stain its glories. Come in, thou heavenly guest, even though each footstep on our floor should crush a thousand of our earthly joys. Thou art thyself more than sufficient recompense for all that thou canst take away. Come in, thou brother of our souls, even though thy rod come with thee. We would rather have thee, and trials with thee, than lament thine absence even though surrounded with all the wealth the universe can bestow.

OH! how jealous we once were lest one divine ordinance should be neglected, or one rule violated. Nothing pained us more than our own too frequent wanderings, and nothing gratified us more than to be allowed to hew wood or draw water at his bidding. Why is it not so now with us all? Why are those wings, once outstretched for speedy flight, now folded in sloth? Is our Redeemer less deserving? or is it not that we are less loving?

TRIED saints are constrained to love their redeemer; not only on account of deliverance out of trouble, but also because of that sweet comfort which he affords them whilst they are enduring the cross. They have found adversity to be a wine press, in which the juice of the grapes of Eschol could be trodden out; an olive-press, to extract the precious oil from the gracious promises. Christ is the honeycomb, but experience must suck forth the luscious drops; he is frankincense, but fiery trials must burn out the perfume; he is a box of spikenard, but the hard hand of trouble must break the box and pour forth the ointment.

THERE are degrees of punishment; but the highest degree is given to the man who rejects Christ. You have noticed that passage, I dare say, that the liar and the whoremonger, and drunkards shall have their portion—who do you suppose with?—with *unbelievers*; as if hell was made first of all for unbelievers —as if the pit was digged not for whoremongers, and swearers, and drunkards, but for men who despise Christ, because that is the preeminent sin, the cardinal vice, and men are condemned for that. Other iniquities come following after them, but this one goes before them to judgment. Imagine for a moment that time has passed, and that the day of judgment is come. We are all gathered together, both quick and dead. The trumpet-blast waxes exceeding loud and long. We are all attentive, expecting something marvelous. The exchange stands still in its business; the shop is deserted by the tradesman; the crowded streets are filled. All men stand still; they feel that the last great business-day is come, and that now they must settle their accounts forever. A solemn stillness fills the air; no sound is heard. All, all is noiseless. Presently a great white cloud with solemn state sails through the sky, and then—hark! the twofold clamor of the startled earth. On that cloud there sits one like unto the Son of Man. Every eye looks, and at last there is heard a unanimous shout—"It is he! It is he!" and after that you hear on the one hand, shouts of "Hallelujah, Hallelujah, Hallelujah, Welcome, Welcome, Welcome Son of God." But mixed with that there is a deep bass, composed of the weeping and the wailing of the men who have persecuted him, and who have rejected him. Listen; I think I can dissect the sonnet; I think I can hear the words as they come separately, each one of them tolling like a death knell. What say they? They say, "Rocks, hide us, mountains, fall upon us, hide us from the face of him that sits upon the throne." And shall you be among the number of those who say to the rocks "Hide us?"

My impenitent hearer, I suppose for a moment that you have gone out of this world, and that you have died impenitent, and that you are among those who are weeping, and wailing, and gnashing their teeth. Oh! what will then be your terror! Blanched cheeks, and knocking knees are nothing, compared to thy horror of heart, when thou shalt be drunken, but not with wine, and when thou shalt reel to and fro, with the intoxication of amazement, and shall fall down, and roll in the dust for horror and dismay. For there he comes, and there he is, with fierce, fire-darting eye; and now the time is come for the great division. The voice is heard, "Gather my people from the four winds of heaven, mine elect, in whom my soul delighteth." They are gathered at the right hand, and there they are. And now saith he, "Gather up the tares, and bind them in bundles to burn." And you are gathered, and on tho left hand there you are, gathered into tho bundle. All that is wanted is the lighting of the pile. Where shall be the torch that shall kindle them? The tares are to be burned: where is the flame? The flame comes out of his mouth, and it is composed of words like these—"De part, ye cursed, into everlasting fire, in hell, prepared for the devil and his angels." Do you linger? *"Depart!"* Do you seek a blessing? *"Ye are cursed!"* I curse you with a curse. Do ye seek to escape? *It is everlasting fire.* Do ye stop and plead? No! *"I called, and ye refused; I stretched out my hands, and ye regarded me not; therefore I will mock at your calamity, I will laugh when your fear cometh."* "*Depart*, again, I say; depart forever!" And you are gone. And what is your reflection? Why, it is this: "Oh! would to God that I never had been born! Oh! that I had never heard the gospel preached, that I might never have had the sin of rejecting it." This will be the gnawing of the worm in your conscience—"I knew better, but I did not do better."—As I sowed the wind, it is right I should reap the whirlwind; I was checked, but I would not be stopped; I was wooed, but I would not be invited. Now I see that I have murdered myself. Oh! thought above all thoughts most deadly. I am lost, lost, lost! And this is the horror of horrors: I have caused myself to be lost; I have put from me the gospel of Christ; I have destroyed myself.

WE think every Christian will be corrected in due measure; we should be the last to deny that God's people are a tried people. They must all pass through the furnace of affliction, and he has chosen them there; but still we believe that religion is a blessed and happy thing."

AGED and mellow saints have so sweet a savor of Christ in them that their conversation is like streams from Lebanon, sweetly refreshing to him who delights to hear of the glories of redeeming love. They have tried the anchor in the hour of storm, they have tested the armor in the day of battle, they have proved the shadow of the great rock in the burning noontide in the weary land; therefore do they talk of those things, and of Him who is all these unto them, with an unction and a relish which we, who have but just put on our harness, can enjoy, although we cannot attain unto it at present. We must dive into the same waters if we would bring up the same pearls.

THE Lord's prisoner in the dungeon of Aberdeen thus penned his belief in the love of his "sweet Lord Jesus," and his acquiescence in his Master's will: "Oh, what owe I to the file, to the hammer, to the furnace, of my Lord Jesus! who hath now let me see how good the wheat of Christ is, which goeth through his mill, to be made bread for his own table. Grace tried is better than grace, and more than grace—it is glory in its infancy. "When Christ blesses his own crosses with a tongue, they breathe out Christ's love, wisdom, kindness, and care of us. Why should I start at the plough of my Lord, that maketh deep furrows upon my soul? I know that he is no idle husbandman; he purposeth a crop. Oh, that this white, withered ground were made fertile to bear a crop for him, by whom it is so painfully dressed, and that this fallow ground were broken up! Why was I (a fool!) grieved that he put his garland and his rose upon my head—the glory and honor of his faithful witnesses? I desire now to make no more pleas with Christ. Verily, he hath not put me to a loss by what I suffered; he oweth me nothing; for in my bonds how sweet and comfortable have the thoughts of him been to me, wherein I find a sufficient recompense of reward!"

AS fire grows by the addition of fuel, so does our love to Christ increase by renewed and enlarged discoveries of his love to us. Love is love's food. If, as parents, we make known our love to our children, and deal wisely with them, it is but natural that their affections should become more and more knit to us; so it seems but as in the common course of things that where much of divine love is perceived by the soul, there will be a return of affection in some degree proportionate to the measure of the manifestation.

IT is a lovely spectacle to behold the timid and feeble defending the citadel of truth: not with hard blows of logic, or sounding cannonade of rhetoric— but with that tearful earnestness, and implicit confidence, against which the attacks of revilers are utterly powerless. Overthrown in argument, they overcome by faith; covered with contempt, they think it all joy if they may but avert a solitary stain from the escutcheon of their Lord. "Call me what thou wilt," says the believer, "but speak not ill of my Beloved. Here, plough these shoulders with your lashes, but spare yourselves the sin of cursing him! Aye, let me die: I am all too happy to be slain, if my Lord's most glorious cause shall live!"

NEARNESS of life towards the Lamb will necessarily involve greatness of love to him. As nearness to the sun increases the temperature of the various planets, so close communion with Jesus raises the heat of the affections towards him.

A BABE'S fondness of its mother is as pleasing to her as the strong devotion of her full-grown son. The graces of faith, hope, and love are to be estimated more by their honesty than by their degree, and less by their intellectual than by their emotional characteristics.

AN honored saint was once so ravished with a revelation of his Lord's love, that feeling his mortal frame to be unable to sustain more of such bliss, he cried, "Hold, Lord, it is enough, it is enough!" In heaven we shall be able to set the bottomless well of love to our lips, and drink on forever, and yet feel no weakness. Ah, that will be love indeed which shall overflow our souls forever in our Father's house above! Who can tell the transports, the raptures, the amazements of delight which that love shall be get in us? and who can guess the sweetness of the song, or the swiftness of the obedience which will be the heavenly expressions of love made perfect?

IT has become fashionable to allow the title of "intellectual preachers "to a class of men, whose passionless essays are combinations of metaphysical quibbles and heretical doctrines; who are shocked at the man who excites his hearers beyond the freezing-point of insensibility, and are quite elated if they hear that their homily could only be understood by a few. It is, however, no question whether these men deserve their distinctive title; it may be settled as an axiom that falsehood is no intellectual feat, and that unintelligible jargon is no evidence of a cultured mind. There must be in our religion a fair proportion of believing, thinking, understanding, and discerning, but there must be also the preponderating influences of feeling, loving, delighting, and desiring. That religion is worth nothing which has no dwelling in man but his brain. To love much is to be wise; to grow in affection is to grow in knowledge, and to in crease in tender attachment is to be making high proficiency in divine things.

THERE are many fair and enchanting spots in the highway of salvation—spots which angels have visited, and which the saints have sighed to behold again and again. But some other parts of the way are not so inviting; we love not to enter the Valley of the Shadow of Death, nor to approach the mountains of the leopards, nor the lions' dens, yet must all of them be passed.

OH, mourner, say not that *thou* art a target for all the arrows of the Almighty; take not to thyself the preeminence of woe; for thy fellows have trod den the valley too, and upon them are the scars of the thorns and briers of the dreary pathway.

SONNETS will never cease for want of themes, unless it be that the penury of language should compel our wonder to abide at home, since it cannot find garments in which to clothe its thoughts. "When the soul is led by the Holy Spirit to take a clear view of Jesus in his various offices, how speedily the heart is on fire with love! To see him stooping from his throne to become man, next yielding to suffering to become man's sympathizing friend, and then bowing to death itself to become his ransom, is enough to stir every passion of the soul. To discern him by faith as the propitiation for sin, sprinkling his own blood within the veil, and nailing our sins to his cross, is a sight which never fails to excite the reverent, yet rapturous admiration of the beholder. Who can behold the triumphs of the Prince of Peace and not applaud him! Who can know his illustrious merits, and not extol him?

ALL men have their times of sadness, but some seem to be always in the deep waters—their lives, like Ezekiel's roll, seem written within and without with lamentations. They can just dimly recollect happier days, but those are past long ago. They have for sometime been the children of grief. They seldom eat a crust unmoistened by a tear. Sorrow's wormwood is their daily salad.

O THE savour of the name of Jesus, when heard by the ear which has been opened by the Spirit! O the beauty of the person of Jesus, when seen with the eye of faith by the illumination of the Holy One of Israel! As the light of the morning, when the sun ariseth, as "a morning without clouds," is our Well-Beloved unto us. The sight of the burning bush made Moses put off his shoes, but the transporting vision of Jesus makes us put off all the world. When once he is seen we can discern no beauties in all the creatures in the universe. He, like the sun, hath absorbed all other glories into his own excessive brightness. This is the pomegranate which love feeds upon, the flagon wherewith it is comforted.

HEAVEN itself, although it be a fertile land, flowing with milk and honey, can produce no fairer flower than the Rose of Sharon; its highest joys mount no higher than the head of Jesus; its sweetest bliss is found in his name alone. If we would know heaven, let us know Jesus; if we would be heavenly, let us love Jesus.

THAT sweet name "brother" is like perfume to the believer, and when he lays hold upon it, it imparts its fragrance to him.

THE best enjoyments of Christ on earth are but as the dipping of our finger in water for the cooling of our thirst; but heaven is bathing in seas of bliss: even so our love here is but one drop of the same substance as the waters of the ocean, but not com parable for magnitude or depth. Oh, how sweet it will be to be married to the Lord Jesus, and to enjoy forever, and without any interruption, the heavenly delights of his society! Surely, if a glimpse of him melteth our soul, the full fruition of him will be enough to burn up with affection. It is well that we shall have more noble frames in heaven than we have here, otherwise we should die of love in the very land of life.

IT is the ambition of most men to absorb others into their own life, that they may shine the more brightly by the stolen rays of other lights; but it is the Christian's highest aspiration to be absorbed into another, and lose himself in the glories of his sovereign and Savior.

LOOK to thy love, O Christian! and let the carnal revile thee never so much, do thou persevere in seeking to walk with Christ, to feel his love, and triumph in his grace.

IT is the highest stage of manhood to have no wish, no thought, no desire, but Christ—to feel that to die were bliss, if it were for Christ—that to live in penury, and woe, and scorn, and contempt, and misery, were sweet for Christ—to feel that it matters nothing what becomes of one's self, so that our Master is but exalted—to feel that though, like a sere leaf, we are blown in the blast, we are quite careless whither we are going, so long as we feel that the Master's hand is guiding us according to his will; or, rather, to feel that though like the diamond, we must be exercised with sharp tools, yet we care not how sharply we may be cut, so that we may be made fit brilliants to adorn *his* crown.

EARTHLY joys are continually failing us; and cisterns, one after another, are dried up. A hot, dry wind steals away every drop of comfort, and, hungry and thirsty, our soul fainteth in us. No fruit of sweetness grows here. It well answers the description of Watts:

> "It yields us no supply,
> No cheering fruits, no wholesome trees,
> Nor streams of living joy."

THE vale of tears is very low, and descends far be neath the ordinary level; some parts of it, in deed, are tunnelled through rocks of anguish. A frequent cause of its darkness is that on either side of the valley there are high mountains, called the mountains of sin. These rise so high that they obscure the light of the sun. Behind these Andes of guilt, God hides his face, and we are troubled. Then how densely dark the pathway becomes! Indeed, this is the very worst thing that can be mentioned of this valley: for, if it were not so dark, pilgrims would not so much dread passing through it.

IF there be an inner chamber in which the king doth store his choicest fruits, let us enter, for he bids us make free with all in his house; and if there be a secret place where he doth show his loves, let us hasten thither and embrace him whom our soul loveth, and there let us abide until we see him face to face in the upper skies.

TRUE grace may be in the soul without being apparent; for, as Baxter truly observes, "grace is never apparent and sensible to the soul but while it is in action." Fire may be in the flint, and yet be unseen except when occasion shall bring it out.

THE air from the sea of affliction is extremely beneficial to invalid Christians. Continued prosperity, like a warm atmosphere, has a tendency to unbind the sinews and soften the bones; but the cold winds of trouble make us sturdy, hardy, and well braced in every part. Unbroken success often leads to an undervaluing of mercies and forgetfulness of the giver; but the withdrawal of the sunshine leads us to look for the sun.

BETTER walk on rugged rocks than on slippery ice. If we lose our roll it is in the harbor of ease, not in the valley of Baca. Few Christians backslide while under the rod; it is usually when on the lap of plenty that believers sin.

SAY, poor soul, what do you get from Christ whenever you go to him? Can you say, Oh! I get more love for him than I had before; I never approached near to him but I gained a large draught and ample fill of love of God. Out of his fullness we receive grace for grace, and love for love. In a word, by faith we behold the glory of the Lord as in a glass, and are changed into the same image—and the image of God is love.

STARS may be seen from the bottom of a deep well When they cannot be discerned from the top of a mountain: be are many things learned in adversity which the prosperous man dreams not of. We need affliction as the trees need winter, that we may collect sap and nourishment for future blossoms and fruit. Sorrow is as necessary for the soul as medicine is to the body:

> "The path of sorrow, and that path alone,
> Leads to the land where sorrow is unknown."

WHEN eastern shepherds travel, if they find no water, they dig a well, and thus obtain a plentiful supply of water for themselves and for their cattle. So did Isaac, and so also did the rulers for the people in the wilderness. When we are thirsty and there is no water to be found in the pools, we must dig deep for it. Calvin translates it—

"They, traveling through the valley of weeping, will dig a well,..."

AS we pour water into a dry pump when we desire to obtain more—so must we have the love of Christ imparted to the heart before we shall feel any uprisings of delight in him.

WE are bound to use every Scriptural means to '"obtain the good we need. The sanctuary, the meeting for prayer, the Bible, the company of the saints, private prayer and meditation—these revive the soul. "We must dig the wells. If there be rocky granite we must bore it; we must not be disturbed from perseverance by the labor of our duties, but continue to dig still; and what a mercy! if the well has ever so small a bore the water will flow.

OH, child of grief, remember the vale of tears is much frequented; thou art not alone in thy dis tress. Sorrow has a numerous family. Say not, I am *the* man that has seen affliction, for there be others in the furnace with thee. Remember, more over, the King of kings once went through this valley, and here he obtained his name, "the Man of sorrows," for it was while passing through it he be came "acquainted with grief."

SO long as mere reason is the only listener, the melody of the cross will be unheard. Charm we never so wisely, men cannot hear the music until the ears of the heart are opened.

IT certainly is not possible for us to be in a position where Omnipotence cannot assist us. God hath servants everywhere, and where we think he has none his word can create a multitude. There are "treasures hid in the sand," and the Lord's chosen shall eat thereof. When the clouds hide the mountains they are as real as in the sunshine; so the promise and the Providence of God are unchanged by the obscurity of our faith, or the difficulties of our position. There is hope, and hope at hand, therefore, let us be of good cheer.

TRAVELERS have been delighted to see the footprints of man on a barren shore, and we love to see the way-marks of the pilgrimage while passing through the vale of tears. Yea, the refuse and *debris* of the receding camp often furnish food for the stragglers behind.

WHEN heaven smiles and pours down its showers of grace, then they are precious things; but without the celestial rain we might as much expect water from the arid waste, as a real blessing in the use of them. "All my springs are in Thee," is the believer's daily confession to his Lord—a confession which until death must ever be upon his lips.

AS Isaac met his bride in the fields at eventide, so do true souls frequently find their joy and consolation in the loneliness of solitude, and at the sunset of their earthly pleasures. He who would see the stars sparkling with tenfold luster must dwell in the cold regions of snow; and he who would know the full beauties of Jesus, the bright and morning star, must see him amid the frosts of trouble and adversity.

AFFLICTION is often the hand of God, which he places before our face to enable us, like Moses, to see the train of his glory as he passes by. The saint has had many a pleasant view of God's loving kindness from the top of the hills of mercy; but tribulation is very frequently the Lord's Pisgah, from which he gives them a view of the land in all its length and breadth.

PIOUS Brooks writes, "Oh, the love-tokens, the love-letters, the bracelets, the jewels that the saints are able to produce since they have been in the furnace of affliction!" Of these they had but one in a season before, but now that their troubles have driven them nearer to their Savior, they have enough to store their cabinet.

IT is often remarked that after soul-sorrow our pas tors are more gifted with words in season, and their speech is more full of savor: this is to be accounted for by the sweet influence of grief when sanctified by the Holy Spirit. Blessed Redeemer, we delight in thy love, and thy presence is the light of our joys; but if thy brief withdrawals qualify us for glorifying thee in cheering thy saints, we thank thee for standing behind the wall; and as we seek thee by night, it shall somewhat cheer us that thou art blessing us when thou takest away thy richest blessing.

OUR faith is the center of the target at which God doth shoot when he tries us, and if any other grace shall escape untried, certainly faith shall not. There is no way of piercing faith to its very marrow like the sticking of the arrow of desertion in it; this finds it out whether it be of the immortals or no. Strip it of its armor of conscious enjoyment, and suffer the terrors of the Lord to set themselves in array against it, and that is faith indeed which can escape unhurt from the midst of the attack. Faith must be tried, and desertion is the furnace, heated seven times, into which it might be thrust. Blessed is the man who can endure the ordeal.

CHOICE discoveries of the wondrous love and grace of Jesus are most tenderly vouchsafed unto believers in the times of grief. Then it is that he lifts them up from his feet, where, like Mary, it is their delight to sit, and exalts them to the position of the favored John, pressing them to his breast and bid ding them lean on his bosom. Then it is that he doth fill the cup of salvation with the old wine of the kingdom, and puts it to the mouth of the Christian, that he may in some measure forget the flavor of wormwood and grating of gravel-stones which the draught of bitterness has placed upon his palate and between his teeth.

LET us, in all time of our tribulation and affliction, content ourselves with one Comforter, if all others fail us. Job had three miserable comforters; better far to have one who is full of pity and able to console. And who can do this so truly as our own most loving Lord Jesus?

AS in time of war the city doubles its guards, so does Jesus multiply the displays of his affection when his chosen are besieged by trials.

THE intense desire after Jesus, the struggling of the soul with doubts and fears, and the inward panting of the whole being after the living God, prove beyond a doubt that Jesus is at work in the soul, though he may be concealed from the eye of faith. How should it, therefore, be a matter of wonder that secretly he should be able to afford support to the sinking saint, even at seasons when his absence is bemoaned with lamentations and tears?

WE learn more true divinity by our trials than by our books. The great Reformer said, "Prayer is the best book in my library." He might have added affliction as the next. Sickness is the best Doctor of Divinity in all the world; and trial is the finest exposition of Scripture. This is so inestimable a mark of the love of our blessed Lord that we might almost desire trouble for the sake of it.

A BLIND man is really nourished by the food he eats, even though he cannot see it; so, when by the blindness of our spiritual wisdom, we are unable to discern the Savior, yet his grace sustains our strength and keeps us alive in famine.

LUTHER said Temptation was one of his masters in divinity. We will readily trust ourselves in the' hands of a physician who has been himself sick of our disease, and has tried the remedies which he prescribes for us; so we confide in the advice of the Christian who knows our trials by having felt them. What sweet words in season do tried saints address to mourners! They are the real sons of consolation, the truly good Samaritans.

GOD'S own glory is sometimes his only motive for action, and truly it is a reason so great and good that he who mocks at it must be a stranger to God, and cannot be truly humbled before him. It may be that the sole cause of our sad condition lies in the absolute will of God; if so, let us bend our heads in silence, and let him do what seemeth him good.

THE *Lord Jesus is no fair-weather friend, but one who loveth at all times—a brother born for adversity.* This he proves to his beloved, not by mere words of promise, but by actual deeds of affection. As our sufferings abound, so he makes our consolations to abound.

IF Christ is more excellent at one time than another it certainly is in "the cloudy and dark day." We can never be well see the true color of Christ's love as in the night of weeping. Christ in the dungeon, Christ on the bed of sickness, Christ in poverty, is Christ indeed to a sanctified man. No vision of Christ Jesus is so truly a revelation as that which is seen in the Patmos of suffering.

SUNLIGHT is never more grateful than after a long watch in the midnight blackness; Christ's presence is never more acceptable than after a time of weeping, on account of his departure. It is a sad thing that we should need to lose our mercies to teach us to be grateful for them; let us mourn over this crookedness of our nature; and let us strive to express our thankfulness for mercies, so that we may not have to lament their removal.

WE often miss our Lord's company, because our conversation does not please him. When our Beloved goes down into his garden, it is to feed there and gather lilies; but if thorns and nettles are the only products of the soil, he will soon be away to the true beds of spices.

RIVALS Jesus will not endure; and unless we give him the highest throne he will leave us to mourn his absence. Love not thy wealth, thy name, thy friends, thy life, thy comfort, thy husband, thy wife, or thy children, more than thou lovest him, or even as much; for he will either take *them* from thee, or else his own delightful presence, and the loss of either would be an evil not worthy the idolatry which will surely engender it.

IF we travel slowly, and loiter on the road, Jesus will go on before us, and sin will overtake us. If we are dilatory and lazy in the vineyard, the Master will not smile on us when he walks through his garden. Be active, and expect Christ to be with thee; be idle, and the thorns and briers will grow so thickly, that he will be shut out of thy door.

WEANING is sorrowful work, but it must be done: we must be made to groan in this body that we may be made ready for the unclothing, and the "clothing upon," by which mortality shall be swallowed up of life.

EVIDENCES are like conduit-pipes—they are sometimes the channels of living water, but if the supply from the fountain-head be cut off from them, their waters utterly fail. That man will die of thirst who has no better spring to look to than an empty pitcher of evidences. Ishmael would have perished in the wilderness if his only hope had been in the bottle which his mother brought out with her from the tent of Abraham; and assuredly without direct supplies from the gracious hands of the Lord Jesus, the saints would soon be in an ill plight.

IN proportion as the Master's presence is delightful, his absence is mournful. Dark is the night which is caused by the setting of such a sun. No blow of Providence can ever wound so sorely as this.

A blasted crop is as nothing compared with an absent Redeemer; yea, sickness and the approach of death are preferable to the departure of Emanuel.

CHRIST is a flower, but he fadeth not; he is a river, but he is never dry; he is a sun, but he knoweth no eclipse; he is all in all, but he is something more than all.

CHRIST never, lingers long with dumb souls; if there be no crying out to him, he loves not silence, and he departs and betakes himself to those hearts which are full of the music of prayer. What a marvelous influence prayer has upon our fellowship with Jesus! We may always measure one by the other. Those pray most fervently and frequently who have been constant attendants on the kind Intercessor; while, on the other hand, those who wrestle the hardest in supplication will hold the angel the longest. Joshua's voice stayed the sun in the heavens for a few hours; but the voice of prayer can detain the Sun of righteousness for months and even years.

INASMUCH as the heart is the most important part of man—for out of it are the issues of life—it would be natural to expect that Satan, when he in tended to do mischief to manhood, would be sure to make his strongest and most perpetual attacks upon the heart. What we might have guessed in wisdom is certainly true in experience; for although Satan will tempt and try us in every way, though every gate of the town of Mansoul may be battered, though against every part of the walls thereof he will be sure to bring out his great guns, yet the place against which he levels his deadliest malice and his most furious strength, is the heart. Into the heart, already of itself evil enough, he thrusts the seeds of every evil thing, and doth his utmost to make it a den of unclean birds, a garden of poisonous trees, a river flowing with destructive water. Hence, again, arises the second necessity that we should be doubly cautions in keeping the heart with all diligence; for if, on the one hand, it be the most important, and, on the other hand, Satan, knowing this, makes his most furious and determined attacks against it, then, with double force the exhortation comes, "Keep thy heart with all diligence." And the promise also becomes doubly sweet from the very fact of the double danger—the promise which says, "The peace of God shall keep your hearts and minds through Christ Jesus our Lord."

HAPPY is he whose faith can see in the thick darkness, and whose soul can live in the year of drought; but that man is not far from a curse who slights the fellowship of the Lord, and esteems His smile to be a vain thing. It is an ill sign if any of us are in a contented state when we are forsaken of the Lord; it is not faith but wicked indifference, which makes us careless concerning communion with him.

IS my conscience at peace? For, if my heart condemn me not, God is greater than my heart, and doth know all things; if my conscience bear witness with me, that I am a partaker of the precious grace of salvation, then happy am I! I am one of those to whom God hath given the peace which passeth all understanding. Now, why is this called "the peace of God I" We suppose it is because it comes from God—because it was planned by God—because God gave his Son to make the peace—because God gives his Spirit to give the peace in the conscience—because, indeed, it is God himself in the soul, reconciled to man, whose is the peace. And while it is true that this man shall have the peace—even the Man-Christ, yet we know it is because he was the God-Christ that he was our peace. And hence we may clearly perceive how Godhead is mixed up with the peace which we enjoy with our Maker and with our conscience.

THE boldness of lion-like courage, the firmness of rooted decision, the confidence of unflinching faith, the zeal of quenchless love, the vigor of undying devotion, the sweetness of sanctified fellowship —all hang for support upon the one pillar of the Savior's presence, and this removed they fail.

DIOGENES may tell us to do without everything, and live in his tub, and then think himself happier than Alexander, and that he enjoys peace; but we may look upon the poor creature after all, and though we may be astonished at his courage, yet we are obliged to despise his folly. "We do not believe that even when he had dispensed with everything, he possessed a quiet mind, a total and entire peace, such as the true believer can enjoy. We find the greatest philosophers of old laying down maxims for life which they thought would certainly promote happiness. We find that they were not always able to practice them themselves; and many of their disciples, when they labored hard to put them in execution, found themselves encumbered with impossible rules to accomplish impossible objects. But a Christian man does with faith what man can never do himself. While the poor understanding is climbing up the crags, faith stands on the summit; while the poor understanding is getting into a calm atmosphere, faith flies aloft and mounts higher than the storm, and then looks down on the valley and smiles while the tempest blows beneath its feet. Faith goes further than understanding, and the peace which the Christian enjoys is one which the worldling cannot comprehend and cannot himself attain. "The peace of God which passeth all understanding."

YOU cannot have peace unless you turn your troubles up. You Lave no place in which to pour your troubles except the ear of God. If you tell them to your friends, you but put your troubles out a moment, and they will return again. If you tell them to God, you put your troubles into the grave; they will never rise again when you have committed them to him. If you roll your burden anywhere else it will roll back again, just like the stone of Sisyphus; but just roll your burden unto God, and you have rolled it into a great deep, out of which it will never by any possibility rise. Cast your troubles where you cast your sins; you have cast your sins into the depths of the sea, there cast your troubles also. Never keep a trouble half an hour on your own mind before you tell it to God. As soon as the trouble comes, quick, the first thing, tell it to your Father.

MOST of us have a lover and idol besides our husband, Christ; but it is our folly to divide our narrow and little love; it will not serve for two. It is best then, to hold it whole and together, and to give it to Christ; for then we get double interest for our love, when we lend it to, and lay it out upon, Christ; and we are sure, besides, that the stock cannot perish.

I HAVE seen the Christian man in the depths of poverty, when he lived from hand to mouth, and scarcely knew where he should find the next meal, still with his mind unruffled, calm, and quiet. If he had been as rich as an Indian prince, yet could he not have had less care; if he had been told that his bread should always come to his door, and the stream which ran hard by should never dry—if he had been quite sure that ravens would bring him bread and meat in the morning, and again in the evening, he would not have been one whit more calm. There is his neighbor on the other side of the street not half so poor, but wearied from morning to night, working his fingers to the bone, bringing himself to the grave with anxiety; but this poor good man, after having industriously labored, though he found he had gained little with all his toil, yet hath sanctified his little by prayer, and hath thanked his Father for what he had; and though he doth not know whether he will have more, still he trusteth in God, and declareth that his faith should not fail him, though providence should run to a lower ebb than he had ever seen. There is "the peace of God which passeth all understanding." I have seen that peace, too, in the case of those who have lost their friends. There is a widow—her much loved husband lies in the coffin; she is soon to part with him. Parted with him she has before; but now, of his poor clay-cold corpse—even of that she has to be bereaved. She looks upon it for the last time, and her heart is heavy. For herself and her children, she thinks how they shall be provided for. That broad tree that once sheltered them from the sunbeam has been cut down. Now, she thinks there is a broad heaven above her head, and her Maker is her husband; the fatherless children are left with God for their father, and the widow is trusting in him. With tears in her eyes she still looks up, and she says, "Lord, thou hast given and thou hast taken away, blessed be thy name." Her husband is carried to the tomb; she doth not smile, but though she weeps, there is a calm composure on her brow, and she tells you she would not have it otherwise, even if she could, for Jehovah's will is right.

IF we are ever privileged to receive Jesus under our roof, let us make haste to secure the door that he may not soon be gone. If he sees us care less concerning him, and cold towards him, he will soon arise and go hence. He will not intrude himself where he is not wanted; he needs no lodging, for the heaven of heavens is his perpetual palace, and there be many hearts of the contrite where he will find a hearty welcome.

I ONCE remember to have heard a woman say when I was passing down a lane—a child stood crying at the door, and I heard her calling out—"Ah, you are crying for nothing; I will give you something to cry for." Brethren, it is often so with God's children. They get crying for nothing. They have a miserable disposition, or a turn of mind always making miseries for themselves, and thus they have something to cry for. Their peace is disturbed, some sad trouble comes, God hides his face, and then they lose their peace. But keep on singing, even when the sun does not keep on shining; keep a song for all weathers; get a joy that will stand clouds and storms; and then, when you know how always to rejoice, you shall have this peace.

AGAINST the child of God conscience brings no accusation, or if it brings the accusation, it is but a gentle one—a gentle chiding of a loving friend who hints that we have done amiss, and that we had better change, but doth not afterwards thunder in our ears the threat of a penalty. Conscience knows full well that peace is made between the soul and God, and, therefore, it does not hint that there is any thing else but joy and peace to be looked forward to by the believer.

THERE is Martin Luther standing up in the midst of the Diet of Worms; there are the kings and the princes, and there are the bloodhounds of Rome with their tongues thirsting for his blood—there is Martin rising in the morning as comfortable as possible, and he goes to the Diet, and delivers himself of the truth, solemnly declares that the things which he has spoken are the things which he believes, and God helping him, he will stand by them till the last. There is his life in his hands; they have him entirely in their power. The smell of John Huss's corpse has not yet passed away, and he recollects that princes, before this, have violated their words; but there he stands, calm and quiet; he fears no man, for he has naught to fear; "the peace of God which passeth all understanding keeps his heart and mind through Jesus Christ." There is another scene: there is John Bradford in Newgate. He is to be burned the next morning in Smithfield, and he swings himself on the bedpost in very glee, and delights, for tomorrow is his wedding day; and he says to another, "Fine shining we shall make tomorrow, when the flame is kindled." And he smiles and laughs, and enjoys the very thought that he is about to wear the blood-red crown of martyrdom. Is Bradford mad? Ah, no; but he has got the peace of God that passeth all understanding. But perhaps the most beautiful, as well as the most common illustration of this sweet peace, is the dying bed of the believer. Oh, brethren, you have seen this sometimes—that calm, quiet serenity; you have said, Lord, let us die with him. It has been so good to be in that solitary chamber where all was quiet, and so still, all the world shut out, and heaven shut in, and the poor heart nearing its God, and far away from all its past burdens and griefs—now nearing the portals of eternal bliss And ye have said, "How is this? Is not death a black and grim thing? Are not the terrors of the grave things which make the strong man tremble? Oh yes, they are; but, then, this one has the "peace of God which passeth all understanding."

WE never live so well as when we live on the Lord Jesus simply as he is, and not upon our enjoyments and raptures. Faith is never more likely to increase in strength than in times which seem ad verse to her. "When she is lightened of trust in joys, experiences, frames, feelings, and the like, she rises the nearer heaven, like the balloon when the bags of sand are emptied. Trust in thy Redeemer's strength, thou benighted soul; exercise what faith thou hast, and by and by he shall rise upon thee with healing beneath his wings.

OH! true believer, is there no strange god with thee? Make a thorough search. Bid even thy beloved Rachel rise, for the teraph is often concealed beneath the place where she sitteth. Say not in haste, I am no idolater. The approaches of this sin are insidious in the extreme, and ere thou knowest it thou art entangled in its iron net. The love of the creature has a bewitching power over men, and they seldom know the treachery of the Delilah until their locks are shorn. Oh, daughters of Zion, let King Solomon alone have your love; rehearse his name in your songs, and write his achievements on your memories; so will he dwell in the city of David and ride through your midst in his chariot paved with love for *you*; but if ye pay homage to any save himself, he will return unto his place and make your beauteous city a by-word with the enemy.

REMEMBER, that in proportion to the fullness of thine heart will be the fullness of thy life. Be empty-hearted and thy life will be a meager, skeleton existence. Be full-hearted and thy life will be full, fleshy, gigantic, strong, a thing that will tell upon the world. Keep, then, thy peace with God firm within thee. Keep thou close to this, that Jesus Christ hath made peace between thee and God. And keep thy conscience still; then shall thy heart he full and thy soul strong to do thy Master's work. Keep thy peace with God. This will keep thy heart pure. Thou wilt say if temptation comes, "What dost thou offer me? Thou offerest me pleasure; lo! I have got it. Thou offerest me gold; lo! I have got it; all things are mine, the gift of God; I have a city that hands have not made, 'a house not made with hands, eternal in the heavens.' I will not barter this for your poor gold." "I will give you honor," saith Satan. "I have honor enough," says the peaceful heart; "God will honor me in the last great day of his account." "I will give thee everything that thou canst desire," saith Satan. "I have everything that I can desire," says the Christian.

HE will never lack appetite for spiritual things who lives much on them. The poor professor may he content with a few of Christ's pence now and then, but he who is rich in grace thinks so small an income beneath his station, and cannot live unless he has golden gifts from the hand of his Lord; he will covet earnestly this best of gifts, and be a very miser after the precious things of the cross.

WHEN our wondering eyes have admired the beauties of our Savior for millions of years we shall be quite as willing to continue the meditation, supremely blessed with that heaven which our eyes shall drink in from his wounded hands and side. The marrow of heaven is Jesus; and as we shall never be surfeited with bliss, so we shall never have too much of Jesus. Fresh glories are discovered in him every hour; his person, work, offices, character, affection, and relationships, are each of them clusters of stars which the eye of contemplation will view with unutterable astonishment as they are in their order revealed to the mind.

ANGELS' visits are few and far between: when we have the happiness of meeting there with, let us, like Jacob, manfully grasp the angel, and detain him, at least until he leaves a blessing. Up, Christian, with a holy bravery, and lay hold on the mercy while it is within reach! The Son of Man loves those who hold him tightly. He will not resent the familiarity, but will approve of thine earnestness. Let the loving bride of the Canticles teach thee by her example, for she glories in her deed when she sings, "I found him whom my soul loveth, I held him, and I would not let him go."

HAPPY are the spirits who have ended their fight of faith, and now live in the raptures of a sight of Him; yea, thrice happy are the lowest of those seraphs who fly at his bidding, and do forever behold the face of our Father which is in heaven. The drought of these dry plains stirreth us to desire the river of the water of life; the barren fig trees of this weary land urge us to pursue a speedy path to the immortal trees upon the banks of the river of God; our clouds exhort us to fly above this lower sky up where unclouded ages roll; the very thorns and briers, the dust and heat of this world's pilgrimage and strife, are powerful orators to excite our highest thoughts to the things which are unseen and eternal.

LOOK! look! look with solemn eye through the shades that part us from the world of spirits, and see that house of misery which men call hell! Ye cannot endure the spectacle. Remember that in that place there are spirits forever paying their debt to divine justice; but though some of them have been for these four thousand years sweltering in the flame they are no nearer a discharge than when they began; and when ten thousand times ten thousand years shall have rolled away, they will no more have made satisfaction to God for their guilt than they have done up till now. And now can you grasp the thought of the greatness of your Savior's meditation when he paid your debt, and paid it all at once; so that there now remaineth not one farthing of debt owing from Christ's people to their God, except a debt of love. To justice the believer oweth nothing; though he owed originally so much that eternity would not have, been long enough to suffice for the paying of it, yet in one moment Christ did pay it all, so that the man who believeth is entirely justified from all guilt, and set free from all punishment, through what Jesus hath done. Think ye, then, how great his atonement if he hath done all this.

BLESSED be God, the green pastures and the still waters, the shepherd's crook and pleasant company, are objects which are quite as familiar to the believer's mind as the howling wilderness and the brandished rod.

THE meanest lamb of the blood-bought flock shall be preserved securely by the "strength of Israel" unto the day of his appearing, and shall, through every season of tribulation and distress, continue to be beloved of the Lord.

FIRE will not tarry in a single coal, but if many be laid together it will be long before it is clean gone. A single tree may not afford much shelter for a traveler, but he will rest beneath the thick boughs of the grove: so will Jesus often sit longer where many of "the trees of the Lord" are planted. Go to the assemblies of the saints, if you would keep the arm of the King of saints. Those who dwell most with the daughters of Jerusalem are most likely to have a goodly share of Emanuel's company.

A LITTLE filth acquired daily, if left unwashed, will make us as black as if we were plunged into the mire; and as sin upon the conscience turns Christ's joy out of the heart,—it's impossible for us to feel the delights of communion until all our everyday sins have been washed from the conscience by a fresh application of His atoning blood.

AS plants thrive not when the light is kept from them, but become blanched and unhealthy, so souls deprived of the light of God's countenance are unable to maintain the verdure of their piety or the strength of their graces. What a loss is a lost Christ!

WHEN the Lord Jesus is present in the soul, and is beheld by it, ambition, covetousness, and worldliness flee apace; for such is his apparent glory that earthly objects fade away like the stars in noon day; but when he is gone they will show their false glitter, as the stars, however small, will shine at midnight.

TRUST the Lord much while he is with you. Keep no secrets from him. His secrets are with you; let your secrets be with him. Jesus admires confidence, and if it be not afforded him, he will say, "Farewell," until we can trust him better.

IF thou desirest Christ for a perpetual guest, give him all the keys of thine heart; let not one cabinet be locked up from him; give him the range of every room, and the key of every chamber; thus you will constrain him to remain.

I HAD rather put my foot upon a bridge as narrow as Hungerford, which went all the way across, than on a bridge that was as wide as the world, if it did not go all the way across the stream.

PRINCES have melted pearls into the wine where with they entertained monarchs; let us do the same. Let us make rich offerings to Jesus; let our duties be more faithfully discharged, our labors more willingly performed, and let our zeal be more eminently fervent.

WHATEVER our frame or feeling, the heart of Jesus is full of love—love which was not caused by our good behavior, and is not diminished by our follies—love which is as sure in the night of darkness, as in the brightness of the day of joy.

WHEN Christ is with the Christian, the means of grace are like flowers in the sunshine, smelling fragrantly and smiling beauteously; but without Christ they are like flowers by night, their fountains of fragrance are sealed by the darkness.

JESUS will never linger in a divided heart. He must be all or nothing. Search thy heart; dethrone its idols; eject all interlopers; chastise all trespassers; yea, slay the Diabolians who thy soul.

THERE is a story told, that in the olden times, Artaxerxes and another great king were engaged in a furious fight. In the middle of the battle a sudden eclipse happened, and such was the horror of all the warriors, that they made peace there and then. Oh, if an eclipse of trouble should induce you to ground arms and seek to be reconciled unto God! Sinner, you are fighting against God, lifting the arm of your rebellion against him. Happy shall you be if that trouble which is now fallen upon you should lead you to throw down the weapons of your rebellion, and fly to the arms of God and say, "Lord have mercy upon me a sinner." It will be the best thing that thou hast ever had. Thy trouble will be far better to thee than joys could have been, if thy sorrows shall induce thee to fly to Jesus who can make peace through the blood of his cross.

A PORTION of the Lord's family live usually in the shade: they are like those sweet flowers which bloom nowhere so well as in the darkest and thickest glades of the forest.

THE SUN will shine on the dunghill, but Christ will not shine on the back-slider while he is indulging in his lusts.

IF there be a place under high heaven more holy than another, it is the pulpit whence the gospel is preached. This is the Thermopylæ; of Christendom; here must the great battle be fought between Christ's church and the invading hosts of a wicked world. This is the last vestige of anything sacred that is left to us. We have no altars now; Christ is our altar: but we have a pulpit still left, a place which, when a man entereth, he might well put off his shoes from his feet, for the place whereon he standeth is holy. Consecrated by a Savior's presence, established by the clearness and the force of an apostle's eloquence, maintained and upheld by the faithfulness and fervor of a succession of evangelists who, like stars, have marked the era in which they lived, and stamped it with their names, the pulpit is handed down to those of us who occupy it now with a prestige of everything that is great and holy. Yet I have seen the wicked come and go from it. Alas! if there be a sinner that is hardened, it is the man that sins and occupies his pulpit. We have heard of such a man living in the commission of the foulest sins, and at length has been discovered; and yet such is the filthiness of mankind, that when he began to preach to the people again, they clustered round the beast for the mere sake of hearing what he would say to them. We have known cases, too, where men, when convicted to their own forehead, have unblushingly persevered in proclaiming a gospel which their lives denied. And perhaps these are the hardest of all sinners to deal with. But if the garment be once defiled, away with all thoughts of the pulpit then! he must he clean who ministers at the altar. Every saint must he holy, but he, holiest of all, who seeks to serve his God. Yet, we must mourn to say it, the church of God every now and then has had a sun that was black instead of white, and a moon that was as a clot of blood, instead of being full of fairness and beauty. Happy the church when God gives her holy ministers; but unhappy the church where wicked men preside. I know ministers to this day, however, who know more about fishing rods than they do about chapters in the Bible; more about fox-hounds than about hunting after men's souls; who understand a great deal more of the spring and the net than they do of tho net for catching souls, or earnest exhortations for men to flee from the wrath to come. We know such even now: still uproarious at a farmer's dinner, still the very loudest to give the toast and clash the glass, still mightiest among the mighty, fond of the gay, the wild, and the dissolute. Pity on the church that still allows it! Happy the day when all such persons shall be purged from the pulpit; then shall it stand forth "clear as the sun, fair as the moon, and terrible as an army with banners."

YOU need not dispute divine decrees, but sit down and draw honey out of this rock, and wine out of this flinty rock. Oh, it is a hard, hard doctrine to a man who has no interest in it, but when a man has once a title to it, then it is like the rock in the wilderness; it streams with refreshing water whereat myriads may drink and never thirst again. Well does the Church of England say of that doctrine, it "is full of sweet, pleasant, and unspeakable comfort to godly persons." And though it he like the Tarpeian rock, whence many a malefactor has been dashed to pieces in presumption, yet it is like Pisgah, from whose lofty summit the spires of heaven may be seen in the distance.

ONE reformation will never serve the church; she needs continually to be wound up, and set agoing afresh; for her works run down, and she does not act as she used to do. The bold, bald doctrines that Luther brought out, began to be a little modified, until layer after layer was deposited upon them, and at last the old rocky truth was covered up, and there grew upon the superficial subsoil an abundance of green and flowery errors, that looked fair and beautiful, but were in no way whatever related to the truth, except as they were the products of its decay. Then there came bold men who brought the truth out again, and said, "Clear away tins rubbish; let the blast light upon these deceitful beauties; we want them not; bring out the old truth once more!" And it came out. But the tendency of the church perpetually is, to be covering up its own naked simplicity, forgetting that the truth is never so beautiful as when it stands in its own unadorned, God-given glory. And now, at this time, we want to have the old truths restored to their places. The subtleties and the refinements of the preacher must be laid aside. We must give up the grand distinctions of the school-men, and all the lettered technicalities of men who have studied theology as a system, but have not felt the power of it in their hearts; and when the good old truth is once more preached by men whose lips are touched as with a live coal from off the altar, this shall be the instrument, in the hand of the Spirit, for bringing about a great and thorough revival of religion in the land.

LITTLE do we know when we look hero from this pulpit—it looks like one great field of flowers, fair to look upon—how many a root of deadly henbane and noxious nightshade groweth here; and though you all look fair and goodly, yet "I have seen the wicked come and go from the place of the holy."

SOLDIER of the cross! the hour is coming when the note of victory shall be proclaimed through out the world. The battlements of the enemy must soon succumb; the swords of the mighty must soon be given up to the Lord of lords. What! soldier of the cross! in the day of victory wouldst thou have it said that thou didst turn thy back in the day of battle? Dost thou not wish to have a share in the conflict, that thou mayest have a share in the victory? If thou hast even the hottest part of the battle, wilt thou flinch and fly? Thou shalt have the brightest part of the victory, if thou art in the fiercest of the conflict. Wilt thou turn and lose thy laurels? Wilt thou throw down thy sword? Shall it be with thee as when a standard-bearer fainteth? Nay, man, up to arms again! for the victory is certain. Though the conflict be severe, I beseech you, on to it again! On, on, ye lion-hearted men of God, to the battle once more! for ye shall yet be crowned with immortal glory.

THE END

YOU'LL ALSO LOVE THESE BOOKS BY C.H. SPURGEON

Available from www.greatchristianbooks.com

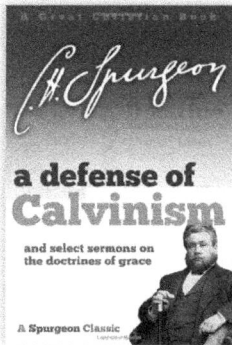

There are many books explaining and defending the doctrines known as Calvinism but there is none like that of this volume from C. H. Spurgeon, the Prince of Preachers. Spurgeon was not only a theologian but a Pastor, and it is with the heart of a pastor that he defends the doctrines of grace. This quintessential classic work by Spurgeon is fortified with select sermons on the individual doctrines as well as a bonus sermon on the issue of whether extolling the grace of God as taught in Scriptures leads to sin. A must have for every Christian's library.

ISBN 978-1610101301 $12.99

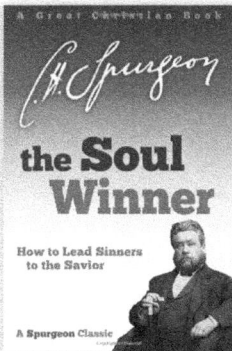

Who better to teach "How to be Soul-Winner" than C. H. Spurgeon. Known the world over as the "Prince of Preachers", Spurgeon is the master of the evangelical sermon and perhaps the most prolific communicator of the gospel in history. In this classic manual on evangelism, he lays out the most biblical, and therefore effective, methodologies for leading sinners to the Savior. Before buying into any of the so-called "new & innovative" systems of evangelism— learn the basics of sound Bible teaching on how to share the good news from the pen of a master evangelist.

ISBN 978-1610101806 $8.99

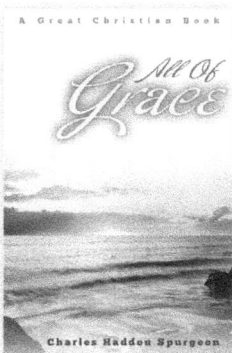

All of Grace is wonderful, evangelistic presentation of the gospel of Jesus Christ. The jailer cried "What must I do to be saved?" C. H. Spurgeon answers the question in the style all his own; he presents the gospel in a thoroughly biblical manner easily understood by even a child. Since its original publication over a century ago—*All of Grace* has never been out of print. It is truly a Christian classic. This edition is newly typeset in a fresh modern typeface for the easy reading pleasure of the modern reader.

ISBN 978-1610100304 $7.99

THE MISSION OF GREAT CHRISTIAN BOOKS

The ministry of Great Christian Books was established to glorify The Lord Jesus Christ and to be used by Him to expand and edify the kingdom of God while we occupy and anticipate Christ's glorious return. Great Christian Books will seek to accomplish this mission by publishing Gospel literature which is biblically faithful, relevant, and practically applicable to many of the serious spiritual needs of mankind upon the beginning of this new millennium. To do so we will always seek to boldly incorporate the truths of Scripture, especially those which were largely articulated as a body of theology during the Protestant Reformation of the sixteenth century and ensuing years. We gladly join our voice in the proclamations of— Scripture Alone, Faith Alone, Grace Alone, Christ Alone, and God's Glory Alone!

Our ministry seeks the blessing of our God as we seek His face to both confirm and support our labors for Him. Our prayers for this work can be summarized by two verses from the Book of Psalms:

"...let the beauty of the LORD our God be upon us, And establish the work of our hands for us; Yes, establish the work of our hands." —Psalm 90:17

"Not unto us, O LORD, not unto us, but to your name give glory."
—Psalm 115:1

Great Christian Books appreciates the financial support of anyone who shares our burden and vision for publishing literature which combines sound Bible doctrine and practical exhortation in an age when too few so-called "Christian" publications do the same. We thank you in advance for any assistance you can give us in our labors to fulfill this important mission. May God bless you.

For a catalog of other great
Christian books including
other books by
C. H. Spurgeon—

contact us in
any of the following ways:

write us at:
**Great Christian Books
160 37th Street
Lindenhurst, NY 11757**

call us at:
(631) 956-0998

find us online:
www.greatchristianbooks.com

email us at:
mail@greatchristianbooks.com

www.ingramcontent.com/pod-product-compliance
Lightning Source LLC
Chambersburg PA
CBHW030824090426
42737CB00009B/867